Dispatches from
MY SOUTH

Reflections and Recipes from a Southern Food Scribe

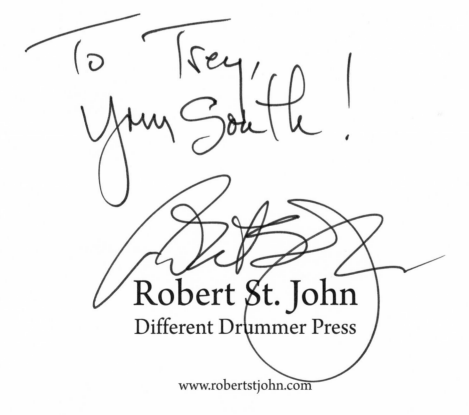

Robert St. John

Different Drummer Press

www.robertstjohn.com

Different Drummer Press
Hattiesburg, MS

Layout and Design by The Gibbes Company

ISBN-10: 061532410X

ISBN-13: 978-0-615-32410-4

First Edition

Printed in the United States of America

Front cover photo Joey DeLeo
Back cover photo Joey DeLeo
Title page photo Michael Goldsholl
Inside flap photo Michael Goldsholl

To Jill, Holleman, and Harrison
in remembrance of good times shared
and in enthusiastic anticipation of good times to come
(thanks for ten years of good subject matter)

Previous books by Robert St. John

A Southern Palate (Different Drummer Publishing)
*Deep South Staples or How to Survive in a Southern Kitchen
Without A Can of Cream of Mushroom Soup* (Hyperion)
Nobody's Poet (Different Drummer Publishing)
My South A People, a Place, a World All Its Own (Rutledge Hill Press)
Deep South Parties (Hyperion)
Southern Seasons (Different Drummer Publishing)
New South Grilling (Hyperion)

Visit Robert's restaurants at www.nsrg.com
The Purple Parrot Cafe
The Crescent City Grill
The Mahogany Bar
3810 Hardy Street
Hattiesburg, MS 39402
601-264-0656

Visit Robert's website www.robertstjohn.com

To make a difference in your community, visit www.extratable.org

To book speeches, or schedule Robert for cooking demos
and fundraising events: 888-315-6774

GIVING CREDIT WHERE CREDIT'S DUE

Thanks

To The Big Guy Upstairs for giving me more blessings than I deserve and for making it all possible.

To my family for their continued love and support.

To all of my friends who keep me pointed in the right direction. My grandfather used to say, "You can judge a man's wealth—not by the size of his bank account, but—by the depth and breadth of his friendships." Thanks for making me feel wealthier than Bill Gates.

To Denton Gibbes, Anne Jernigan, and all of the crew at the Gibbes Company for producing this book—especially to the über-talented Wade Rico for his expert design and layout.

To Stacey Andrews for keeping my life and career in line, in order, focused, and on time.

To Maria Keyes who keeps me in the black.

To Linda Nance for steering the culinary ship.

To Clint Taylor, Dusty Frierson, and the staff and management of the Purple Parrot Cafe, Crescent City Grill, and Mahogany Bar for holding down the fort.

Last, but clearly not least, to all of the restaurant patrons and column readers for their continued support and devotion through the years.

CONTENTS

Dispatches from
MY SOUTH

Reflections and Recipes from a Southern Food Scribe

Chapter 1

Childhood

Of Bells and Dogs

It was a time before reality TV, before Watergate, and Contragate, and *Frontgate*. The Cold War was in full bloom, Jimi Hendrix was alive, and the Beatles were still together. Captain America had morphed from a World War II comic book superhero with a star-spangled shield to a counterculture icon on a Harley-Davidson. Dr. King and Bobby Kennedy were gone, but Jim Crow was still here. Elvis was alive, skinny even, and only went to Vegas to get married. It was a time before AIDS, and low-carb diets, and New Orleans was still the city that care forgot. Television had Carson and Cronkite and Little Joe Cartwright. A war was being lost, and a cultural shift was occurring, though Berkeley and Kent State were light years away. Hair was long and days were longer. Doors were left unlocked, and I knew every dog in the neighborhood.

The Hillendale subdivision of Hattiesburg, Mississippi, was being constructed as the babies boomed. It was filled with the low-rate mortgages of Depression-born parents and the tall pines native to my corner of the South. Hillendale stretched from Howling Wolf's Highway 49 on the east, to Eisenhower's Interstate 59 on the west. My mother, brother, and I moved into a small house on a small lot midway between those two roads in 1968.

There were two-car garages, no sidewalks, and homes filled with discernment and dysfunction. Summers were spent on bikes, in creeks, and wrestling on St. Augustine.

Neighborhood boys ran alongside dogs while squeezing every ounce of sunlight out of the long summer days. Appetites were earned. My love for food and my love for dogs were shaped and solidified in the same moment and the same place.

The ladies of my neighborhood were brilliant cooks. They prided themselves on the dishes they prepared. There were no microgreens or infused vinegars, no baby vegetables or precooked entrees. Everything was made from scratch, simple, honest, pure. Families sat together at the same table—television off—and shared a meal. A mother called her children to supper and they ran to the table.

The third meal of the day was always called "supper." The term "dinner" was reserved for a more formal midday meal. In earlier decades, the call to supper had been a whistle, not a metal coach's whistle, but a sweet, airy birdlike whistle from the pursed lips of a woman who was too polite to scream her son's name from the front porch. Each mother had a different whistling style and tune. Fifty years later, my friend Bill can replicate, to an exact note, the whistle of his mother. The birdlike change in pitch and tenor of a mother's whistle can bring a tear to the eye of the grown man who recalls it. The birdcall whistle was unassuming and sedate, like the decades that spawned it.

The call to supper in the late 1960s and early 1970s was different. In my neighborhood most mothers had a bell. The bell was the clarion call for supper. Every bell had a different tone and each could be heard from blocks away. Most bells were of the come-and-get-it handheld variety, no larger than a mayonnaise jar, and every child knew the sound of his mother's bell.

In the early evening, just before dusk, as the asphalt started to cool, bells could be heard from back doors and back porches in all directions. The neighborhood became a sporadic symphony of chimes—the mother's opus, an unorganized and unintentional handbell ensemble.

In the middle of a heated Wiffle Ball game, a bell would ring from blocks away, and the conversation would go something like this: "Pat, that's your bell. See you tomorrow." "No, that's Stan's bell." "No, it's Robby's bell. His little brother broke their old one and his mom got a new one."

"That's my bell, guys; I gotta get home for supper."

Every boy knew the sound of his mother's bell. My mother—a devout disciple of all things Early American—opted for a miniature version of the Liberty Bell, minus the crack. She purchased it on a Colonial Dames field trip to Williamsburg. It had a Williamsburg yellow handle and rang long and true, with a deeper tone than all of the others. And when it rang, I ran.

A friend whose dad kept a large boat on the Gulf Coast was called home to the sound of an air horn that could be heard all the way to

Eisenhower's interstate. The mother of another friend who had recently moved into town used a cowbell.

Most boys had a bell, Ernest had Cokie. Cokie was an elderly black woman who had moved down from a Mississippi Delta plantation when Ernest's mother married into the neighborhood. She lived in a converted garage and served as the family's nanny, cook, maid, babysitter, and town crier. While other mothers were ringing bells, Cokie walked up and down the pine-lined streets yelling, "Ernest. Ernest." After ten minutes and a few blocks, the cry changed to a more longing, "Ernest, come home!" If we quietly moved from street to street, avoiding Cokie's detection, we could usually elicit a remark such as, "Ernest, get your little white ass home! Supper's getting cold!"

Occasionally, when bells didn't get the job done, mothers would drive around the neighborhood—a scotch and water in one hand, the steering wheel of the Vista Cruiser station wagon in the other—playing an ever-moving game of cat and mouse–style hide-and-seek. The mother, an unwilling participant in the game, bellowed her son's name as she slowly drove from block to block one step behind the group.

Just as I knew everyone's bell, I knew everyone's dog. It was a time before leash laws and pooper scoopers, and the dogs of my neighborhood—like the kids of the day—ran free and with abandon. William Dunlap says, "Some civilizations worship dogs, some work them, others put them on the menu." Hillendale fell into the first category.

The dogs of my neighborhood were more like those of a commune than pets of individual houses or owners. I belonged to the neighborhood and all of the dogs belonged to me.
Buffy and Sue—a cocker spaniel and an English setter—lived in my house. Lucky lived across the street and was a mixed breed with one blue eye and a limp. Scooter was a dachshund. Cappy was a cocker, too, named after his owner, Cathy. Cola was a poodle named after her seller.

Sam and Caesar were black labs who lived one block apart. Caesar was the neighborhood Don Juan and prone to random bouts of leg humping. He is primarily responsible for creating the first, and only time, I ever saw a romance broken up by a garden hose. Sam, on the other hand, kept his love life to himself.

There were Festus, and Rastus, and Rufus—all mutts—and Frank, a golden retriever that would fetch a stick out of the lake until your arm got so tired you could no longer throw.

Son was a trembling Chihuahua with a vicious growl and Frosty was an Eskimo spitz who once bit my face when I sat on his tail. Dynamite was a poodle, Bijou was an Afghan, and Piper was an incessantly yapping terrier. Bertha Butt was a small mutt I found and gave to the wife of a preacher, and Sheba was an English sheepdog who always seemed miserable living in the heat and humidity of South Mississippi. At one or more times in my life, I befriended all of them.

Willie Morris once wrote, "The dog of your boyhood teaches you a great deal about friendship, and love, and death." I believe that the neighborhood dogs taught me and my friends how to live together and how to interact with one another, through fights, and breakups, and times we felt lost or alone. They taught us the virtues of loyalty within friendship and gave us an early glimpse into pain and loss and unrequited love. They ran all day long, and like us, they ran with purpose when they were called home.

Today a mother calls, "supper," and kids run—not to a table—but to a minivan. Soccer has replaced Wiffle Ball and cell phones have replaced bells. I still live within eight blocks of the small house on the small lot. I don't know the dogs in my neighborhood. I don't know my neighbors, and I am ashamed that I never took the time to learn Cokie's full name.

The dusk of my youth was filled with barks and bells. As the sun set on my neighborhood, a carillon rang through the streets. The clangs were interrupted by the occasional bleat of a boat horn, clank of a cowbell, or the frustrated cry of a housekeeper. Birds fell silent as smoke from backyard barbeques dissipated and televisions were tuned to *Mannix* and *Hawaii Five-O*. One by one the bells surrendered to crickets and bullfrogs as darkness fell on Hillendale.

Methodists and the Art of Cat Flossing

In the South, parties come in all shapes, forms, sizes, and scope. They are held in apartments and homes, on lawns, patios, porches, and verandas.

Whether city or country, beachside or poolside, Southerners are just as comfortable at a barbeque, crawfish boil, or pig picking as they are a seated brunch, cocktail party, formal gala, or black-tie ball.

Parties are also held in churches, not just holiday teas in the parsonage, and post-nuptial wedding receptions in the church parlor, but the ultimate, end-all, and coup de grace of Southern cooking: the covered-dish supper.

I am a Methodist, and we Methodists love a covered-dish supper.

A covered-dish supper is a mass-feeding event in which a select group of people each bring a portable dish for many to share. Enough dishes are brought so that a collection of families have plenty of food from which to choose. In the South, it is an opportunity for the home cook to shine. Though in a church, the covered-dish supper has a definite party atmosphere surrounding it.

At my church, every mother in every family brought a dish. Some ladies excelled in desserts, some in vegetables, others in the main course. No one ever brought chain-store chicken or grocery-store cakes. The food was always made from scratch and always good. The atmosphere at these gatherings was light, festive, and full of hope and eager expectation.

Tables ran the entire length of the fellowship hall for the once-a-week feast and every red-checkered inch was filled with a homemade specialty. My church never hosted a we'll-supply-the-meat-you-bring-the-vegetables-and-dessert covered-dish supper. The ladies in my church brought center-of-the-plate items, too: fried chicken, meatloaf, main-course casseroles, side-dish casseroles, and dessert casseroles.

Casseroles have become the redheaded stepchild of the Southern larder. In these days of micro greens, boutique vinegars, and designer foams, casseroles have taken a backseat to the trendy foods-of-the-moment. It is a sin, indeed.

An honest casserole is true comfort food. As long as we can wean ourselves off of canned-soup fillers and other shortcut additions, the Southern casserole is as legitimate as any French cassoulet.

The casserole sits in an honored place of reverence at a covered-dish supper. The tables are a Pyrex jungle of casseroles. From elaborately prepared entrees to cream-soup-laden vegetables, the dishes come in all sizes, shapes, and colors. Aromas rise from beneath the tinfoil, fuse, and drift through the room, teasing the arrival of the imminent feast. It is at that moment—just before the foil is lifted and the single-file line begins to move forward—that the entire room smells Southern.

There is always a slight health risk involved in covered-dish suppers, due to the fact that most of the items are being held at room temperature for long periods of time. But Methodists—not known for living on the edge—would never let something as trivial as a bacteria-laden food-borne illness get in the way of a successful covered-dish supper.

The covered-dish supper is also about fellowship. Sitting down with one's family, friends, and neighbors and enjoying a shared meal is a treat that has unfortunately become less common over the years. We pull through the drive-through window and bring home a paper sack full of fast-food fried chicken, and eat it on a TV tray while watching reality TV programs, and call it "dinner." Not so, the covered-dish supper.

Some of my fondest food memories from childhood are centered in the fellowship hall of the Main Street United Methodist Church in my hometown of Hattiesburg, Mississippi. In my church, I knew who the best cooks were, and I always kept a close eye on the door when those women made their entrance. I knew who cooked the best fried chicken and who baked the finest homemade cakes. I arrived at church early on covered-dish supper night and sat at a strategic location that offered a full and unobstructed view of the food tables. From my perch, I watched closely to note the exact placement of the best-tasting dishes, making detailed mental notes so I could return to load my plate with those items.

There is a certain conversational roar that covers a room when a crowd is gathered and waiting to eat. The banter level gains a tinge of excitement. On covered-dish supper night, the room was always alive and in full conversational roar. From my seat, I listened to the volume of the room as it raised and lowered depending on which woman entered and which dish she was carrying. The entrance of a gifted cook bearing a banana cream pie with homemade meringue piled eight inches above the custard made the room's conversation level swell in noisy anticipation. A woman lugging a Cool Whip–topped strawberry shortcake made with leftover cornbread brought the noise level down a few decibels as an audible disappointment covered the room.

In my church, there was an elderly woman who had a houseful of cats. I will call her Mrs. Lancaster, may she rest in peace. Mrs. Lancaster's cats were known to climb all over her kitchen counters and in and out of her cabinets. They ran wild in the streets and lived in, on, under, and on top of her house. It was not unusual to find a few dozen cat hairs in any casserole Mrs. Lancaster brought to a covered-dish supper.

When the Widow Lancaster walked into the fellowship hall on covered-dish supper night, the conversational roar came to a halt, and the crowded room fell instantly silent. All eyes focused on her. The entire membership watched in measured stillness as she slowly shuffled across the room and placed her casserole on the table among the other offerings. The room's silence was quickly replaced by frantic whispers. "Pass the word; it's a congealed green-bean ring tonight." Once the location of the dish was noted, the room once again filled with chatter and the parade of casseroles entering the room resumed.

I pitied the latecomers who weren't in the room when Mrs. Lancaster arrived. For they were clueless when it came to trying to figure out which dish was hers. Later, I watched with great delight as the uninformed and out-of-the-casserole-loop church members ate, occasionally pulling strands of a thin, stringlike substance from between their teeth. I called this covered-dish-supper practice "cat-flossing."

Up North, covered-dish suppers are called potluck dinners. The food is bland and tasteless. Northerners sit around eating unseasoned meat and talk about how much snow they shoveled that morning. Down here, in the epicenter of the Bible Belt, we have parties in churches where we eat fried chicken, potato salad, green-bean casserole, broccoli casserole, chicken and dumplings, chicken pie, barbeque ribs, butter beans, peas, cornbread, yeast rolls, assorted pies, homemade ice cream, and coconut cakes, while simultaneously keeping a close eye on church members who own more than three cats.

The Bug Truck

Yesterday I was on my way home from the office and passed an ice cream truck just two blocks from my house.

I can't remember the last time I saw an ice cream truck in my neighborhood. It was probably sometime around 1974.

When I was a kid growing up in the thick heat of the South Mississippi summers, the circuslike jingle of the ice cream truck creeping down the street was always a welcome sound. It could be heard from blocks away and a mad dash always followed, with dozens of neighborhood kids running frantically to make sure they ended up on the same street as the truck before it passed.

There was an excited eagerness that preceded the advent of the truck that was unique only to that occasion. Hot and sweaty kids anxiously waiting for ice cream is an unrivaled enthusiasm. Those who anticipated the truck's arrival earlier in the day were already packing pocket change. Others, unprepared, had to run beg money from their mother and hurry back before the ice cream man bolted. When the truck finally stopped, a swarm ensued.

The only other sound that generated as much excitement in my neighborhood was the hum of the bug truck ambling down the street.

The bug truck was a city-owned vehicle and the lone soldier in the battle for a mosquito-free neighborhood. It had a large white tank on the back that spewed a thick white fog as it slowly ambled down the block, sort of a crop duster on wheels. In those days, the fog that billowed from the back of the truck was laced with DDT and highly poisonous.

Wherever the bug truck traveled, a crowd of at least half a dozen kids riding their bikes in and out of the fog would certainly follow. No matter what was happening elsewhere in the neighborhood, weaving in and out of the thick white mist was *the* place to be at that moment.

The bravest of our crew would stand on the bumper of the bug truck, their faces only inches away from the source of the insecticide, eyes watering, toxic fog blowing furiously in their faces. I am fully prepared to grow a second head and a third eye by the time I am in my sixties, just for breathing in a few summers' worth of DDT.

My mother, a single mom, was an early warrior in the battle to save the environment. She subscribed to environmentally conscious magazines and had read a theory that the fog from the bug truck did, indeed, kill mosquitoes, but then the birds ate the mosquitoes and died, the cats ate the birds and died, the dogs ate the cats and died, and eventually everyone on our block was going to croak because the bug truck passed in front of our house.

One summer evening, my brother and I were eating an early supper when we heard the seductive sound of the bug truck turning the corner at the end of our street. We looked at each other, and just as we were about to jump out of our chairs and head outside, our mother yelled, "No! You boys sit back down. I've had enough of this!"

She stormed out the front door and stood in the middle of our street, feet planted, left arm outstretched in a Tiananmen Square–style tank-halting protest. My brother and I watched wide-eyed from inside the house as she walked toward the driver's-side window and began shaking her finger, lecturing the driver on the long and drawn out birds-eating-the-mosquitoes theory. The kids cycling behind the truck scattered.

The mosquito lectures continued for a few consecutive nights, until, after a few weeks of environmental sermons, the bug man finally started avoiding our street altogether. Consequently all of the mosquitoes moved into our neighborhood and the St. John boys were the ones who returned to school at the end of the summer looking like they had a chronic case of chicken pox.

Nowadays they have removed the DDT from the bug truck's tanks. The vehicle that travels in front of my house today spits out a weak stream of a barely visible mist, certainly nothing that could be considered fog. There are no children peddling their bikes behind the truck or riding on the bumper. Consequently, all of the dogs and cats are healthy and accounted for; they might have my mother to thank for that.

We do, however, have an ice cream truck, and the next time I hear its alluring call, I'll grab my two children and a handful of change and join in the chase.

Screaming Yellow Zonkers

In 1969 my mom, a widowed art teacher raising two small boys on a limited income, taught painting classes out of a small studio room in our attic. Her students—various ladies from the neighborhood—learned how to paint mushrooms onto small blocks of wood using shades of avocado green and harvest gold.

Occasionally, I was asked to model while she demonstrated portrait painting. I usually found it hard to sit still for longer than ninety seconds, so mostly I planted fake vomit and rubber dog poop around the studio for her students to find.

Mildred Puckett, a doctor's wife—tall, fun, with a great sense of humor and a contagious laugh—was one of her students. One night Mrs. Puckett showed up with a black cardboard box and asked me if I had ever eaten Screaming Yellow Zonkers. "No, ma'am," I said.

"Well try these," she said. I did, and I was hooked.

Screaming Yellow Zonkers are my all-time favorite snack food. They hit the market in 1969, two years removed from the Summer of Love, and smack-dab in the middle of the psychedelic era. A counterculture snack aimed directly at the stoner crowd with a bad case of the munchies.

At eight years old, I didn't know what the munchies were—Mrs. Puckett probably didn't either—but I knew that the Screaming Yellow Zonkers' box filled with light butter-toffee-glazed popcorn tasted good.

For years I thought that Screaming Yellow Zonkers had been discontinued. Last week I learned that they are still being produced by Lincoln Snacks, the same company that manufactures Fiddle Faddle and Poppycock. I Googled "Screaming Yellow Zonkers" and found an outfit that would mail-order a few boxes to me.

The box was black. It still is. Actually, Screaming Yellow Zonkers were the first food ever to be packaged in a black box. The font on the box is pure vintage 1969. Best of all, Screaming Yellow Zonkers still taste great.

In 1969, there were two things I wanted to be when I grew up: an astronaut and a hippie. When I learned that being a hippie took a lot less math and training, I decided to move in that direction. While most kids wanted a new bike, I wanted sideburns and a mustache. I actually ordered a pair of lamb-chop sideburns and a Dennis Hopper–style mustache from the back of an *Archie* comic book. I wore them to school and made it through three periods of the third grade before my teacher sent me, my sideburns, and my box of Screaming Yellow Zonkers to the principal's office.

The counterculture intrigued me. I didn't know where Haight-Ashbury was, but I knew it was a long way away from Hattiesburg, Mississippi. Being eight years old, and learning that mail-order sideburns were not the solution, I figured Screaming Yellow Zonkers were the closest I could get to hippiedom.

I would retreat to my room, crank up Iron Butterfly's *In-A-Gadda-Da-Vida*, turn on the black light, light some incense, and eat handfuls of Screaming Yellow Zonkers. Move over, Peter Fonda.

While the country was turning on and dropping out, I was doing my part. Little did I know that for the next few years, the closest I was going to get to being "turned on" to anything would be the offer of Screaming Yellow Zonkers by Mrs. Puckett.

Alas, the obstacles of becoming the world's first, and youngest, hippie astronaut.

Somewhere out there, my principal, Mr. Russell, is probably still locked in his office, strobe light on, *In-A-Gadda-Da-Vida* blaring over the school sound system, wearing the confiscated fake sideburns and mustache, dancing wildly, and eating my box of Screaming Yellow Zonkers.

The Payback Party of 1976

My mother loves all things Early American and would, if given the chance, travel back to the eighteenth century to live in Colonial Williamsburg.

She is a devout member of the Daughters of the American Revolution and the Colonial Dames, and Williamsburg is her Mecca, the center of her universe. It guides her travel, it influences her reading. It is the basis for every decorating decision she has ever made or will ever make. No matter what the problem is, the way they did it in Colonial times is the solution.

She loves Williamsburg almost as much as she hates dirty hands. She is not a rupophobiac, but she watches too much television, committing every news report involving germs or dirt to memory, and within hours publishes lengthy theses on cleanliness and Godliness which she passes out—double spaced, typed, and in three-punch folders—to every member of the family.

Her love of all things Early American is in her bloodstream and molds her philosophical being. She wanted her two sons to grow up and attend the College of William and Mary, not because of any concern for our education, but for its proximity to Colonial Williamsburg.

So on that fateful day in 1976 when she announced that she was planning a party, my brother and I already knew the theme.

Three years earlier she'd drag us along on one of her many pilgrimages to the Early American Promised Land. We went willingly, but only based on the promise that we would also be able to go to Busch Gardens and ride the roller coaster.

We arrived in Colonial Williamsburg at the crack of dawn. Nothing had opened yet, but she didn't want to risk missing a single thrill that might lay waiting in a simulated replica of an Early American village. As we walked through the streets, I witnessed a transformation in her demeanor. She was wide-eyed and in awe. Weaving our way through the James Geddy House, she spoke under her breath, to no one in particular, "Things were just better back then."

"But Mom, they peed in a bowl and kept it on a table in their room overnight."

"It's called a chamber pot, and just look at the craftsmanship and artistry of the bowl. It's beautiful. Anyone would be proud to urinate in such a work of art. I'll bet they always kept their hands clean."

"But Mom, they had no air-conditioning."

"It was cooler back then, boys. Those were the days before global warming." My mother, like the colonists, was early into environmental issues.

She bought us tricornered hats and made us wear them. It was 1973—the year in which bell bottoms reached their largest circumference and stack shoes attained their highest elevation—but there we were, at twelve and sixteen years old, wearing tricornered hats and souvenir-shop baby-blue waistcoats with our names stitched on the chest.

After the obligatory photograph of my brother and me locked in the stocks, and a visit to the town pillory, we went to the blacksmith shop where she bought me a horseshoe. "Did you wash your hands? You don't know where that horseshoe has been."

"But I do know where it has been, Mom. It's been with us in the un-air-conditioned blacksmith shop for the last two-and-a-half hours."

After visiting a basket maker, a shoe maker, a brick maker, and a wig maker, we ended up watching a woman churn butter. No Busch Gardens. "You boys can ride a roller coaster anytime. This is history. Now go wash your hands."

Three years later this trip would pay off as we prepared for the Williamsburg party. The Colonial theme would be easy to create as the house would need no decorating. We lived in my mother's own private Williamsburg.

The house was painted Colonial yellow and all rooms were adorned with antiques and reproductions from the Early American era. While our friends had posters of Dennis Hopper, Peter Fonda, and the Beatles hanging in their rooms, our rooms were filled with framed prints of minutemen, Ben Franklin, and Thomas Jefferson. The bathroom my brother and I shared was a patriotic tribute to the founding fathers—a blue lavatory, a white shower, and a red commode. Yes, a red commode.

I can trace 42 percent of my difficulties in adjusting to adulthood—and a full half of the emotional problems I've endured—to having to use a fire-engine red commode for the first eighteen years of my life. Immediately after she built the house, I tried to explain to her that the citizens of Colonial Williamsburg never had to sit on red toilets.

"They were extremely patriotic," she replied. "If they had ever had the chance to sit on a red commode, I'll just bet they would have."

On the day of the party, my mom found the hiding place where we had hidden the tricornered hats. She made us wear them during the event. My brother opted for his brown leisure suit, figuring it would at least make him look like a modern-day American statesman.

The party was a payback party. A payback party is a social gathering one holds to pay back all of the people who have invited one to a party over the course of the previous year. Mom was three years overdue in her payback, as she had been waiting for the perfect time to host her next party—the Bicentennial.

The rooms were themed: The living room became the Boston Tea Party, where her silver tea service was placed on a mahogany secretary. Constitution Hall was the entry hall where my brother manned the coat closet. The Raleigh Tavern and Public House was the breakfast room where the bar was set up, and the dining room was the Governor's Palace.

My brother made an eight track mixed tape—his version of Colonial-themed music—for the occasion. The party mix included such hits of the day as "Play That Funky Music" by Wild Cherry, "Afternoon Delight" by The Starland Vocal Band, "Car Wash" by Rose Royce, "Don't Go Breakin' My Heart" by Elton John and Kiki Dee, "Muskrat Love" by the Captain and Tennille, and "Free Bird" by Lynyrd Skynyrd. I loaned him my forty-five single of Edwin Starr's "War" to add to the lineup in the hope that it might conjure up images of the American Revolution. *"War! Huh! Good God, y'all. What is it good for? Absolutely nothing!"* The mood was now set.

I was churning butter in the Governor's Palace as the guests began to arrive. The house filled quickly due to the three-year delay in party payback.

While the rooms were crowded, it was mostly quiet on the food front. Colonial food having its roots in the cuisine of Mother England, it didn't lend itself to memorable dining. The cloth-draped table was full of such Early American delectables as salt mackerel, pickled cabbage, rice pudding, preserved fruit compote, corn pone, fermented-lemon chess pie, something called George Washington cherry surprise, Monticello gingerbread, and six different recipes using cranberries as the main ingredient.

"Mom, I don't think that George Washington Cherry Surprise is a true Colonial dish."

"Well, they would've eaten it had they known about it. Did you wash your hands before churning that butter?"

The typical bone china, crystal, and sterling silver had given way to the more true-to-theme pewter and copper.

As KC and the Sunshine Band played over the hi-fi system, cocktails were being served in large pewter mugs that weighed at least three pounds each. The sheer weight of the drinks forced serious pleasure seekers to stay seriously close to the bar, which in turn allowed them to get seriously drunk. Those brave enough to venture through the house with a weighty mug full of faux ale and a bulky pewter plate full of salt mackerel and cranberries were so tired by the time they reached the family room that they called it quits and went home to eat a more fitting, and less exhaustive, supper.

Many of the guests weren't into the Colonial theme. Most skipped the ale and headed straight for the scotch—another import from the British Isles—and never complained.

Over the years my mother had purchased and inherited an impressive collection of Early American antique furniture. Unfortunately most of the pieces were old and delicate and off limits for sitting, not to mention uncomfortable. As the evening wore on, and the scotch and ale began to produce their desired effects, my mother nervously scurried around the house trying to keep drunken—and now rowdy—guests from dancing on the small handmade chairs and tables.

From my spot at the butter churn, I could see my brother dancing the robot in his tri cornered hat as "Play that Funky Music" blared over the tinny speakers in the Market Square (family room).

"You'll never get into William and Mary acting like that," my mother yelled to him as she pulled a pressed-tin lampshade off of a neighbor's head in the corner of the Raleigh Tavern.

With the food being a major disappointment, the highlights of the party appeared to be the endless supply of scotch from the liquor cabinet and the red commode in the front bathroom, which hosted a steady stream of gawkers for most of the evening. "Come see, Sarah, they have a red commode!"

Overall, the payback party served its purpose. The corner grocery finally got rid of their three-year-old salt mackerel inventory, our friends' parents learned how to dance the robot, my brother and I gained a newfound respect for our red toilet, and we were finally able to mothball the tri cornered hats where they've remained for thirty years.

My mother recently moved into a condominium, "a townhouse just like the Guardhouse in Williamsburg," she says. It is filled with all of the Early American antiques that survived the Payback Party of 1976.

This Christmas, while most kids were opening handheld video games and robotic dinosaurs, she gave my eight-year-old daughter and four-year-old son a set of "authentic" Early American pressed-tin mobiles and an automatic soap dispenser. Thirty-three years after my brother and me—my kids, too, ended up watching a lady churn butter instead of going to Busch Gardens.

Stable Staple

Every home has a stable staple.

A stable staple is an item that is almost, if not always, in an individual's home kitchen. It varies from home to home and is usually located in an heirloom cookie jar, or a favored Pyrex dish, tucked away on a special shelf in the pantry, or highlighted front and center in the refrigerator.

It is the singular food item that is ever-present in your home. It's usually kept in the same place, and it is the one item that is served when someone visits your home, and the item that will be there when you visit someone else's home.

Your best friends always know where the stable staple is kept, and they feel free to help themselves when they visit.

Sometimes the stable staple is a snack, every now and then a cake or pie; it can be store-bought or homemade. In a few families the item changes with the holidays; in others the stable staple is ever-changing regardless of the season or occasion.

As a kid I committed to memory all of my friends' stable staples. When playing outside in the Mississippi summer heat it was important to know which friend's house to visit to eat a certain snack.

One friend always had chips and picante sauce; another had off-brand generic cookies that he would personally dole out—one to each friend—while his mouth was crammed full with a dozen of the cookies. In between those two lived a friend whose parents owned several grocery stores. They didn't have a lone stable staple, but a treasure trove of snacks, drinks, and frozen treats that we raided on a daily basis. Their pantry was kid-snack heaven.

My mom always had oatmeal cookies and Hawaiian Punch in her house. They were her stable staples.

Today, my wife's stable staple is a pan of warm, freshly baked chocolate chip cookies. My kids love them and their friends annihilate them as soon as they are removed from the oven.

My paternal grandmother almost always had a pound cake under a glass dome. Occasionally she would have an angel food cake, but most times it was a pound cake. Kids don't get too excited about pound cake. I like it. It's good. It's better than tea cakes or scones. But it's not an iced cake, pie, or cobbler. It's more of a little-old-lady tea-party stable staple than a snack or treat.

My paternal grandmother excelled when it came to entertaining and serving a large formal lunch or dinner, but when it came to goodies in the pantry, we were left with pound cake topped with strawberries and Cool Whip.

My maternal grandmother always had a Tupperware container of fudge cake squares. She was known for two recipes: pancakes and fudge cake. I have written at great length about her pancakes and have actually formed a food products company in which her pancake recipe is sold in mix form all across the country. Her stable staple, though, was fudge cake.

My grandmother's fudge cake was neither fudge nor cake, though it was more closely related to cake than fudge. The recipe was one that probably came from her childhood home of Nashville and followed her to Danville, Kentucky, Macon and Atlanta, Georgia, the Upper East Side of Manhattan, and finally, my hometown of Hattiesburg, Mississippi.

Fudge cake squares are more like brownies than cake, but fudgier than a normal brownie. I loved the recipe as a kid and I love eating fudge cake squares today. Homemade fudge cake might be the coup de grâce of stable staples.

Nowadays my stable staple is oatmeal. Not oatmeal cookies— oatmeal—the breakfast gruel that is eaten with a spoon. It's the item that is always in my pantry, not fudge cake, or pound cake, or even angel food cake—oatmeal. Sometimes middle age and responsibility stink.

Icees, Bikes, and Brain Freezes

Over the past few weeks my family has been catching up on movies, sometimes seeing two films in one day.

I love movies. As a matter of fact, the two things I love most about owning my own business are—getting to wear whatever I want to work (no neckties, ever) and being able to see a matinee in the middle of the day.

During the summer we bring our children to matinees, and lately, I have devised an effective method that turns the average movie visit into a well-oiled and precise system which puts us in our seats just as the previews start.

After parking, I go to the ticket counter to purchase tickets. My wife flanks me and—with the kids in tow—heads immediately for the concession stand line. Once I arrive with the tickets, I replace her in line and she and the children find our seats (first row above the walkway in front of the rail). Fast, efficient, effective.

Our concession order is the same every time—a large Diet Coke for me, water for my wife, a small popcorn for the family to share, Milk Duds for me, an orange drink for the girl, and a cola-flavored Icee for the boy.

Yesterday, as I was making my way to our seats carrying all of the concession-stand booty, I took a sip of my son's Icee. I hadn't had an Icee in years. It was good. I took another sip and another. I was instantly transformed to the hot summers of my youth, riding my Schwinn bicycle around the Hillendale neighborhood of my hometown, Hattiesburg, Mississippi. I took another sip, this time a bigger and longer one. By the time I reached our seats the Icee was half-gone and I had a brain freeze.

My son took one look at his Icee (or what was left of it) and sent me back to the concession stand.

I purchased most of the Icees of my youth at a convenience store called the Minit Mart. It was the junk-food capital of our neighborhood and the central meeting place for both bicycling kids and teenagers with driver's licenses. The Minit Mart was made famous in a Jimmy Buffett song that told a story of the composer and his friends—during their college days at the University of Southern Mississippi—utilizing a five-finger discount with peanut butter and sardines. In the song, the name was changed to "Mini Mart" I assume to protect the not-so innocent.

Icees were a great portable drink. In those days most soft drinks came in glass bottles, not the safest vessels to be drinking while riding a bicycle. An Icee—cold and sweet—was served in a paper cup with a long stroon.

A stroon was a half straw/half spoon that could be used for slurping and spooning in alternate steps. I always felt the stroon was included to prevent brain freeze. If one slowly spooned the Icee into one's mouth, the chances of a full-scale brain freeze decreased dramatically, though most kids still sucked Icees through a straw, quickly delivering the cool sugary liquid to the stomach, and consequently a burning freeze to the brain.

The brain freeze, sometimes known as an ice cream headache, is a medical phenomenon that, according to my research (read: ten minutes on Google), has no medical explanation. I never knew anyone who could get through a hot Mississippi summer without contracting at least one severe, but quickly dissipating, case of brain freeze. A fan of Icees would deal with the brain freeze almost every time he or she drank one.

Sno-cones were summer treats, but they always seemed more like ice cream than a beverage. Cokes in the little bottles were good, but only when stationary, and in those days not many days or nights were spent in a stationary position.

As adults we stop doing things that we did daily as kids—rolling in the grass for no reason, running so long and so hard that it took several minutes to regain your breath, and not on a treadmill or stair climber but in the schoolyard and through the woods. We rode bikes and played board games, and tackle football in friends' front yards, and we drank Icees.

Today a gynecology clinic stands where the Minit Mart did, we don't roll in the grass for fear of staining our clothes, and bicycles mostly stay parked. We have turned into calorie counters and self-appointed food police. We have traded in our Icees for fruit smoothies and we might just be the lesser for it.

Beautiful Swimmers

When I was a child my family owned a small, rickety fish camp on the Pascagoula River near the Gulf Coast of Mississippi.

When the year's final school bell rang, shorts were put on, shoes were kicked off, and the slow pace of summer kicked in. I spent those days fishing, trolling for shrimp, and water-skiing.

In an era before catch-limits, we filled ice chests full of redfish—this, a full decade before Prudhomme blackened one in a skillet and started the national craze that created the subsequent redfish shortage. Other days we attached a small shrimp trolling net to the back of our boat. We trolled slowly all afternoon, hauling in the net every hour or so and separating shrimp from the other sea life that had been netted. Most of the other species were tossed back into the water except for the occasional flounder or sheepshead. We then returned to the small camp and boiled the shrimp just minutes out of the water.

All summer we kept crab traps in the water. No matter where we were traveling on the river, or into the Gulf, we stopped on our way home to check the crab traps. The day's crab catch was added to the ice chest and the crabs were boiled and picked that evening.

The refrigerator was always full of crabmeat, usually in the form of West Indies Salad. My mother loved West Indies Salad and was never too far from a Tupperware bowlful and a box of crackers.

West Indies Salad is a simple creation of crabmeat with a light vinaigrette dressing and is said to have been created by Bill Bailey, a Mobile restaurateur who operated a long-running establishment on the Dauphin Island Parkway. My mother used a recipe from the 1964 Mobile Junior League cookbook, *Recipe Jubilee!*

As Labor Day drew nearer, afternoon showers became lighter, the days grew shorter, and the crabs traveled upriver with the brackish water. I can remember using hand nets to scoop crabs out of the shallows of the tiny beach near our swimming hole, always returning the sponge crabs (those bearing eggs) to the water. On some days, ice chests could be filled in mere minutes.

The generic and specific name for the Gulf blue crab is *Callinectes sapidus*, and according to the Mississippi Department of Marine Resources website, "Its generic name, *Callinectes* is a combination of two Latin words meaning 'beautiful swimmer,' while its specific name, *sapidus*, means 'savory.'"

I have always loved the term "beautiful swimmer," and though the blue crab's swimming motion is more of a herky-jerky sideways scamper than a graceful and fluid movement worthy of the title beautiful swimmer, I think the name is befitting if only for the crustacean's wonderful flavor, unmatched versatility, and culinary stature in the Gulf South.

The three most beautiful words in the Mississippi cooking lexis are: jumbo lump crabmeat. The majority of my restaurant career has been filled using dishes featuring crabmeat. It is the first and foremost ingredient in my larder. One would have a hard time finding more than a dozen savory seafood dishes that couldn't be improved substantially by the addition of crabmeat. It is sweet, and delicate, and versatile.

Since childhood I have associated the month of August with crabs. It is the most plentiful and economical month for purchasing crabmeat, and to this day, the abundance allows me and my chefs to focus on developing dishes featuring the Gulf's most versatile delicacy. At the Crescent City Grill in Hattiesburg we use over four-hundred pounds of fresh crabmeat each week during the annual August crabmeat promotion. The slow and tedious effort of picking through the fragile lobes in search of stray shell or cartilage is worth every man hour of overtime.

My mother sold the fish camp twenty years ago. A few years after my son was born, I drove down to see if I might be able to buy the property back from its current owners. The old camp, the neighboring camps— the entire area was in such a state of disrepair that I immediately lost the desire to return, and haven't.

Today, summer is shorter and the pace is faster. My kids don't have the luxury of a Memorial Day–to–Labor Day vacation as school now starts in the middle of August. Something seems wrong about a world that makes a kid sit in a hot classroom while there are so many beautiful swimmers to be caught.

I Am Not on Al Gore's Christmas Card List

I stirred up a lot of trouble when I was a kid.

Possessing an overactive imagination and a hyperactive disposition, I was responsible for a fair share of the havoc created in and around my school and neighborhood.

Most of the parents in the neighborhood had, on at least one occasion, found the need to admonish me about my actions and activities. Whether I was running over Dr. Phillips's newly planted shrubbery on my bicycle, or soaking Dr. Ross's important medical papers by giving an impromptu demonstration of his new underground sprinkler system, I was responsible for countless acts of unintentional destruction and mayhem through the years.

Most of the incidents were unintended and harmless. I never flushed a M-80 down a toilet or ran over someone in my car. As a matter of fact, I don't think I have ever inflicted deliberate physical harm on anyone.

I have made it 47 years without destroying too much around my hometown. But I have just recently learned that I may be responsible for the end of the world as we know it.

The end of the world—that's a heavy burden to bear. Maybe my principal, Mr. Curry, was right when he told my ninth-grade class that I was "Nothing but trouble" and "would never amount to anything."

Growing up, I always thought that the end of the world would come from a nuclear holocaust instigated by the Russians. They'd bomb us, we'd bomb them, and both countries would continue to bomb each other while we squatted in school corridors with our heads tucked between our knees.

Today I learned that the end of the world won't come from mutual nuclear annihilation, or terrorist attacks, or any of the fun stuff we always imagined. No. The world will cease to exist because I am fat.

I just read a *New York Times* story that quoted a British scientist who believes that fat people are causing global warming. I can't cite the science behind the fat-people-are-going-to-kill-us-all theory, but you can Google it and take the time to read the study if you like.

A man named Dr. Phil Edwards in London makes his case by stating that fat people eat more (really?) and are more likely to drive instead of walk, creating more CO_2 gas emissions and causing the earth to warm (note to reader: I deserve columnist credit here for skipping the obvious fat-people-and-gas-emissions joke).

So if fat people are causing global warming, and if my home state of Mississippi is the perennial statistical leader as the most obese state in the country, that means that I am writing this column from Armageddon headquarters. No wonder I'm not on Al Gore's Christmas card list.

Remember, Mississippi, the next time you ask for seconds on pork chops, a little more of the polar ice cap will melt away. Eat blackberry cobbler for dessert and watch sea levels rise. Biscuits for breakfast—deforestation in the Amazon.

We Mississippians are used to 98 percent humidity on hundred-degree afternoons. We laugh in the face of global warming. Of course, we are laughing with our mouths full.

Mr. Curry always said, "You boys better stop eating all of those hamburgers and pizza. It'll kill you." Who knew?

I survived childhood. My neighborhood is still standing. Today, Dr. Phillips's shrubs—notwithstanding recent holes in the ozone layer—are over eighteen feet tall. Dr. Ross's sprinkler system is in perfect working condition and his grass is greener than ever. It seems that I have made it through all of the challenges of growing up, only to learn that I have been eating us into oblivion.

Pass the potatoes, please.

The Invasion of the Whores de Orvrays

"They're gonna have Mexican prostitutes there," said Forrest.

"How do you know?" I said.

"I heard Mrs. Wagner on the telephone. They're bringing them in from some town south of the border. Mexico, probably. A town called Orvrays, I think it was."

"That's not necessarily in Mexico," said Chris. "Orvrays could be any Latin American country." Chris was our intellectual. His father was a college professor.

So began the most memorable episode of the summer of 1972—my sixth-grade year—the two-week period our entire neighborhood spent in anticipation of busloads of love-sick floozies invading our town from somewhere south of the border.

The eavesdropee, Mrs. Wagner, was a native of Hungary. It was said that she came from the same town from which the Gabor sisters hailed. Even though she had lived in South Mississippi for eighteen years, her accent was thick and awkward. She pronounced "with" as "weet" and "the" as "dee" and had an affinity for goulash and paprika. Accent or not, there was no mistaking the word "whores." It was the world's oldest profession and, along with it, the world's oldest pronunciation. There was no doubt in anyone's mind that they were talking about exotic and lustful Latin ladies and they were probably en route to our town at that exact minute.

It was widely understood that Mrs. Wagner, being European, had a different sensibility than the other mothers in the neighborhood. "She's more open-minded," Chris said. "She has a laissez-faire attitude."

"You mean she likes girls?"

"No. She's liberal. And she asked who was bringing the whores de Orvrays. I heard it. She said 'de,' but my sister said that 'de' means 'of' in Spanish. They're whores of Orvrays, Mexico, and they're coming to the Johnsons' party. Just think, Mexican hookers in our neighborhood."

"I wonder if Hugh Hefner will be there, too," I said.

"Are you sure she didn't say Norway?"

"Nope, she said Orvrays and they'll be here in two weeks."

The news spread from brother to brother, brother to sister, sister to mother, mother to father, and within a matter of hours word of the upcoming Johnson party had traveled to the outermost reaches of the Hillendale subdivision.

For the next two weeks, every woman in a twelve-block radius had a telephone cocked and loaded between her shoulder and ear, every father was meeting another father in the backyard, bridge clubs were abuzz, and beauty parlors were rife with scandalous scuttlebutt. All were covering the same subject: the painted ladies that were coming to the Johnsons' party. The Bible Belt gossip line in our small Southern town was on all-out full-bore ringing-off-the-hook red alert.

In a town where the local district attorney had banned *Last Tango in Paris* from being shown in local theaters, a busload of whores was a noteworthy event. At the grocery store, at the ballpark, and at church—male, female, young, and old—everyone was talking about the upcoming Johnson party.

Three days before the party, Mildred Baker passed away while sitting in the dryer chair at Marilyn's Beauty Parlor. She had gone under the dome around 8:30 a.m., had a massive coronary, then sat—stiff and unattended, beehive baking—until closing time, when the nail girl realized Mildred "hadn't moved in a while." The coroner was never able to pinpoint the exact time of death due to the elongated exposure to the heat of the dryer, but most believe she passed sometime around 9:30 a.m., after Celia Rhodes and Betty Chapel came in talking about the Johnson party.

The men of the neighborhood were uncharacteristically low-key. There was a different air about them—a flicker of hope. Some publicly disparaged Mr. Johnson; some secretly wished they could trade places.

The event was turning out to be more scandalous than the Franklin Christmas Tree Controversy six months earlier. The Franklin family was from "somewhere up north," my mother used to say. I later found out that they were from Kentucky... a northern state to most in the area. On their first Christmas in town, the Franklins had committed the cardinal Yuletide sin: blue lights on a metallic silver Christmas tree. My mother wrote it off as the act of Catholics, others blamed the Franklins' Northern breeding, most chalked it up to a lack of good taste. Phones were busy for weeks.

Like the Franklins, the upcoming party's host, Dick Johnson, was an interloper. He had arrived two summers prior after being hired as the new marketing manager at one of the town's banks. "Marketing," my mother said. "He's probably from New York." He and his two sons moved in to the old Tyler home two blocks from my house. The Tylers had moved out after getting the first divorce ever granted in Forrest County, Mississippi—an event, as it turned out, even more scandalous than a silver and blue Christmas tree.

Mr. Johnson was a Jack Cassidy look-alike who sported tiny Speedo bathing suits around the country club swimming pool, kept *Playboy* on his bedside table, and wore a goatee. His teenage sons tortured cats and shot at neighborhood kids with BB guns. Over the years, there had been rampant stories of wild key-parties, skinny-dipping, swinging, and all manner of sinful and hedonistic debauchery at the Johnsons'. Certainly a party with exotic Latin ladies of the evening shipped in from Mexico wouldn't be a stretch.

The Johnson party was a turning point in our adolescence. Until then the highlight of our hot Mississippi summers had been prank calling neighbors on the telephone, the main victims being the family of a college professor named Dr. Orange. "Is Dr. Apple there?" we would ask, stifling giggles. "I'm sorry, you've got the wrong fruit," an Orange on the other end would reply. It was always good for a laugh, and I think for at least the first two-hundred times, the Orange family got a kick out of it, too.

On the day of the party we awoke early and the entire day was spent in the neighborhood tree house across the street from the Johnsons'. We wanted to see the whores from Orvrays arrive, watch them pile out of the limousine, and sashay half-dressed into the house. The music would then be turned up, the lights would be turned down, and all manner of sexual depravity would ensue.

As night fell, teenagers looking for action, frat boys in search of cheap thrills, and most of the uninvited men of the neighborhood loaded into Jeeps, vans, and station wagons and cruised up and down the street trying to catch a glimpse of a real, live hooker. At 7:30 pm guests had begun arriving and there wasn't a whore in sight.

Had we not gotten out of bed early enough? Had we missed the floozies' arrival the night before? Did Mr. Johnson smuggle them into the house in the catering van? At 9:15 p.m. we sent Chris over to get answers.

As he walked across the street, Chris recognized a catering waitress on a smoke break in the garage. He pulled the girl, a friend of his sister's, aside and whispered, "When are the whores gonna get here?"

"What?"

"The whores? Mrs. Wagner said that there were going to be whores from Orvrays, Mexico, here."

The caterer looked puzzled for a minute, paused, and then grimaced, "You idiot. What Mrs. Wagner said was: h-o-r-s (or) d-'-o-e-u-v-r-e-s (derves). Hors d'oeuvres, not whores de Orvrays, or whores from Orvrays."

"You mean they're not coming." Chris said.

"Who?" said the caterer.

"The whores."

"No. You want a cheese straw?"

Chris wasn't listening. Despondent, he walked back over to the tree house and gave us the news.

The neighborhood slowly slipped back into its predictable routine. Ladies found new telephone-gossip topics, the Franklins fell into lockstep and switched to Scotch pine, and finger foods became finger foods again— although, for some strange reason, the term canapé fell into favor. My friends and I entered junior high at a new school, and spent the next three years in search of female foreign exchange students from Mexico. Mr. Johnson took a job in Dallas and, according to Mrs. Wagner, abandoned the banking trade to become a male model—that, or a frail bottle.

For years afterward the men of the neighborhood could be seen cruising the streets at night in the family Chevrolet, always slowing at the Johnson house—a distant look of longing in their eyes. None ever stopped; they always kept on driving.

The Mississippi Legislature Is Banning Fried Foods from Our School Cafeterias.

At least we're better off than Rhode Island. Up there, they've banned talking in the school cafeteria during lunch. Well actually only one school has barred talking, but you know how these things work—once one falls the others are sure to follow.

The legislature has been trying to outlaw soft drinks, too. Fried steak fingers and imitation veal cutlets, I can understand, but I might have to draw the line at Diet Coke.

The legislature is citing our number-one-in-the-nation obesity rate as reason for the fried-food ban. Go figure, we're always number forty-nine or fifty in every other statistical category, then we finally reach number one and the politicians want to take the designation away from us. We're fat. So what, where's the Lard Lobby when you need them?

My elementary school, Thames Elementary, had a great line-em-up-in-the-back-of-the-room-and-grab-your-tray-for-butter-beans-and-lime-Jell-O-and-a-yeast-roll cafeteria. We ate vegetables, cornbread, strawberry shortcake, and turnip greens on days when they mowed the playground. I don't remember an inordinate amount of fried food being served, but that was in the 1960s, maybe things have changed.

In the sixth grade I was sent to a small private school in town. There, free of state regulations, we ate hamburgers and pizza and something called a steak sandwich, though I don't think any form of steak was used in its preparation.

Note: The statement you are about to read is 100 percent accurate (I have friends who will verify it): For four consecutive years of high school I ate a small frozen pepperoni pizza, two Coca-Colas, and an oatmeal cream pie every day, day in day out. Occasionally I would eat a Richeyburger (named after the lunch lady Mrs. Richey) with hot fries. Not French fries that were sliced from real potatoes and fried in grease, but light crunchy fried bits of potato parts, formed into French fry shapes and seasoned with some type of spicy powder, a side item in which—in the words of John Lennon—nothing is real.

The Richeyburger was cooked from a frozen state in one of the earliest examples of a microwave. The school microwave was as large as a desk, and most of the mothers were a little suspicious of it. "How can it cook so quickly? It can't be good for you. Don't watch the food cook, you'll go blind."

My high school years were during the Cold War. No one had a microwave in their home kitchen in those days. The father of a friend believed that microwaves were a communist plot to embed radioactivity into everyday American civilization. My friend brought his lunch every day.

The pizzas were made by a food vending company; they were frozen, and then shipped to the school to lay in wait in the deep freeze before being placed into the communist cooking apparatus. My friends at the public school were eating fish sticks, chicken-fried steak, and fried burritos with a wiener in the middle. We were surviving on a steady diet of Richeyburgers, hot fries, oatmeal cream pies, and Coca-Cola.

The man who owned the local Coca-Cola bottling plant was on the board of directors at the school, and all three of his children were enrolled there. We had Coke machines and snack machines in every hallway and break room. It was great. Public schools didn't have vending machines in those days. Oatmeal cream pies were there for the taking, along with tubular packets of peanuts for adding to your bottle of Coke. There was no Diet Coke in those days, although some of the teachers drank Tab.

Ten years ago, I would have had a field day writing a column against this new piece of legislation. Today I, as a father of two children and in the middle of a three-month diet, think it seems like sound reasoning, though I could be suffering from a lack of sustenance.

I don't want my kids eating hot fries, microwave pizza, and burritos with a wiener in the middle. Could we amend the bill to include a once-a-month serving of fried chicken? Actually, that should be a requirement in every Southern school, though I will officially go on record as being in favor of doing away with steak nuggets forever.

At least our children can talk while they eat, hopefully not with their mouths full.

For Whom the School Bell Tolls

I am now the father of two school-aged children. This week my daughter enters fourth grade and my son enters kindergarten (let's all bow our heads and say a prayer for Mrs. Prine, his teacher).

Back to school means returning to the daily routine of getting to bed early, waking up early, the before-school scramble, and waiting in a long line for the after-school pickup. It also means lunches away from home.

Throughout the summer my children eat late breakfasts and large lunches. Lunch might be eaten at 11:30 a.m. or at 2:45 p.m. It depends on several factors: how hot they get while playing outside, what's on television, which friend is visiting, or what's being served. Not so in the school year. Back to school means back to a daily routine that will be followed—with the exception of a few brief holiday interruptions—until next May.

I love the fall. Though Mississippi won't see a hint of fall-like weather until the middle of October, it is my favorite season. The excitement that comes with returning to school—a new teacher, new books and supplies, the possibility of making new friends—is an excitement that we never relive in our adult years. Fall just smells different.

The sense of smell, like the sense of taste, has strong connections with our memories. Today, the scent of pencil shavings from a pencil sharpener will instantly take me back to Mrs. Smith's fourth-grade class at Thames Elementary School. Nowhere in my average workday do I encounter the smell of pencil shavings; these days it's all rolling-ball pens with precise grips and Microsoft Word with dull and odorless keyboards and screens.

In my youth, the aroma of yeast rolls wafted through the corridors of school signaling the approaching lunch hour. My elementary school had an honest-to-God line-them-up-in-the-back-of-the-room, grab-a-tray-and-a-carton-of-warm-milk, we-only-eat-greens-on-the-days-they-mow-the-grass cafeteria.

The school cafeteria is an important place for childhood socialization.

One is not supposed to talk in a classroom; recess is usually spent running, playing, or competing in kickball or basketball games. In the lunchroom the pressure is off. That is where the art and politics of conversation is learned, friends are made, urban legends are spread, and meals are shared.

Sharing a meal with friends is one of the few elementary school activities that we carry into adulthood. We no longer dust the chalk off of erasers, or line up in single-file lines, we don't turn in homework, take tests, or carry a lunch box. I haven't played kickball in several decades, but I share a meal with friends all of the time, and I don't do it much differently than I did when I was ten years old.

In those days lunch boxes were—like today's bumper stickers—a statement or extension of one's personality or views. I had a Charlie Brown and Snoopy lunch box. It was lame and didn't really make a bold statement about who I thought I was, or what I believed, but it was on sale when my mom bought it, and that was that. As a kid I always wanted a Beatles lunch box. In retrospect I had more in common with Charlie Brown than John Lennon, but a kid has to dream.

A few years ago I compiled a list of the items that I longed for as a kid but never got. The list was long and extensive. Most were toys that I no longer wanted or material junk that no longer mattered. Though, sitting at the top of the list were a Beatles lunch box and a lava lamp.

I write this column surrounded by three large lava lamps and a Beatles lunch box, reminiscing about the school cafeteria, yeast rolls, and the many hours I spent dusting erasers, a punishment then, but a fond memory today.

Bake Sales

Many of our childhood school activities fall by the wayside as we grow older.

Today I don't play tetherball or box hockey. I haven't roller skated in years. I don't think I've played an all-out game of dodgeball since the Carter administration, and I haven't played tackle football since I was in my early twenties, though I'd love the opportunity to go back out there and tear a few of my tendons, pull some muscles, and break a few of my bones.

Some activities I miss, others not so much. If I never attend another pep rally, or work on an algebraic equation, I'll be OK.

One school activity that played a fairly important role in my youth is: the bake sale. Nowadays, I never happen upon a bake sale and I am a lesser man for it.

I loved a bake sale. It seemed like there were two or three a week in my school. The thing that made bake sales in my junior high and high school so memorable was the mothers who baked the product. I grew up in a neighborhood filled with excellent and dedicated cooks. They baked well and they baked often.

The bake sales of my youth were held in the hallways of my school. They were mostly low-key affairs. All one needed was a card table, poster board, Magic Markers, a shoe box for the money, and the store was open. The table was always filled with homemade sweets of all types.

Caramel apples were available, but they tended to stick to braces and headgears. Cakes and pies were not popular bake sale items as one needed a fork and plate to eat them and most bake-sale foods needed to be eaten on-the-run between classes. The Rice Krispie treat was the most popular item at my school's bake sales, and they were always the first to sell out. Brownies were a close second, cookies came in third, but nothing ever surpassed the goshamighty Rice Krispie treat.

I was on the road last week, returning home late from a speaking engagement, and stopped in a convenience store to load up on caffeine and a snack. I didn't want a candy bar, chips, or a microwave sandwich, and I'm not quite dedicated enough to eat a protein bar, granola, or mixed nuts. As I browsed the aisle, there it was—the zenith of the high-school bake sale—a Rice Krispie treat. I didn't know they packaged them for sale in stores.

I read the nutritional information on the back of the package and was surprised to learn that the treats were relatively low in saturated fat, cholesterol, and sugar. Who knew we were eating fairly healthy at bake sales in the 1970s?

I bought one.

As I drove home, the Rice Krispie treat took me back to the days at my school. One bite and I was instantly dusting erasers, sharpening pencils, and nervously waiting outside the principal's office.

We need more bake sales in our adult lives. We tend to gravitate towards black-tie galas, draw-downs, and wine tastings; but I would gladly trade them all for a rickety card table loaded with sweets.

If I were holding a bake sale today, I would sell nothing but Rice Krispie treats and sweet potato brownies. My sweet potato brownie recipe was in my most recent cookbook. It was one of the most popular recipes in the book.

A famous New Orleans restaurateur once said, "Do you know why kids love peanut butter and jelly sandwiches? It's because peanut butter and jelly sandwiches are good." Ditto Rice Krispie treats.

Chapter 2
Fatherhood

Blue Rabbits
A Lamentation

I dismantled a baby bed today. Took the screwdriver and wrench out of the drawer—a location where they have probably resided since the bed was constructed—sat on the floor of the boy's room and took apart the small bed, bolt by bolt.

A millisecond ago I was sitting in the same spot, assembling the bed. The nursery was new. Even though we knew it was to be a girl, we opted for the blue wallpaper decorated with Victorian-era rabbits. The nursery, at that time, was pristine. Every pillow and Lamaze toy was carefully placed in an aesthetically strategic location to sit and wait on the arrival of the new addition to the family, the first addition to the family.

Pictures, many pictures, were taken of the room the night before the girl arrived. Many more were taken after her return from the hospital. Not as many were taken when the boy came home. It's true, you know, what they say about the second child and pictures. I will regret not having those pictures one day. I know it, yet I still don't take the pictures.

The room will soon take on a new look. It will have to be redecorated. The Victorian rabbits will be out of our lives forever, the rabbits that have been there since the beginning of this new chapter. The rabbits that watched us play on the floor and splash in the tub. Mostly they watched us in the rocking chair. They were close then.

Maybe I will leave a strip of blue-rabbit wallpaper in a dark corner by the baseboard or behind a piece of furniture—a dresser or the new bed. Maybe I will wallpaper the inside of a cabinet so, when pictures won't suffice for memories lost, the wife and I can sit on the floor, open the cabinet, like a portal to another time, and remember a place when crying and laughing occurred within moments of each other. A time when sweet songs were sung, first words were spoken, and whispers were heard, on occasion. A time of soft, classical lullabies, lavender-perfumed baby-wash, and creaking doors. A time, the first time, that the huge undiscovered box that had theretofore been hidden deep inside my soul, was opened, and I learned of my enormous capacity to love, to give love and receive love, and how good it felt to be truly needed. A wonderful time, a happy time, the time of the little Victorian rabbits.

The wife has been thinking lately. We'll see a baby in his mother's arms and we are struck by a growing feeling of melancholy. Not a groundswell of emotion, but a gentle sadness. We have fleeting thoughts of how good it feels when a baby is cradled in your arms. Maybe we didn't take full advantage of all of the baby-holding opportunities given to us. I wonder if I will regret not holding babies as much as I regret not having pictures.

The bed will now go to the attic, a place where memories live, or go to die. It will be placed alongside the bins of baby clothes, strollers, high chairs, and infant toys. A place where it will stay until, many years from now, another little one will be brought into our lives with the single mission of opening yet another undiscovered box hidden deep inside our souls.

And then we will play on the floor next to the bed, and splash in the lavender beside the creaking door, and open the cabinet to the Victorian rabbits.

Bathroomitis and the Joys of Lavender Soap

My four-year-old son used to be an extremely rowdy restaurant customer.

Early on, he screamed like a banshee while eating in restaurants. Later, during his terrible twos, he graduated to holding conversations with customers seated at surrounding tables while they were hopelessly trying to finish their meal. Today, in terms of enjoying a peaceful meal away from home, we are miles ahead of where we were in his early years. He no longer yells and screams at the table and rarely, if ever, disturbs neighboring patrons.

Nowadays he has a strange new affliction. I call it bathroomitis. He has traded in his large voice for a small bladder.

For some strange reason, restaurants make him want to go to the bathroom. I can't explain this phenomenon but it's real. Five minutes after we are seated in a restaurant, something clicks in his brain, then travels southward, and out of his mouth comes, "Daddy, I have to go to the bathroom."

"But you just went five minutes ago, before we left the house."

"I know, but I have to go again." And he does.

Early on, I assumed his multiple restroom visits were a crafty ploy he had devised to keep us away from the table, allowing him to wander through restaurants. But every time I took him to the restroom, he did, in fact, need to go.

One trip to the lavatory per restaurant visit wouldn't be bad. But, as with everything in our family, this isn't done in moderation. He often makes four trips in one restaurant stay.

I began to think that it might be a medical problem, but this strange phenomenon only occurs in restaurants. At home he's a camel. He can go hours without ever stepping foot in a bathroom. In a restaurant he develops a bladder the size of an English pea.

Consequently, I have become an expert on restaurant bathrooms. I know what every restaurant lavatory looks like from Jackson to New Orleans. I know which eatery offers the best soap, who mops their floor regularly, and who never restocks the paper towels.

"How was your meal today, sir?"

"The meal was fine. However, that mint-green hue you chose when painting your bathroom walls makes one look a little peaked when washing one's hands for the fourth time. Also, you soap is a little fruity. Try something with lavender or herbs."

"Will you be having dessert today, Mr. St.John?"

"Yes, I'll take mine in stall number three. And could you please restock the paper towels."

These days, at the end of a meal, I have visited the bathroom sink so often that by the time dessert arrives, my overly washed hands have morphed into that I've-been-swimming-for-hours prune look.

I've tried everything. I talked to a pediatrician friend who assured me that nothing was out of order. I had the boy checked for diabetes, I even changed my son's restaurant beverage of choice—Sprite—to water, thinking that the lemon-lime combination acted as a diuretic in his system. To no avail—I still heard those four familiar words multiple times during a restaurant visit: "Daddy I gotta go!"

I have become quite the connoisseur when it comes to paper towels. I know a three-ply from a pseudo-two-ply, and can spot a single-ply towel from a mile away. I have developed a deep hatred for those old-fashioned pull-the-towel-down-from-inside-the-machine-while the-used-cloth-loops-back-into-the-machine gas-station-style towel dispensers. As luck would have it, my son loves those contraptions. I turned around once and found that he had crawled up into the towel loop and was hanging by his feet, upside down in the bathroom. "Look, Daddy, no hands!"

Having a son with a chronic case of bathroomitis makes one appreciate the little things in life such as adequate restroom ventilation, distance from the dining room to the washroom, and low-to-the-ground child-friendly urinals.

Ultimately, I have come to believe that his Bathroomitis is nothing more than a Pavlovian response directly related to the excitement of visiting a restaurant and the sheer anticipation of enjoying a restaurant meal. In the end, he's just like his old man, he loves food and he gets excited when he's about to eat a mess of it.

The Sword, the Bathroom, and the Pirate

My son has a the bladder the size of an English pea.

He also likes pirates.

These two seemingly diametrically opposed statements converged during one fateful incident in a restaurant bathroom.

I have often written of my son's bouts with bathroomitis. Bathroomitis is a malady that strikes early in life and usually affects boys in the three- to five-year-old age group. It is not a condition recognized by the American Medical Association, but it is surely experienced by fathers of young boys everywhere. The symptoms are easily detected and the condition is effortlessly diagnosed. During any restaurant visit, my son makes multiple trips to bathroom.

He might not need to go for hours while at home. But take him to a restaurant and he's up every five minutes.

What does any of this have to do with pirates, you say? Read on, dear reader, read on.

My five-year-old son chooses a favorite toy as some might choose a pair of underwear. It is a random procedure that usually involves picking up the first thing he sees in his toy chest or the toy nearest the back door on the way out of the house. No deep thought goes into the process and he likes it that way.

During a forty-eight hour period in June his favorite toy happened to be the Elite Operations Medieval Fantasy Sword, Barberia design, from Toys "R" Us, $5.95. Granted, an ancient Celtic sword is out of place in the world of pirates and buccaneers, but five-year-olds don't split hairs when playing games; it was the toy that was at the top of the pile when he was in search of a pirate weapon, and one sword is as good as another when forcing someone to walk the plank.

The sword is approximately thirty-six inches long and is made of hard, shiny plastic. If one didn't know it was a harmless toy, it might look like an intimidating weapon. At a quick glance, it might even look like a real sword. In the hands of my son, a swashbuckling kindergartener, it can be the cause of much grief and embarrassment.

While driving my daughter to camp last month, we were to meet my mother-in-law, who was going to babysit the five-year-old buccaneer for a week. The rendezvous point for the obligatory child trade-off was a restaurant just off of the interstate in Vicksburg, Mississippi.

At this point I should note that when my son chooses his toy-of-the-moment, the choice is made and he doesn't turn back. At least until the next toy catches his fancy. Nevertheless, the toy, whatever it may be, stays in his hands. He doesn't let go. Whether it is a small rubber ball, a *Star Wars* action figure, a *SpongeBob* pencil eraser, or a pirate sword, it goes everywhere with him. It is the parental path of least resistance. Better to let the boy keep his toy—whether in church or in a restaurant—than to deal with the alternative. As parents we choose our battles. His affection for the toy-of-the-moment is a battle we choose not to fight.

Back to the mother-in-law trade-off.

So, we were in the rendezvous point making the exchange when the wannabe pirate was struck with his usual case of bathroomitis. I took him to the restroom, sword in hand, to do what needed to be done. Unfortunately it was a small restroom and there was only one stall, and what needed to be done, needed to be done in that stall. As fate would have it, the stall was occupied. I know this because my son said, "Look, Daddy, cowboy boots." He had done as we all do—the universal method to make sure the stall door isn't stuck and there's actually someone inside—the bend-down-and-peek-under-the-stall-door maneuver.

While we were waiting for the stall to empty, nature called. Daddy was struck with a case of bathroomitis, and I went to the urinal to stand and do what one does at a urinal. While standing, I turned around to check on my son.

The boy was bent over with his arm reaching under the bottom of the adjacent stall. Unfortunately it was the arm that held the aforementioned pirate sword and he was waving it back and forth on the other side of the stall wall.

I was stunned for a moment and baffled to the point of speechlessness as I tried to figure out why my son was waving the sword under the stall. Then I remembered the cowboy boots.

For some strange reason the man on the other side of the stall wall remained silent. Maybe he was struck speechless as he sat in his most private of private moments, dumbfounded as a thirty-six inch sword appeared under the stall wall swishing back and forth, cutting the air.

My son had a strange look on his face as he was up to his elbow in swordplay. It wasn't a look of mischievousness, but rather a look of determination to try and make contact with whatever might be on the other side of the wall. To my knowledge he never did.

"Stop!" was the only word that would come across my lips. He looked up at me puzzled. It was a look that said "Why in the world would I stop doing this? It's too much fun."

I grabbed him and ran out of the men's room, shoved him toward my mother-in-law, and said, "Run! Good luck! See you next week!"

In conclusion, to the cowboy-boot-wearing man who was nearly assaulted by the Elite Operations Medieval Fantasy Sword in the stall of the Shoney's restaurant in Vicksburg, Mississippi, around noon on June the 3rd, 2006, wherever you are, just blame it on a chronic case of bathroomitis.

Restaurant Bathrooms and Parenting

I was having lunch with my family in a very nice restaurant on the North Shore of Lake Pontchartrain the other day. The dining room was packed and everyone was dressed in their Easter finest.

Halfway through the appetizer course, my six-year-old son came walking out of the bathroom fastening his belt and zipping up his pants.

Typically, walking through a formal restaurant's dining room with one's pants unzipped would be written off as a slight breach of etiquette and chalked up to a first grader's eagerness to leave the restroom and return to the table, but for one minor detail—he hates to wear underwear.

The not-wearing-underwear dilemma has caused a few problems in his six short years—a trip to the principal's office in kindergarten after bragging to the third graders that he was "going commando," and a few notes from his teacher—but to date, no breach of decorum has been quite as severe as walking through the La Provence dining room letting it all hang out.

And when I say "all," I mean *all*. He flashed a good portion of the dining room. He returned to the table and continued to eat as if nothing unusual or out of the ordinary had occurred.

Welcome to my world.

In my short, yet eventful, parenting career, the Easter Flashing Incident is second only to the Mexican Restaurant Fiasco in terms of noteworthiness and impact.

During my son's terrible twos (which seemed to last all the way into his frightful fours), we were dining in a local Mexican restaurant. On this particular evening he was feeling fearless and independent and asked if he could go to the bathroom on his own. The restaurant was safe and the bathroom was not located near an exit, so the proud father in me replied, "Why, that's a big step, son. Of course you can go to the bathroom on your own." His mother frowned, but on this occasion, Dad's rule won the day.

After several minutes my son hadn't returned. My wife began to worry, but I assured her that everything was fine. After several more minutes she told me to go check on him, but I told her to hold firm, this was a big step for him. After several more minutes I gave in and excused myself to go find out what had happened.

The restroom was located on the far side of the restaurant adjacent to the main dining room. While walking, I noticed people seated in booths and tables staring at me and chuckling. As I got closer to the restroom, people were looking at me and laughing out loud. I wondered what could have happened in the five short minutes my son had been in the restroom to incite this reaction. As I drew even closer to the bathroom, I could hear his voice. I let out a sigh of relief. He was OK.

As I turned the corner, I saw my son, his reddened face peeking out of the bathroom door, his pants to his knees, screaming loudly into the dining room, "Will somebody wipe me?"

My brief relief turned to shock.

Understandably, the answer to his request—which had been shouted over and over and over and over, for the last three minutes—had been "NO." Each petition for assistance had elicited more laughter and anxiousness from the restaurant's customers. I did the dirty work and the two of us snuck out of the side door.

Today's lesson: If you have a son, escort him to the bathroom until he graduates from high school.

Keep me in your prayers. I need all of the help I can get.

The Elementary Vegan

The other day my eight-year-old daughter told me she had become a vegetarian.

A vegetarian? Oh, the betrayal. What hath my sins wrought? She comes from a long line of devout carnivores, what have I done to make God so angry?

She might as well have told me that she had just enlisted in the Symbionese Liberation Army. It was a skewer to the heart, a gut shot. I felt exactly how Ronald Regan must have felt when his daughter told him that she was a Democrat.

In a flash I saw my precious little daughter as a future member of PETA, splashing paint on her mother's fur coats, protesting on the streets dressed in nothing more than leopard-skin body paint, and driving around in a broken down Volkswagen van. In an instant she traded in her frilly dresses and pigtails to become a holistic healer in dirty jeans and dreadlocks.

I did what any carnivorously supportive father would do and said, "That's great, honey."

For a moment I thought about throwing the yes-but-Hitler-was-a-vegetarian jab, but my eight-year-old has no idea who Hitler was. Then I started thinking about Paul McCartney. He's a vegetarian. He's done OK for himself. Maybe this isn't the end of the world.

Her four-year-old little brother is nearly a vegetarian by accident. He almost exclusively eats yogurt, bananas, and snack crackers. His eating patterns have never bothered me. Maybe it's the label.

Later that day I asked, "But sweetie, your favorite food is cheeseburgers. Vegetarians don't get to eat cheeseburgers."

"I know," she said, and that was that.

I began to think of my family's future. No more bacon in the morning. No more ham and cheese sandwiches on Saturday afternoons. Thanksgiving is coming. Would I have to cook a tofu turkey to go along with the roasted turkey? And what about summer?

When I'm cooking steaks on the grill, will my daughter ask for soy burgers and veggie dogs?

Two days later, I noticed her eating chicken strips. "I thought you were a vegetarian," I said.

"I am a modified vegetarian."

"What is that?"

"The only meat I eat is fish or chicken."

"I don't think Paul McCartney gets to eat chicken strips, sweetie. Anyway, I thought the whole vegetarian thing was about not eating anything with a face."

"Yes, but fish and chickens have ugly faces."

I see. We only eat the ugly animals. You are *that* type of vegetarian. A glimmer of hope emerged. Now, with the aforementioned and ugly-faced fish and chicken back in the diet, I thought I would take a shot at the potential future inclusion of cows and pigs.

Looking forward to a weekend cookout in the backyard, I spent the next few days trying to point out how unsightly cows are. "Look at that Holstein, honey. Don't you think that's about the ugliest animal you've ever seen?" I searched for a rodeo on television, figuring that seeing bulls violently buck poor defenseless cowboys would conjure up visions of rib eyes and T-bones, but there was nothing on but *SpongeBob* reruns and NASCAR.

Next I looked for a video of the running of the bulls in Pamplona, hoping that the sight of mad and charging bulls chasing thousands of panicked Spaniards down the street would warrant, at least, a cheeseburger. To no avail.

Next on my agenda were pigs. I love bacon and sausage, and she used to. I knew that Wilbur the pig from the book *Charlotte's Web* was going to be my biggest obstacle, so I rummaged through all of her shelves looking for books with ugly and mean pigs in them. Did you know that it is almost impossible to find a children's book with an evil pig in it? All of the pigs in fairytales are innocent victims who get their houses blown down and lay around sleeping all the time.

"Look here, sweetie, Jack Spratt's wife ate nothing but fat. Do you think that was pig fat or beef fat?"

"Eating fat is gross," she said.

A slight miscalculation on my part, but I recovered with: "Yes, but it's the 'lean' that's so tasty, especially with a baked potato."

She didn't budge. She obviously inherited her mother's will.

Feeling defeated, I left the subject alone, choosing to let sleeping pigs lie. Eventually I came to the realization that she might be healthier in the long run if she never again ate meat.

And then, just as quickly as it came, it went away. One day she was watching her brother eat a cheeseburger (in between bites of yogurt and bananas) and asked for a bite.

I will have to admit that I was actually a little disappointed. My daughter's two-week bout with vegetarianism had added a worldly sophistication—along with a streak of thoughtful independence—to her personality. I was growing accustomed to it.

I sort of miss my little vegan and her independent thinking. Maybe I'll cook a tofu turkey for Thanksgiving after all... Nah.

After-School Snacks

One day last year, while my wife was out of town, I picked my daughter up from school.

On our way home we stopped by one of my restaurants to deliver some paperwork. While there, my daughter and I sat down in the dining room, shared a plate of French fries, and talked about school, church, work, and the joys of being a third grader. It was a spur-of-the-moment occasion and a good opportunity for a meaningful visit.

Last week, my daughter asked if I would pick her up from school again. "But what about your mom," I said. "She's not out of town and she always picks you up." My wife usually bakes cookies for the kids after school while they do their homework.

"Dad, I want you to pick me up so we can go eat French fries again like we did last year."

Wow. The first thing that hit me was that she remembered that afternoon. The second was that it had been over a year since the two of us sat down in my restaurant and shared a plate of fries.

Don't get me wrong, I spend a lot of time with my children, but that time is usually spent with my wife and son, too, all of us together. It was a treat to have my daughter make the request and was even more special that we spent the time in the dining room of my restaurant.

I picked her up that afternoon and we sat at a small table upstairs with a full view of the dining room. We ordered fires and soft drinks. It was three in the afternoon and the lunch traffic in the restaurant had long since cleared. While she dipped her fries in a ramekin of bleu cheese dressing we overheard a manager interviewing a potential employee at the next table.

I took the opportunity to explain the job-interview process and what a potential employer looks for when hiring someone. I told her about the benefits of a higher education and the importance of graduate degrees, and then we played a game in which we interviewed each other.

Although most of the mock interviews were spent joking and making up funny backgrounds and personal histories, she was able to think on her feet and deliver some extremely creative answers.

As a kid I ate a lot of oatmeal after school. I made bowls of instant oatmeal, baked oatmeal cookies, ate oatmeal cream pies, and drank a lot of Hawaiian Punch. My father died when I was six and my mom was usually in school or teaching school. My after school snacks were usually eaten in front of the television or running out of the door on my way out to play neighborhood football.

I don't know what it was about oatmeal and after school, but it—along with the occasional Milky Way bar—was my after-school snack of choice. In those days, French fries would have been a special occasion food.

Eating fries after school with my daughter was significant because the conversation was fun and the company was exceptional, but it was made even more special because she initiated it. We laughed, and ate, and enjoyed each other's companionship. She picked up a few pointers on applying for a job and begrudgingly learned the benefits of a master's degree.

It's good for a father to share a plate of fries with a daughter—for no other reason than to slow down and catch up—and if you can throw in a few laughs and a couple of life's lessons at the same time, it will serve as a memorable and magical moment.

Food Fight!

In the cafeteria scene of the 1978 movie *Animal House*, John Belushi pops up from behind a table and yells, "Food fight!" Chaos ensues. That was my first exposure to the phenomenon of thrown food.

There is a cafe near an outlet mall in Alabama where the employees of the restaurant throw yeast rolls at the customers. They don't do this in a fit of anger, or in an inspired moment of college hijinks, but they throw hot bread at paying customers on purpose.

A town in Spain hosts a food fight every year in which hundreds of citizens throw tomatoes at each other. They throw tomatoes at an annual festival in Colombia, South America, too. Italy is home to a festival where people throw oranges at one another.

My father-in-law—a man with the maturity level of your average eighth grader—once threw a roll at me in a backwoods catfish house. He missed and hit a large pulpwooder at a neighboring table. We both escaped to tell the tale, but barely.

My wife cooked a clean-the-cooler dinner last night. A clean-the-cooler dinner is a meal where one gets all of the old, passed-over, and mishmashed food items out of the refrigerator and freezer, and cooks them in one meal. It should be done approximately four times each year. Unfortunately, it only happens once a decade in my house.

My wife is a pack rat when it comes to food and spices. Shelf lives and expiration dates mean nothing to her. I constantly throw away all manner of outdated food in our cabinets.

Last night, there were two tins of leftover dinner rolls in the freezer. I am not exactly sure how old the rolls were, but they had probably been hiding behind the chopped spinach since Bill Clinton's first term.

She served two tins of the Clinton-era rolls for dinner.

"These rolls taste funny," my son said.

"What's up with the rolls, Mom?" said my daughter.

I made a joke and my daughter acted like she was going to throw her roll at me. I, in turn, actually threw one at her. My son howled. My daughter threw a roll at him. He threw one back at her. My son ran into the kitchen and grabbed the entire cookie sheet of rolls.

A full-scale food fight ensued. It was *The Three Stooges* on steroids. The breakfast room looked like an out-of-control episode of *Jerry Springer.*

It was a blast. The look on my kids' faces was sheer joy. It was one that said—*I can't believe they are letting me do this.* It soon changed to—*I can't believe Daddy's actually doing this with us.*

My wife sat unaffected and watched as the six-year-old, the ten-year-old, and the forty-six-year-old acting like a six-year-old pelted one another with rolls. There was bread everywhere. There were crumbs everywhere. There was laughter everywhere.

Typically, I advocate the use of proper manners in this column. I was taught good manners at an early age. My mother and grandmother kept *Emily Post's Etiquette* book next to the family Bible. When I was growing up, nothing was done without consulting Mrs. Post. Though every once in a while it is liberating and exhilarating to throw decorum to the wind, especially while throwing rolls at your dining companion.

I am not endorsing the act of throwing food. As a restaurant owner, I am grateful that food never flies in any of our dining rooms. If you decide to throw caution to the wind and heave a roll at your dining companion, it should be done in the confines of your family home (or in one of my competitors' restaurants).

I am, however, letting you know that some of the deepest belly laughs I've enjoyed recently came from a stale-roll war between my children and me. Maybe it's healthy to act like a child every once in a while, no matter what Emily Post says.

Baseball, Red Dirt, and Apple Pie

Baseball and food are numinously entwined. The two go together like peanuts and Cracker Jack.

Times have changed from the popcorn, peanuts, and hot dog days of our youth. Today's major-league ballparks feature servers who take your order while you sit in your seat, enter the order on a wireless computer device, and deliver the food directly to you. From San Diego, to Seattle, to Maryland, baseball fans are eating fish tacos, tofu hot dogs, and crab cake sandwiches.

In Hattiesburg the local baseball parks are still serving the all familiar peanuts, popcorn, and candy bars. I know this because I am now officially entering the next phase of my life: the always-at-the-soccer-field-or-baseball-park phase.

My four-year old son is playing five- to six-year-old coach-pitch baseball. It is his first ever exposure to the sport.

At the conclusion of his first practice, the coach gathered the team in the dugout and asked, "What's the number one rule of baseball?" My son's hand shot into the air. It was the only hand raised.

"Harrison," the coach said, nodding in his direction, "what's the number one rule in baseball?"

"Don't hit dogs."

"Well, Harrison, that's a good rule, but that's not rule number one. Rule number one is 'Don't throw dirt.'" I had to pull the coach aside later and tell him that my son wasn't an animal abuser. He walks around the house with his bat, and his mother and I are constantly telling him not to swing the bat anywhere near the dog.

Driving home after practice, I was trying to figure out the logic behind rule number one. I could come up with at least a thousand other baseball rules that were more important than not throwing dirt—keep your eye on the ball, keep your other hand above your glove when fielding a grounder—then I attended the second practice. It was a red-dirt throwing-and-kicking free-for-all. I became a huge fan of rule number one that day.

I have also learned that five- to six-year-old baseball can turn into a full contact sport. There is an innate desire imbedded in these children to chase the ball, wherever on the field it might be. Every time a ball is hit into the outfield, there is a mad dash of at least six boys chasing it down. They run from all areas of the infield and then jump onto a pile. At the second practice, my son, the right fielder, was chasing down foul tips behind home plate.

His baseball team is Piercon, named for a local construction company. His soccer team's mascot was a panther. Yesterday he asked what type of animal a Piercon was. He has a friend who plays for the Hattiesburg Clinic's Gynecology Group. Luckily, they don't have a mascot either.

I was worried about my boy playing coach-pitch this season for several reasons: him being the youngest on the team and having not yet turned five years old, him not having played T-ball last year, and the fact I hadn't worked with him much on baseball until a few weeks ago. After watching him in the batter's cage minutes before his first game, I realized that he'd only hit one out of thirty pitched balls. In a game, the batter only gets seven pitches. As he stepped up to the plate, I was already composing my "father speech," which would be delivered in the hopes of cheering him up and making sure he held his head high after he swung and missed the seventh ball. Then he got a hit! He was excited. I was ecstatic.

We are currently three games into my son's baseball career. He has six hits, forty-seven errors, and three tackles, and I've never had more fun in my life.

On July 20, 1969, I was eating popcorn and peanuts in Yankee Stadium watching a double header between the Yankees and the Washington Senators when an announcement was made, "America has just landed on the moon!" Everyone stood and cheered. The game was stopped and the national anthem was played. Until last Saturday, that was my most memorable baseball moment.

I am proud to say that, to me, America landing on the moon can't hold a candle to Harrison getting his first base hit.

Please keep Darian Pierce, coach of the Piercon Dirtkickers, in your prayers. He needs all the help he can get.

Campfire Food, Crawling Insects, and Things That Go Meow in the Night

I love cooking outdoors.

One of the best hamburgers I ever enjoyed was cooked in Omaha, Nebraska in a public park on a small, portable barbeque grill. There was nothing special about the method, ingredients, or cooking equipment. The meat was bought from the closest grocery store we could find, the buns were of the standard white-bread variety, and we used disposable salt and pepper to season the meat. Nevertheless, that burger stands to this day as the tastiest burger I have ever eaten.

So, with that twenty-year old remembrance in mind, I struck out to create another memory: camping out and cooking s'mores with my four-year-old son and eight-year-old daughter in our backyard.

Santa Claus brought a tent for Christmas and we—make that I—have been waiting all year for the perfect opportunity to set up camp.

The perfect opportunity arrived last Friday. Although I had pitched the tent several weeks earlier, and it had been up so long the grass beneath it was brown and dying, the timing was right.

At this point I should make it clear to the reader that neither my son—who has more pent-up energy than the Southern Company—nor my daughter—who loves clean sheets, and all things soft and pretty—have ever camped out in their short, air-conditioned, goose-downed lives. For that matter, I haven't slept under the stars since the Carter administration.

Nevertheless, after a late supper and a bowl of ice cream, we trekked into the backyard to light the fire pit.

It was too hot to cook s'mores. This was not a major defeat as I have never been a fan of s'mores, anyway. I have always had trouble getting the chocolate to melt. There is no way to toast a graham cracker over an open flame and get it hot enough to melt the chocolate without burning the underside of the graham cracker. Some say to roast the marshmallow and place the hot marshmallow on top of the chocolate, but a hot marshmallow won't completely melt a chocolate bar. Unless one has a microwave oven in the woods, the chocolate will always be hard, and much harder than the cracker. It makes more sense to eat the ingredients of a s'more separately as individual components.

The evening was doomed from the start. The tent, having been pitched several weeks earlier, was full of water. A slight item I didn't notice until all of the sleeping bags, pillows, and blankets were laid down inside.

Maybe it was a blessing that it was too hot to light a fire in the portable fire pit, as the sugar in the ice cream kept my son bouncing off of the tent walls for the first two hours of the evening.

The evening was also educational, as it served to highlight my son's newfound insect phobia. Every time a grasshopper, cricket, fly, or mosquito landed on the tent's mesh netting he screamed like a banshee. I would bet that the average reader has no idea how many different bugs can land on a tent while its occupants—not to mention anyone located in a three-block radius—are trying to fall asleep.

After two hours of tossing, turning, and screaming, my son thought it would be a good idea to let the cat inside the damp, muggy tent. I didn't argue, since the cat had been standing immediately outside the tent loudly meowing the entire time. Having a tame house cat inside the close quarters of a tent is probably not usually a problem. However, this particular house cat had been banished to the great outdoors and hadn't received her daily allotment of petting for six months. The cat continued to meow, but now it rubbed against my waterlogged legs and damp back, trying to make up for a half year of neglect.

It was hot in the tent, much too hot for late April. Did I mention that there were hailstorms and tornadoes on the way? Unfortunately, Daddy forgot to check the Weather Channel before picking the perfect night for camping out. The still, humid evening turned out to be the calm before the storm.

Sometimes a thunderstorm starts with the slow, pitter-patter of small raindrops dancing about, gradually building into a measured crescendo of falling water, intermingled with the gentle rolling of thunder in the distance, and the occasional flash of faraway heat lightning. Then again, sometimes the bottom drops out without warning; this, my friends, was one of those nights.

We made a mad dash into the house, soaking wet, carrying our pillows but leaving everything else in the tent. Put it this way: Hail hurts.

The first outdoor cooking event of the season was a bust, the tent floated away to a different section of the backyard, where it still holds a few hundred gallons of water, sleeping bags, flashlights, and possibly an attention-starved cat.

As for s'mores, I think we'll all stick to ice cream for the rest of the summer.

Pineapple Sherbet

One day last week the weatherman at my local television station reported the day's heat index as 117 degrees.

Earlier that afternoon I had been running errands for my wife. My children were with me. One of our errands placed us near Kamper Park in my hometown of Hattiesburg. As a child I spent countless days in that park during the summer months. Funny thing, I don't ever remember being too hot. Running, swinging, sliding, and jumping in the Mississippi heat with more energy than I'll ever know again never slowed me down, the temperature outside never mattered.

However, last week's heat slowed my pace considerably. Maybe it was age. I was certainly feeling all of my forty-four years, maybe more.

As we drove down the road that led to the park, I showed my children—a nine-year-old girl and a five-year-old boy—the place where I ate ice cream as a child. It was an ice cream parlor owned by the Seale-Lily Ice Cream Company.

The "Seale-Lily," as it was known around town, was a soda fountain of the standard 1950s/1960s variety, which served ice cream in bowls and cones, sundaes, splits, milk shakes, and light sandwiches. I held the place in high regard.

At the Seale-Lily I only ate pineapple sherbet. It was my favorite then and it is my favorite today, when I can find it. When making homemade ice cream, my family usually prepared vanilla or peach. To me, homemade peach ice cream tastes like summer, but pineapple sherbet tastes like my youth.

I am not sure what it was about pineapple sherbet that steered me away from the typical childhood choices of chocolate and strawberry. It has only occurred to me as I write this column that pineapple sherbet might be a strange choice for a kid.

Today a liquor store occupies the space where the employees of the Seale-Lily scooped thousands of cones.

My children asked about the Seale-Lily and wanted to know if there was a place in town that served pineapple sherbet. Hattiesburg has several ice cream shops, which offer excellent gourmet ice creams, varieties in every color and flavor, places where exotic candies and fresh fruits are mixed by hand into one's selection. I am a regular at the Marble Slab Creamery, and my waistline is a testament to those visits. However, I couldn't think of one place that serves pineapple sherbet.

At forty-four, I might not be as active as I was at six years old, but I am much more resourceful. After thinking for a minute, I walked over to the Sunflower grocery store that anchors the shopping center that housed the Seale-Lily and bought a quart of pineapple sherbet and a box of hard-plastic spoons.

I drove my children next door to the park and took them to the giant gazebo that has been there as long as I have been alive. We sat at a picnic table in the sweltering August heat, no cones, no air-conditioning, no worries, and ate pineapple sherbet straight out of the box.

In an instant I forgot about the heat. I watched as my children ate with abandon and wondered if one day they would tell their kids about the joys of pineapple sherbet in the hot Mississippi heat.

Do yourself a favor, today: Buy your young son, daughter, niece, nephew, grandson, granddaughter, or friend some ice cream. Whether it's in a cone or straight out of the box, you'll be making memories for you and them. Pineapple sherbet or not, you're likely to forget about the heat and humidity, but you'll never forget the joy of eating ice cream with a child.

Food for Thought

"If I was a doughnut, I'd eat myself."

Those words were spoken by my six-year-old son as I sat watching him eat doughnuts yesterday. Our family talks about food a lot. My daughter talks about what we should have for supper while we are eating lunch. It's genetic.

"Daddy, Jesus is like a doughnut hole."

"How is that, son?"

"Well, a heart is like a doughnut. It can have a hole in it. But Jesus is like a doughnut hole. He can fill the hole in your heart."

No seminary necessary, just one year of kindergarten. How could I argue with that? It's doughnut logic. I am not sure if they are teaching food-related Sunday school lessons at our church, but the sugar-fueled religious philosophy is getting through in the First United Church of Krispy Kreme.

Many of the world's problems are being solved over newsprint, coffee, and a few dozen glazed, every morning in doughnut shops all across the country. It's the same with my family.

I guess it's mostly my fault that a lot of my family's thoughts and plans are centered around food, though it is food that often brings families together.

A few years ago I wrote a column about the five tenets I have tried to incorporate into my daily life—faith, family, friends, food, and fun, in that order. My wife and I have structured our parenting philosophy around those principles.

When I speak to large groups or associations, I always cover the Five Fs, one-by-one, in great detail. When I reach the food part, people tend to chuckle. But food is serious stuff. I am not talking about treating food seriously as so many of the stuffy food scholars and historians do, but the simple process of sharing a meal with family and friends. That, my friends, is a dwindling ritual that is seriously needed.

As a society we have gotten too used to pulling up to a drive-through window, picking up a paper sack of food, taking it home, and eating it on a TV tray in front of the TV. That's not supper.

When I was growing up, moms came to back doors and yelled, "Supper," and everyone ran to the dinner table. Today a mom yells "Supper" from the back door and everyone hops into the minivan.

We have lost something through the years. For my family, the simple process of sitting down—television off—and sharing a meal is one of the most important parts of our day. In addition to being able to share our outlook and experiences with our children, we get to listen.

Listening within families is underrated. There is so much to hear, from serious cases of schoolyard drama and hiccups in the social interaction process, to statements such as, "Daddy, do you want to feel my booty muscles?"

"No, son, I do not."

Three years ago I began writing down a lot of the things my children were saying, with the intent of publishing a book. The most recent entry: "What time is eight-seven-central?"

Of the seven books I have written so far, this would be the only one that wrote itself. Many of the quotes are about food, some are just food-related.

My wife was walking through the grocery store the other day and turned down an aisle just in time to see our son approach a perfect stranger, "Hey, do you want to smell my nose air?" he asked, as he tilted his head back and quietly blew air out of his nostrils. Seconds earlier, he had sprayed Febreze air freshener directly into his nose. Funnily enough, his dry, exhaled "nose air" did smell like lavender and vanilla.

Now if I could just come up with some food-related advice that would make him wear underwear.

Cookies for Sale

Everything is changing and I don't like it.

I am slowly turning into one of those old curmudgeons who spend half of their time talking about the good old days. The music was better, the movies were better, the cars were better, the television shows were better, even the Girl Scout Cookies were better.

Actually, the Girl Scout Cookies didn't taste better than they do today, but the method by which they were sold was better.

When my wife told me that our daughter would be selling Girl Scout Cookies, I was pleased. My first thought was that she would be learning the all-important life lessons of managing money, making a sale, and delivering a product in a timely manner based on the long-standing, faith-based buyer-seller relationship. Well, truthfully, my first thought was *Ooh, peanut butter cookies and shortbread,* but my second thought was about all of that responsibility and money stuff.

"Which of us will drive her around to sell the cookies?" I asked.

"Oh, you don't drive around and sell cookies anymore," she said.

"What? Then how do the cookies get sold?" I asked.

"We will buy the cookies and then sell them. It's the way everybody does it now."

"When did they change the process?" I said. "When I was a kid, Girl Scouts knocked on our door all of the time, they were like miniature Amway salespeople. We placed an order for cookies, and in a few weeks, they delivered them to the house."

"That's the old way," she said. "Doing it that way, the girls had to keep up with who bought which cookies, how many they bought, who had paid, who had not, and things like that."

"Isn't that the whole point of the cookie-selling exercise? Isn't that what they have to do to get their cookie-selling merit badge or whatever it is that they get?" I asked.

"You are too old-fashioned. You don't know how things work nowadays. You're stuck back in the seventies; why don't you just go put on some of those Led Zeppelin records and let me take care of the Girl Scout business. Step up to the twenty-first century, buster."

Ouch. Playing the geezer card, it works every time.

So, we bought eight cases of cookies. One for each cookie flavor the Girl Scouts produce.

All eight cases are still in my pantry two months after I wrote the check. Actually, not eight full cases. The peanut butter and shortbread are mostly gone.

The Girl Scout website has an entire section on "Learning Life Skills." It states, "Many successful business women today say they got their start selling Girl Scout Cookies. Girls practice useful life skills like planning, decision-making, and customer service. During cookie activities, girls are members of a team working towards a common goal, with each girl striving to do her best."

The only "team" that was at work in my house was the mother-daughter team that teamed up on me and conned me into buying eight cases of Girl Scout Cookies—in advance—without a customer in sight. The "planning, decision-making, and customer service" lesson fell flat on both of them. I, on the other hand, leaned a lot.

My daughter is a Brownie Scout now. In a few years she'll be promoted to full-fledged Girl Scout status. By then she and her mother will have perfected their cunning cookie con. But they'll have to swindle the grandparents, aunts, uncles, and cousins. I've learned my lesson.

My daughter was originally recruited into the Daisy Scouts while in kindergarten. I don't remember Daisy Scouts when I was growing up. Before long they will have a Girl Scout recruiter standing watch in the maternity ward waiting to sign up the newest cookie seller immediately after she pops out of the womb.

"Dad, do you want to cut the umbilical cord?"

"Sure, Doc, would you like to buy some Thin Mints?"

To this day I have a pantry filled with boxes of Girl Scout Cookies. Plastered on the cookie-box covers are frolicking Girl Scouts in varying states of activity. All of the young ladies are laughing. The website states that the boxes show the girls "having fun and growing strong." Wrong. I know that look. It's not the look of a young girl growing strong and having fun. It's a look that says, "I just got my dad to buy eight cases of cookies, and didn't have to knock on one single door!"

Welcome to the twenty-first century.

The Basket and the Box

My friend Wyatt became a grandfather last week.

I am beginning to come to grips with the fact that I am old enough to have friends that are eligible grandparents.

Before driving to Jackson to be present at the birth, I grabbed a large wicker basket from my house and traveled to the drugstore to fill it with candy, chips, and cookies.

A basket full of junk food might seem like an unorthodox baby gift, but the basket wasn't for the baby, but the mother, Wyatt's daughter.

When my daughter was born, the best gift my wife and I received while in the hospital was a similar basket filled with candy, chips, and cookies. The basket was placed on a table in the corner of the room next to a pile of other gifts—flower arrangements, pink baby blankets, rattles, and booties—and went mostly unnoticed until 2 a.m. on the first night.

The baby was brought in for one of her many late-night feedings and my wife and I realized we hadn't eaten all day. In the excitement of the birth, we had forgotten about food. We tore into the junk basket with abandon. Potato chips never tasted better. It was a simple, yet wonderful, gift from someone who had been in the same situation a few years earlier. After two long nights of multiple feedings, we had emptied the basket.

I love being a father. It is the best job I will ever have and, by far, the most important. I had wanted to be a father since I was a kid. My father died when I was six, and I guess I felt like I could fill a void by playing the role of something that I was never able to experience.

Even though I wanted badly to be a father, it didn't happen until I was thirty-six years old. In all of the years I had dreamed about being a father—thinking about what it would be like, and how it would feel to have a child of my own to raise—there was no doubt in my mind that I would love my child. I had no idea.

When they placed my daughter in my arms it was like a box that had been hidden deep inside of me opened for the first time, and my capacity to love another human being became stronger and deeper than I ever could have imagined. Parents know exactly what I am talking about.

I knew I would love my children, though I had no idea of the depth of that love until the box was opened. There is no joy like the sheer joy that is the privilege of parenthood.

Last week in that Jackson hospital room, I was taken back to a moment almost nine years ago. My wife and I were sitting on a hospital bed, I was holding my daughter in my arms—a brand-new life with fresh, pink skin, tiny fingers, wisps of dark hair, toes like her mama's, and a head that smelled of lavender. We were eating chocolate chip cookies and staring at this wonderful little human being that seemed to have come from nowhere. Nothing in the world existed outside of that moment.

For Wyatt and his family, the box is open, again. Welcome to the world, Dylan Cade.

A Fruitful Day Off

For forty-six years I have been blessed with excess energy.

I seem to have been born with enough vitality and drive for two people. Though lately, I have been feeling my age.

Sunday I experienced my first "true" day off in six weeks. I planned to stay in bed most of the afternoon and treat myself to a full day of football for the first time since September.

My wife had to take my son to a birthday party, and my daughter needed to stay home to work on a school project. Around 1:30 p.m. my daughter came into my bedroom wanting to know what we were having for lunch. I asked her what she would like, and she couldn't decide.

As an offhand remark, I said, "Why don't you go into the kitchen and make us a sandwich," and turned my attention back to the football game.

When on tour or giving a speech, the most frequent question I am asked is, "Who does the cooking in your home?"

The answer is always the same, "My wife cooks for the family, and I cook for company." It's not written in stone. The roles reverse on occasion. If my wife decides to sleep late, I am happy to make a "Daddy Breakfast" for the children, or if she's putting on makeup before the movie, I don't mind throwing together a chicken casserole and salad. She, too, makes great lasagna, spaghetti, and pasta shells for company.

For the most part, we stick to our roles. Mom cooks for the family. Dad cooks for company and away from home. The children just eat.

Before long my ten-year-old daughter came walking into the bedroom holding a tray. She was beaming. I know all of her expressions. This was one that I hadn't seen before. It was an ear-to-ear smile filled with satisfaction and achievement.

On the tray was a triple-decker peanut butter and jelly sandwich, Fritos, and a glass of milk.

I have eaten thousands of peanut butter and jelly sandwiches in my life. In my first six years on the planet, they were almost all I ate, exclusively. I have eaten peanut butter and jelly sandwiches prepared by my mother, by both of my grandmothers, by my babysitters, by my wife, by friends, and by my own hands. I have taken them to school in lunch boxes. I have eaten them at church and on picnics; I have eaten peanut butter and jelly sandwiches in my formal dining room, and I have eaten them in sparsely decorated bachelor apartments. I can truly say that I have never eaten one that I have enjoyed as much as the one prepared and served by my daughter at 1:47 p.m. on December 9, 2007.

An hour later, she came back into the room with a plate of freshly baked oatmeal cookies and another glass of milk.

"Thank you, precious."

"You're welcome, Daddy."

The cynical reader might say, "What's the big deal? It was a sandwich and a plate of Fritos." That is correct, but it was so much more.

It was a small act of independence born in original thought. The look on her face signaled a sort of self-sufficient culinary rite of passage. She has now reached an age where she can go into the kitchen and prepare food, and she is happy about it.

In the last twenty years, I have eaten at some of this country's finest restaurants. I don't know if any of those meals can match the sheer joy I experienced having a Sunday afternoon lunch in bed, prepared by my daughter.

The smile on my daughter's face was one that I will never forget. It was a look of delight, independence, and accomplishment all at once, and one that could only be surpassed—at that moment—by the look of pride on the face of her father.

Now when I am asked, "Who does the cooking in your home?" I will have to change my answer. My wife cooks for the family, I cook for company, and my daughter cooks for special occasions.

A Different Kind of Date

Last week I invited my eight-year-old daughter on a date.

It was the first in what I hope will become a quarterly event. No mom, no wife, no brother, no son, just my daughter and me.

Earlier in the day I made a reservation at the Purple Parrot Cafe. I told them to give me the best table in the house. They did—not because I own the restaurant—but because they knew how important this night was to me.

After coming in from soccer practice, and finishing her homework, she was ready. I got in my car, pulled around to the front door, rang the doorbell, and opened the car door exactly how a gentleman is supposed to.

We ordered the five-course tasting menu at the Purple Parrot Cafe.

The meal started with an amuse bouche tart of spinach, blue cheese, and bacon. She loved it. This is going to be great, I thought to myself. She'll breeze through these menu items with no problem. I refuse to be a parent that raises one of these children who eat nothing but chicken strips and soda. My daughter has always had a rather sophisticated palate, so the prospects looked good for a new and positive learning experience.

Butternut squash soup was the first official course. She swallowed a couple of spoonfuls and, when asked, said it was good. I could tell that she didn't care for it, but she didn't want to let me know. When the waiter came to check on us, I had him remove the soup and told him that we were pacing ourselves. I want her to have a refined palate, but I don't want to force any foods on her that aren't "her thing." To this day, there are still foods that *I* don't eat and no one forces them on me.

The second course was a warm duck confit salad with a wild mushroom vinaigrette. It was great. Again, she wasn't thrilled with it. She took a few bites and politely laid her fork on the plate. At this point and time I thought about forcing her to eat more, but held back. Instead, we talked about the proper way to transfer butter to the bread-and-butter plate and how to butter a piece of bread.

The third course was a petit filet mignon with fingerling potatoes, wilted spinach, lobster, and Brie. Bingo! She cleaned her plate. I patted myself on the back for not commenting on her lack of enthusiasm for the first two courses. If I had, this course might have had a different end result.

The fourth course was a cumin-dusted rack of lamb with couscous and an ancho-chile demi glace. "Lamb, as in 'Mary Had a Little'?" she asked.

"Yes," I said, and took the opportunity to tell her the story of how I never ate lamb as a child until my mother told me that it was roast beef. The story didn't work. Six weeks earlier, my daughter had decided to become a vegetarian. Though she was only herbivorous for a few days, this jump from "I'm not going to eat anything with a face" to slicing into the medium-rare flesh of an animal whose "Fleece is white as snow" was going to be a huge step.

"But they're so cute," she said.

"Just try one bite. If you don't like it, you won't have to eat another."

On the night of October 20, 2005, another lamb lover was born.

Our fifth course was a pecan-praline bread pudding. She loved it.

After the meal was over, I asked which had been her favorite course. She said that she liked the amuse bouche best, followed by the tenderloin, the lamb, and the bread pudding. Squash soup and duck confit will have to wait for another meal. The final tally was four out of six. Not bad for foods that I didn't eat until I was in my twenties.

I want my daughter to set her goals high. I want her to know exactly how a man is supposed to treat her. Investing this sort of time in our relationship now is going to help with all of the relationships that follow in her life. Especially when it comes to one of the most important steps she'll ever make: choosing a man.

When my children are grown and gone and I am left to sit and remember, there is no doubt in my mind that one of my fondest memories will be of that first date with my daughter. It just might be one of hers, too.

Fathers, do yourself a favor: Make a date with your daughter, tonight.

The Piney Woods Challenge

Yesterday I drove a carload of kids—under the age of twelve—on a seven-hour trek that ended in Arkansas's Ouachita National Forest so they could attend summer camp.

Early on, the van was relatively calm. Most surprising, the van was quiet. I think it's because my wife packed the snacks. The kids were munching on pita chips, cheese crackers, and bottled water. I stopped for gas in some small town an hour from our destination, and the kids went inside by themselves to get their own snacks—ice cream and candy bars.

I learned two things: 1) Even though they might claim to have the capacity, kids have *no* clue how to take care of themselves. 2) Left on their own, they would die from sugar poisoning and daily overdoses of chocolate and corn chips.

The van instantly became raucous. The sugar fueled their madness as arguments began to break out between warring factions of the middle seat versus the way-back seat. Things were being thrown, toys were getting broken, and strange odors began to materialize. The tranquillity that had enveloped the van moments earlier was a distant memory.

I thought back to my youth. Water didn't come in bottles and pita was never chipped. I mainlined sugar through any source available— soft drinks, punch, Kool-Aid; my grandfather used to make glasses of homemade lemonade, which contained probably a half of a cup of sugar.

When snack time came at the park, I bought candy bars (chocolate and sugar), cotton candy (spun sugar), orange soda (liquid sugar), hard candy (hard sugar), and those large plastic straws filled with —you guessed it—colored sugar.

I rarely drank iced tea in my youth, but when I did, it was loaded with sugar. Sweet 'N Low, Equal, and Splenda were nowhere to be found. My mom had some little saccharin pills in a bottle, but I used those as ammunition for my slingshot—not because I was creative when it came to ammo, but because I was so hyped up on sugar at the time, my judgment was clouded and it seemed like a good idea. Artificial sugar? Ha! We used it to kill birds.

My son eats healthy, grown-up cereals like Special K and Kashi. I ate sugary cereal when I was a kid, and if the Frosted Flakes didn't taste sweet enough, I poured on more sugar until there was a layer of thick sugary sludge in the bottom of the bowl (which always made the second bowl of cereal even tastier).

I was the poster child for hyperactivity. I spent most of my days babbling on, twitching involuntarily, and bouncing off of the walls in the classroom. "Robert, finish your Cap'n Crunch, chocolate milk, and sweet rolls. You're going to be late for school."

"Mrs. St. John, Robert won't sit still in class."

"He'll be fine, just give him a few Twinkies and some chocolate milk. That'll settle him down."

I stayed in trouble. I ate sugary stuff all day long, never skipped dessert, and smuggled cookies into my bedroom late at night. With the money I made mowing lawns, I bought whole cases of Sour Apple Jolly Rancher candies.

My youth was filled with sugar-fueled moments that didn't turn out well. Most notably there was the Piney Woods Challenge. I remember that event like it was yesterday (probably because I had a carload of screaming kids yesterday). In my mind's eye, I can see my brother and mother in the front seat of the old yellow Plymouth. I was in the backseat—which smelled like our wet cocker spaniel—eating miniature Milky Way bars and drinking Mountain Dew. I was jabbering a mile a minute and my mother, who was at the end of her rope, issued a challenge: "If you can be totally still and completely quiet until we get to Jackson, I will give you five dollars."

We were passing the Piney Woods School at the time. It would be twenty-five minutes, at the most. Twenty-five minutes of silence for five dollars. I said, "OK you've got a deal," and then took another swig of my soft drink. Five dollars was a ton of money in 1969.

I sat on my hands and looked out the window with my lips drawn in and my mouth closed tightly. I concentrated on the five dollars while I twitched involuntarily. The pressure mounted as the car drove on. The pounding in my head grew louder. Be still. I wanted to tell someone about it. Be quiet. I wiggled and squirmed. Five dollars. Five dollars. Finally, I could take it no longer. Somewhere around Star, Mississippi, I screamed, "Where are my Jolly Ranchers?" And began jumping up and down on the backseat.

I didn't make it five miles. I did my best, but I failed. My brother, whom I think had been pulling for me, said, "That's all right, Robert. Cheer up, you'll get it next time. Here, have my Snickers and Orange Crush."

Anticipation

In the early 1970s, pop singer Carly Simon hit the Top 40 charts with a song called "Anticipation."

A few months after the song's release, a company that manufactures ketchup purchased the exclusive rights to use it in a series of television commercials. It forever changed my connection with the song. Instead of thinking about a slinky, sexy Carly Simon singing, "Anticipation is making me wait. It's keeping me wa-a-a-a-a-aiting," I began to associate a thick glob of ketchup slowly oozing out of a ketchup bottle. Big difference. Music has such strong connections to our memories.

My association with that particular song has changed once again. Yesterday, while driving my daughter though Arkansas on her way to summer camp, "Anticipation" came on the radio. As Carly Simon sang, I watched my daughter's face in the rearview mirror. She was wide-eyed, eager, and excited about going to summer camp. It was the same look her brother had had on his face an hour earlier when we dropped him off at his grandmother's—the excited anticipation of good times to come.

It struck me that there is nothing quite like the anticipation of summer camp and summer activities during one's youth. It is an eagerness that we never seem to recapture with the same intensity once we grow older. The anticipation experienced during one's youth is unlike that in any other period in one's life.

As I write this, I am sitting in a room in the Peabody Hotel in Little Rock waiting to fly to New York to meet with publishers, agents, and publicists. Certainly nothing I am looking forward to with excited anticipation, though the prospects for eating a few good meals have me contemplating the parental summer formula: Son with grandmother + daughter at camp = parents alone. Parents alone + one free week = New York City. New York City + restaurateur/food writer = great dining, squared. I am certainly anticipating a week's worth of excellent meals.

Suddenly it strikes me that Carly might have had it wrong. She sang, "Anticipation is making me wait. It's keeping me waiting." Actually, anticipation is the result of waiting. It is not making one wait, or keeping one waiting, but the by-product of the act.

As we offered our good-byes to our daughter and prepared to leave her in the able hands of the Camp Ozark staff, she gave us the I-don't-want-to show-too-much-affection-to-my-parents-while-the-other-kids-are-watching brush-off. Her friends were urging her to follow them as they hurried off to their first activity of the camp session. She gave us a halfhearted hug, said, "Bye," and ran off with the others. We were a little disappointed but couldn't point the finger too strongly as her mother and I had probably done the same thing to our parents when we were younger.

Slightly dejected, my wife and I began the slow walk up the hill that led to the camp exit—in an instant, my anticipation changed from a culinary field trip to New York, to the joyful reunion with my daughter seven days away. Halfway up the hill—about five minutes after we had said our good-byes—we heard a sweet, but excited, voice, "Momma, Daddy." It was her.

Our daughter had left her friends to come and give us a huge bear hug, a kiss, and a final thank-you for sending her to camp. Somewhere in the middle of the Ouachita National Forest, on the side of a dirt hill that led to a parking lot, I experienced the greatest hug of my life. It was a moment that I will never forget.

The song was still swimming around in the back of my mind as her mother and I finished our walk to the car. Carly was singing, "…and stay right here, 'cause these are the good ol' days." Yes, ma'am, they certainly are.

What a Wonderful World

What a difference a few years make.

When my daughter was born—eleven years ago—my wife and I never slowed down. We ate in the same restaurants, visited the same hotels, and flew the same airlines. Other than getting to move to the front of the line when flying Southwest, our travel plans were never altered.

Our daughter was the perfect restaurant customer. At six months old she ate a meal at Commander's Palace in New Orleans. She never made a peep. She was neat, well mannered, and polite, never dropping a morsel. The floor around her was as clean as her cheeks.

My wife and I spent countless hours patting ourselves on the back in those days. We had obviously mastered this whole parenting thing. While dining in restaurants, we would watch other children running around the dining room, screaming, throwing food, and being all-around bad restaurant patrons. We would turn to our daughter and think to ourselves: *If only those parents could talk to us, we would tell them how it's done. Look at our child. See how well behaved she is. We are masters of parenting. As a matter of fact, I wouldn't be surprised if someday soon someone asks us to write the definitive guide to parenting, and what a breeze that would be.*

And then our son was born and we learned that we had nothing to do with the good nature and refinement of our daughter. It had been the luck of the draw. The second time we shuffled the deck, we drew a joker.

My son was not a good restaurant customer. Actually, we only went out to dinner a few times in his early years. We had suddenly become the parents with the rowdy child terrorizing the dining room. We would see other parents—parents with only one well-behaved child—looking at us the way we used to look at other people. We knew the look. It said: *You poor, poor people. If only you would talk to us. We could give you all of our parenting secrets.*

I wanted to tell them where they could put their secrets, but I was too busy trying to stop my son from swinging on the light fixtures. He had good intentions. He was not mean, or rude, or hurtful, just full of energy and volume.

Fast forward six years. My daughter is eleven years old, my son is seven. The two of them and their mother took me to Commander's Palace for Father's Day brunch. It was a great experience. Other than jumping up once to swat a fly on the windowsill with his napkin, my son was perfectly behaved. My daughter, who is eleven going on forty, was her usual well-mannered self. I thought: *We have finally arrived.*

Two tables over, in the middle of the room, was a young couple with a baby. The baby was loud. He was just being a baby. The parents were obviously embarrassed. The father was looking around the room, giving the universal sign of helplessness—the shrug of the shoulders and a humiliated grin.

Midway through the third course, my eyes met the eyes of the screaming baby's father. He gave me a look that said: *I'm sorry.* I knew the look. I had lived with that look for several years. I shrugged and mouthed the words, "It's OK." I don't think he believed me, but I know that he'll get through it. Things will get better. There are brighter days ahead.

I then turned my attention back to my family. My son was dipping his spoon into his bread pudding soufflé; my daughter was tasting her mother's coffee. The jazz band had drowned out the screaming six-month-old with a wandering three-piece version of a Louis Armstrong classic.

I hear babies cry, I watch them grow.
They'll learn more than I'll ever know.
And I say to myself, what a wonderful world.
It truly is.

Chapter 3
Family

Wise Men Say

LAS VEGAS—Greetings from the Glitter Gulch. I'm here on a business trip, my first visit here since 1993. Since then, celebrity chefs from all around the globe have opened branches of their famous eateries. I arrived at 1:30 a.m. last night ready to eat in as many of those restaurants as I can over the next few days. Details to come.

Much has changed in Las Vegas since 1993. One thing that hasn't changed is the Graceland Wedding Chapel.

In 1988, when I met my future wife, I told her that if I ever got married the service would have to be performed by an Elvis impersonator in Las Vegas. I was adamant about it.

Four years later we were engaged and I compromised. We were married by my uncle in our church in Hattiesburg and then flew to Las Vegas the next day to get remarried by an Elvis impersonator.

In two days we went from getting married by Hugh the Episcopal rector from Virginia to reciting vows to Norm the Elvis impersonator on the Sunset Strip.

The Graceland Wedding Chapel is exactly what one would think the Graceland Wedding Chapel would be: just as tacky as the real Graceland.

I opted for the deluxe ceremony, which came with flowers for the bride (a tacky bouquet of hard plastic red roses similar to the type used outdoors in cemeteries), a red garter for my wife, a complimentary "I Got Married at the Graceland Wedding Chapel" T-shirt, and three songs sung by the king.

I am not a big a fan of Elvis; I just liked the campiness of getting married by someone who is so dedicated to one human being's life and career that he still wears dyed-black lamb-chop sideburns thirty years after they were *en vogue*, if they ever were.

A limousine picked us up at our hotel and drove us to the older part of the Strip where the Graceland Wedding Chapel was located. We were greeted by Norm and a fellow named Stewie, who was there to witness the event and to play the Casio keyboard.

Norm asked us which three songs we would like. I chose "Kentucky Rain" and "In the Ghetto," which weren't exactly wedding songs, but they were my two favorite Elvis songs, and it didn't really matter because we had been officially, legally, and spiritually married the day before.

Stewie escorted my wife down the aisle as Norm the Elvis impersonator broke into "In the Ghetto." I leaned over and whispered to my wife, "At least it wasn't "Hound Dog.""

During the ceremony, my wife and I got tickled and were stifling laughs so as not to offend the Graceland Wedding Chapel crew. It was the type of laughing that one tries to stifle while sitting in the choir loft during church in junior high school. The harder one tries not to laugh, the more one wants to laugh.

I learned on that fateful day, February 7, 1993, that a stifled laugh, when observed by a third party, doesn't look like a stifled laugh at all. A stifled laugh obviously looks like something akin to sheer joy.

Norm the Elvis impersonator mistook the stifled laughs as a sign that we were overjoyed and emotionally moved by our visit to the Graceland Wedding Chapel. Before long, three songs turned into four, four turned into six, and six turned into eighteen.

Almost an hour later, we learned from Stewie that we had just witnessed what he described as, "A real treat." Norm, seeing the "joy" on our faces, had performed his entire nightclub routine for us. "No one has ever looked as happy as you two and he gave you the full treatment."

By the eighth song, "All Shook Up," our stifled-laugh grins had morphed into a panicked looking expression of sheer desperation. That didn't stop Norm.

At the time, Vicki Lawrence, of "The Night the Lights Went Out in Georgia" fame, had a daytime talk show. Norm asked us to stay over two days to get married again during his upcoming visit to Vicki!. Alas, the slopes of Aspen were calling, three wedding ceremonies in four days was too much to ask of anyone, and my wife had barely agreed to get remarried by an Elvis impersonator in the first place.

Now I am back in Vegas. My wife is home with the kids. I don't drink.

82

I don't gamble. I don't like Celine Dion, Wayne Newton, or Tom Jones. Maybe I'll drop by the Graceland Wedding Chapel and say hello to Norm and Stewie. Maybe I'll sit in on a couple of nuptials just for old times' sake.

Reduce Speed Ahead, Life at Work

As a society, we have grown too used to picking up a brown paper sack at the drive-through, bringing it home, pulling it out on a TV tray, watching television, and calling it supper.

It is a shame.

We're too busy. We're too hurried. We're too overscheduled. We're too overcommitted. And life is flying by too fast.

We need to slow down.

The Slow Food Society has over eighty thousand members in more than one hundred countries, dedicated to the principles of "protecting the pleasures of the table from the homogenization of fast food and life. Through a variety of initiatives, it promotes gastronomic culture, develops taste education, conserves agricultural biodiversity, and protects traditional foods at risk of extinction."

The Slow Food Movement began in Paris fifteen years ago. I first heard about it while taking classes at the Culinary Institute of America in Napa Valley in the late 1990s. Slow Food USA was founded in 2000 and is dedicated to preserving our native cuisines and culinary culture. The organization celebrates, supports, and promotes the growing of heirloom fruits and vegetables, artisan breads and cheeses, the purity of animal breeds, and organically grown foods. The members of Slow Food USA are dedicated to saving our culinary heritage one relaxing meal at a time.

When my wife was pregnant with our first child, we witnessed a strange and alarming phenomenon. While out and about, at a party, in the grocery store, or in a restaurant, we ran into friends and acquaintances that had one thing in common: While talking to me and my wife, noticeably pregnant, they would look us in the eyes and say, "It goes so fast. It goes so fast." There was a look of longing in their eyes, and an aching for the past written in the lines of their faces.

After the ninth or tenth time this happened, my wife and I sat down and had a heart-to-heart. We both agreed that we didn't want to reach a point in our lives where we realized that we had missed out on our children growing up. I didn't want to be in my sixties wondering where my children's youth had gone. We agreed to make every moment of parenthood count.

The Slow Food Society is based on the principle of "taking the time to slow down and enjoy life with family and friends." The pact I made with my wife in her third trimester was based on the principle of making the most out of parenthood and enjoying life with our children to the fullest extent. Raising children is the most important job I have, or will, ever have.

Food and family go together like, well, like food and family.

We have strayed from the family dinner table. Sharing a home-cooked meal with family and friends is one of our most ancient and most rewarding customs. When I sit down with my family at night, we talk about what we did that day, what we will do tomorrow, and I always ask, "What was the best part of your day?" The answer is easy for me. The best part of my day has always been: sitting at that table, with those three people, sharing a meal, sharing life, loving, laughing, creating memories, and doing the best I can to slow things down.

Sharing a meal doesn't have to be an event for a mother, father, 2.5 kids, and a dog. Whenever two or more people gather around a table with food and share a meal, relationships are tightened, friendships are strengthened, life slows down a little, and memories are created.

Those that know me know that my life is anything but slow. That is until it comes to my family and food. In those areas I'm moving at a snail's pace, and it's still going by too fast.

Culinary Infidelity

I have been cheating on my wife.

It's true. I've been sneaking around behind her back, and lately my rendezvous have been getting more frequent. I feel guilty and believe it's time to air out my dirty laundry. This might seem like an odd forum to address marital infidelity, but I am not Catholic, so this medium will have to serve as my confession.

Maybe I should clarify that another woman has nothing to do with my unfaithfulness. No. I have cheated on my wife with food.

Raw oysters are my mistress. My wife believes strongly that no one should eat raw oysters. She's read alarmist-authored articles and half-cocked studies that speak to the dangers of consuming raw oysters. I, on the other hand, grew up eating raw oysters. I love them.

One of the biggest disputes in our twenty year relationship was over raw oysters. After that I figured that it would be easier to stop eating them than to deal with the conflict—a man has to pick his battles.

Enter the paramour.

My Hattiesburg bar concept, the Mahogany Bar, began serving oysters on the half shell last year. Originally we were purchasing our oysters from P&J Oysters out of New Orleans. They are the gold standard for oysters. All of the great restaurants and oyster bars throughout New Orleans use P&J. They're great, but I was able to resist them and keep my marriage pure.

Then we changed our oyster supplier.

When we brought in the new company, I had to taste-test the new oysters. After all, I am the executive chef. I never thought we'd be able to best our original supplier. My marriage would be safe. I was wrong. The oysters were amazing. They were—by far—the best I had ever eaten. Plump, clean, salty, cold, and just the right size. I succumbed to the moment, gave in to temptation, and ate two dozen on the spot.

Remorse set in. I felt guilty, but I held on to the hope that this might have been a fluke, and that my time away from oysters had made my taste buds grow fonder. A few weeks later, walking through the bar, I noticed a bartender shucking a dozen. They looked so pretty. As I walked past, they seemed to be giving me a siren call. I gave in to temptation again and ate another two dozen oysters to make sure that the first time wasn't a fluke and that these oysters were, in fact, the most unbelievably tasty oysters on the planet. They were.

I put my staff on full alert. Be on the lookout for my wife. Give me the signal if she comes anywhere close to the building. I did whatever it took not to get caught with an oyster fork in my hand. I made sure not to come home with horseradish on my breath or the smell of cocktail sauce on my collar.

Before long my culinary infidelity intensified and I began having weekly oyster trysts in the afternoon. Then the trysts became more frequent. Now I am riddled with guilt and I have made half of my staff accomplices to my gastronomic adultery.

Recently, it's gotten worse. I have been two-timing my wife *and* my mollusky mistress. The courtesan: mashed potatoes.

Over a month ago, my wife and I started a diet together. Potatoes and bread are not on the "allowed" food list. Unfortunately the beginning of the diet coincided with one of my restaurants—the Crescent City Grill—offering a great new side-dish: home-style mashed potatoes.

I love mashed potatoes. My grandmother made the best. They were light and buttery, with little lumps in them, hearty, wholesome, filling, real, comfort food. Our new home-style like-your-grandmother-used-to-make mashed potatoes replaced a roasted-garlic potato offering that I never liked. They are delicious. Whenever I eat our mashed potatoes, I post two servers at each door. "Tell me if you see her coming."

Lately, I've been thinking about keeping a secret apartment across town—a place to eat oysters on the half shell and mashed potatoes and sweet rolls and maybe even oyster-flavored sweet rolls on a bed of mashed potatoes. Is there a 12-step program for this? "Hi, my name is Robert, and I am a food philanderer."

The Camellia Grill

On a hot August day in 1989, I took a young, beautiful, and adventurous twenty-two-old girl to New Orleans for our first, out-of-town date.

We spent time in the French Quarter and then drove down Canal Street to admire the houses and their architecture. We were at the testing phase of the date to see whether tastes and interests were similar and/or compatible.

At the end of St. Charles Avenue, at the river bend sat the Camellia Grill, the last of a breed—the classic American diner—an icon of a bygone era in the restaurant business, but one that was still going strong in New Orleans. Uptown locals and tourists sat side by side on one of the twenty-eight stools in the small, sparsely decorated room and watched two cooks, four waiters—in white, pressed, jackets—and a few busboys serve some of the best diner food to be found anywhere.

My date ordered and ate a chili-cheese omelet—make that a "yes" in the compatible column. I told myself then and there, *I'm gonna marry that girl,* and I did.

It's not the most romantic beginning in the history of love affairs, but probably appropriate for me nonetheless. My wife and I have returned to the Camellia Grill many times since that hot August day.

The Camellia Grill was another Hurricane Katrina casualty until April 20 of this year. Over the last eighteen months we have traveled to New Orleans many times, each time driving by the diner to check the status of the operation. Each time it was closed.

Someone left a pad of Post-it notes and a pen outside the restaurant. The front door, windows, and walls of the exterior were covered with various handwritten come-back-soon notes from those lamenting the loss of the neighborhood dining institution.

Almost twenty years after I took my future wife on that fateful date, I took my daughter to New Orleans to celebrate her tenth birthday. Over the years she had heard the Camellia Grill-chili-cheese omelet story a dozen times. When I asked where she wanted to eat lunch, the Camellia Grill was her first, and only, choice.

I have a feeling that—like the Civil War and World War II—all future events will be evaluated and remembered as "before" or "after" Hurricane Katrina in this part of the country. Given that, not much has changed at the Camellia Grill since the pre-Katrina days. The walls are mostly bare and are still painted an unusual shade of pink. The artwork is still the same except for the addition of a framed collage of recovered Post-it notes in the shape of a camellia. Linen napkins are still in use. The place seems cleaner. They now accept credit cards, and the hours of operation have been paired down, but they still serve the exact menu right down to the chili-cheese omelet.

As in the pre-Katrina days, there was a line of people on the sidewalk waiting to be seated. The wait for a stool lasted about twenty minutes. My daughter ordered a chili-cheese omelet "like Momma did," an order of fries, and a sweet tea. I nixed the sweet tea and told her about the Camellia Grill's chocolate freeze with ice cream.

Some say that the official drink of New Orleans is the Pat O'Brien's Hurricane, others the Sazerac. I hereby tender my vote for the chocolate freeze with ice cream at the Camellia Grill. A chocolate freeze is a combination of vanilla ice cream, milk, chocolate syrup, simple syrup, and ice, blended and served ice cold. It's a chocolate shake on steroids, and it's delicious, always has been, always will be.

They still grill a mean burger and they still cook pecan pie in a pool of butter right on the flat-top griddle. The service wasn't quite what it used to be, but it wasn't bad. One can't expect to lose service veterans of twenty-plus years and expect the same results.

It was a day of firsts: My daughter's first chili-cheese omelet, her first chocolate freeze with ice cream, and the first day of her eleventh year of life.

As we sat in The Camellia Grill celebrating the occasion of my daughter's first decade on the planet, I couldn't help but think back to that first date in August 1989. If you would have asked me then to write a script of how I wanted my life to turn out, I would have been ashamed to ask for the embarrassment of riches that is my wife, children, and family life. I had no idea what life had in store for me. I am truly a lucky man. Welcome back, Camellia Grill.

The Dining Room

The crystal glassware is individually wrapped in tissue paper and stored in a wooden box in the back of the attic. The sterling silver is in the felt-lined monogrammed mahogany box, or in the dining room sideboard, or in the clothes dryer during out-of-town vacations. The fine china is on permanent display in the glass-fronted china cabinet.

That's the way it is.

We receive all of these nonessential niceties for wedding gifts and through inheritance, yet we show our appreciation by only bringing them out twice a year—at Thanksgiving and Christmas.

If your home has a formal dining room, odds are it's the least-used room in the house. My formal dining room is the second least-used room in the house, coming in just behind the formal living room.

For years my family only went into the dining room during Thanksgiving and Christmas. It was then that we would pull out all of the china and crystal and set the table for one of our two formal meals of the year.

That was then.

Several summers ago I changed my thinking about the formal dining room. I started going to the local farmer's market on Saturday mornings and loading up on foods that had come in fresh that week—sweet corn, pink-eye purple-hull peas, butter beans, peaches. I would take these fresh foods home and spend the rest of the morning cooking summer vegetables.

Around noon I would set the table with all of the china, silver, and crystal and serve friends and family down-home country cooking in an upscale and refined way. We are usually clothed in T-shirts and shorts, the food is casual, but we treat the food—our heritage cuisine—with the respect that it deserves.

Until those summer lunches, I always felt that a family should be dressed up, or that a special occasion/holiday was needed, before one could use the dining room and all of its accouterments. Not so.

Sharing a meal is special. The food doesn't have to be formal, upscale, white-tablecloth food. Neckties and cocktail dresses are never necessary dress for the formal dining room.

Treat food with the respect that it deserves. Throw tradition and long-held rituals to the wind. Start a trend. Do it your way.

Once Thanksgiving is over, keep the crystal out of the tissue paper, leave the china out of the cabinet, and stop putting the silver in the dryer. Use your dining room. Share a meal with friends and family. Treat simple uncomplicated foods as if they are special—they are. Invite your neighbors, invite your grandchildren, and invite your neighbor's grandchildren. Create memories.

Pancakes and Passings

I buried my grandmother today. She was the only one I had left.

I was fortunate to have spent all of my childhood and a good part of my early adult years with both grandmothers, each playing a crucial role in my upbringing. My paternal grandmother passed away seventeen years ago, my grandfather twenty-five years ago, my maternal grandmother, last week. She was ninety-seven years old.

In their respective families, grandparents are usually known among their grandchildren for a few specific deeds or character traits. My grandfather was an avid outdoorsman, sportsman, and history buff. My paternal grandmother was a gracious Southern lady with impeccable manners and a knack for entertaining. The lady we buried today was full of spunk, devoted to her family, an excellent bridge and solitaire player, and the creator of the best pancakes on the planet.

Some cooks are more comfortable cooking specific items such as seafood; others excel on a certain piece of equipment—a barbeque grill or cast-iron skillet. Some cooks pride themselves on elaborate dinners; some are more comfortable with small, intimate lunches. For my grandmother, breakfast was her domain; the early morning kitchen was her kingdom, we were her subjects, a spatula was her scepter, and pancakes were the currency.

When dining at my grandmother's home, no breakfast was complete without her pancakes. The supporting cast of breakfast items might change with each meal—sausage one morning, bacon the next, grits, or no grits—but there were always pancakes.

I am not sure what made her pancake recipe so much better than others, but it is better, much better. It might have been the amount of baking soda, or it could have been the baking powder, possibly a combination of the two with the addition of buttermilk. Most pancakes are dull, flavorless, and too breadlike. Not hers. I am fortunate to have grown up in a home where out-of-the-box pancakes of the just-add-water variety were never served.

Whenever the family traveled, she packed her pancake mix into Ziploc bags and prepared them on site wherever we might be. Her pancakes were the constant in an ever-changing family structure.

I would bet three paychecks that my grandmother cooked more pancakes than any other homemaker of her era. A few years ago, as I was thinking back on so many shared breakfasts, it occurred to me that no one had ever cooked pancakes for my grandmother. All of my life, every time pancakes were served when she was around, it was she that did the cooking. At the time I came to this realization, she was living in an assisted living home. I invited her to my house for pancakes. This time I did the cooking. We sat with my wife and daughter and enjoyed one of the more memorable breakfasts I will ever have.

Today, my wife makes the pancakes in our family. She uses my grandmother's recipe.

There are many options for those who want to leave a legacy to their family. It seems that food, or a particular food item, is a legacy of the utmost significance. Like money, it can be passed down to future generations, but unlike cash, with food the opportunities for creating lasting memories are limitless. Sharing a meal with one's family makes life richer. My grandmother made life richer for us all.

Jennifer

Several years ago I wrote a column about funeral food and how people in the South band together to feed the family of the bereaved when a loved one has passed away.

I never expected to be so close, so soon, to the phenomenon.

A few days ago my wife's thirty-seven-year-old sister lost a long and hard-fought battle with her heart. It was a battle that she fought with guts and grace, always positive, always resilient, and—even in her most weakened state—a battle in which she spent most of her time caring more about the well-being of others more than her own.

Within hours the food began arriving. Fried chicken, potato salad, cakes, cookies, and fruit were the first to show up. The refrigerator filled to capacity in the first hour.

One friend, whose wife was out of town, and who had no idea how this drill worked, dropped by the grocery store and came over with a mixed-bag smorgasbord of groceries and paper products in various sacks—no rhyme, reason, or theme to the gift, just supplies for people in need from someone who truly cared.

Family and friends were all over the house. Some hadn't eaten in days and were ravenous; others had lost their appetite weeks ago. Three of my wife's friends cooked an entire dinner and brought it to the house. One of those same friends came over and washed clothes and cleaned the children's rooms.

It was a beautiful thing to see. At times, it felt as if the entire community had mobilized in honor of this one cause. The chefs at my restaurant were ready to load us up with even more food, but I had to tell them that we had no more refrigerator space.

Four years ago, when writing the original column on funeral food, I stated: "Down here, communities band together during times of tragedy. Food is the common vein that runs through it all. However, my generation doesn't seem to come together like the generations before us. Are we so busy that we have forgotten the importance of community, friends, and family?"

I was wrong. Very wrong. Community, friends, and family are alive and well and living in and around Hattiesburg, Mississippi. My generation stepped up to the plate and knocked it out of the park in this time of need. It does my heart good.

With dozens of out-of-town family and friends traveling in, all of the food will surely be consumed—homemade bread, pies, crudités, sweet rolls, sandwich platters, chips, dips, and more fried chicken—everything but sausage balls. My wife's sister always cooked sausage balls. They were my daughter's favorite. The two of them could eat dozens in one sitting. Every Christmas, Easter, and Fourth of July our kitchen was filled with sausage balls. Whenever my sister-in-law asked my daughter what she would like for her birthday, the answer was always, "Sausage balls."

The sausage-ball recipe wasn't a passed-down family secret, or a much-sought-after prize-winning formula, just a simple recipe off of the side of the Bisquick box. What made the recipe special was the love that went into the preparation of the dish. It was the same main ingredient in the food that recently kept our refrigerator bulging.

We lament the loss of a sister, a daughter, a wife, and an aunt—a woman of exceptional strength and courage. We thank our friends who kept us in their thoughts and prayers. We thank those who kept us fed, and we try to move on with a large, empty, and seemingly endless void in our lives, a space where a courageous young woman used to be.

Chapter 4

Katrina

My Coast
(Written 5 days after Hurricane Katrina made landfall.)

Down around Biloxi
Pretty girls are dancin' in the sea
They all look like sisters in the ocean
The boy will fill his pail with salty water
And the storms will blow from off towards New Orleans
 — Jimmy Buffett

The Gulf Coast is my second home. I grew up one hour due north, in the Piney Woods of Hattiesburg, Mississippi But my childhood summers were spent on the Gulf.

In my youth, I spent countless hours fishing, shrimping, and crabbing in the Mississippi Sound—usually more interested in catching the saltwater bounty than eating it. My adult years have been filled with cooking the plenteousness the warm Gulf waters have to offer.

Cooking and eating on the Mississippi Gulf Coast is unlike doing those things in any other place. There is a certain reverence attached to the process. A definite pride is taken in the simple practice of boiling shrimp or picking crabmeat. Sharing a meal of fresh-out-of-the-water seafood is a pleasure many in this country, especially those who are landlocked, never enjoy. It is one, I am sad to say, I have taken for granted.

Today, the Coast, as I knew it, is gone.

Hurricane Camille, the gold standard for storms in this area, swept through in '69 and made a clean sweep of the Coast. Long-standing restaurants and cafes were instantly wiped out. Many were rebuilt. The casinos blew in twenty years later, and bellwether institutions such as Baricev's and Fisherman's Wharf gave way to behemoth structures filled with blue hairs flown up on junkets from Tampa, playing nickel slots and smoking Salem Lights. Through it all, the food remained.

Food is the common bond.

My Jackson friends, Ben and Dero Puckett, owned one of those century-old majestic homes on Scenic Highway 90 in Pass Christian. For the last thirty-five summers the Pucketts' have spent Memorial Day through Labor Day in that beautiful and stately home. It was purchased just a few months before Camille blew in. Ben rode out that storm in a second-floor closet. Just weeks ago I ate my first lunch in that house. The Pucketts prepared a beautiful meal of crabmeat au gratin, fresh fruit, and a cold shrimp salad—a true Gulf Coast feast.

Seafood is the lifeblood of the area.

Today, more than 50 percent of the restaurants in the three-county stretch from the Louisiana state line to the Alabama border are gone. Another 15 to 20 percent of restaurants in that area sustained major damage and may be out of business for up to six months. All of the other dining establishments on the Coast received, at the least, minor damage.

Upon returning from a three-day trip to the hurricane-ravaged area, Mike Cashion, executive director of the Mississippi Hospitality and Restaurant Association, stated, "There were two things that made a lasting impression on me. The first was the absolute vicious power and enormous size of the storm. The Mississippi Gulf Coast was devastated. The second was the incredible attitude of our restaurant brothers and sisters. In the midst of death, destruction, and despair, the restaurant industry, *to a person*, showed nothing but compassion for their community and fellow human beings."

It's not just restaurateurs, it is everyone. It has been said that only in times of crisis do we discover the true strength of a community.

While eating—what would turn out to be—my last meal in the Puckett house, I thought back to all of the summer lunches that must have been shared in that dining room; all of the shrimp that had been boiled in the kitchen; children, and later grandchildren, who splashed in the salt water just across the street. A row of brick steps—and memories—are all that remain.

My Coast is now a world of brick steps without porches, concrete slabs without houses, fishermen without boats, and restaurateurs without buildings.

However, Mississippians are a resilient people. Our forefathers came to this area—machete in hand—and fought mosquitoes, tics, horseflies, rabid animals, malaria, encephalitis, Lyme disease, stifling clouds of pine pollen, and scorching heat. We have endured war and occupation, floods, storms, depression, recession, tornadoes, hurricanes, all manner of natural and man-made disasters, and we are still here. We have taken the worst of what life and nature have given us and we have prevailed.

In the not too distant future, we will once again share a meal of fresh-from-the-water seafood. Restaurateurs are a hearty lot. The next Baricev's or McElroy's will open their doors ready to feed the world. Mary Mahoney's is still standing, others will rise.

We will prevail.

Sun shines on Biloxi
Air is filled with vapors from the sea
Boy will dig a pool beside the ocean
He sees creatures from his dream underwater
And the sun will set from off towards New Orleans

Notes, Thoughts, Hurricane Fatigue, and Hope

Living one hour north of the Gulf of Mexico has its advantages. Then again...

I hope to never again take electricity and running water for granted.

After seeing hours of bad news on television—people shooting rescue workers and doom-and-gloom talking heads—it's good to know that there are people out there getting the job done. It's good to know that the Red Cross, the National Guard, and hundreds of other agencies are working tirelessly to save and restore lives.

Tens of thousands of electric power workers are working day and night throughout the region, praise the Lord for the power workers.

There are thousands of heart-moving stories out there. Stories like the Kensington Woods Church of Christ in my hometown, where members from all across the country went to work immediately, sending to the area tractor trailers filled with water, food, baby supplies, chain saws, generators, cash, and gas. The members of the church then distributed all of those items throughout the community without care to church affiliation. Just one requirement was needed: being in need.

Neighbors are helping neighbors. Strangers are helping strangers. All with one common goal: the attempt to restore normalcy.

Sometimes it is not until you lose something that you appreciate it.

Two days after the storm, I was sitting in the dark eating a sandwich. It was a sandwich made of cheap, pressed luncheon meat, Bunny bread, and Creole mustard. That simple meal might as well have been prime aged New York strip and a two-pound lobster tail. Actually it might have tasted better than any steak-and-lobster meal has ever tasted. It was at that precise moment that it struck me...Creole mustard is a beautiful thing.

Creole mustard, unadorned. No special seasoning on the meat, nothing extraordinary about the bread, nothing complicated at all, just plain old Creole mustard. Simple, easy, uncomplicated—like life should be. Maybe as life will be, again.

A week after Hurricane Katrina my house is still without electricity. Yet I have a house.

Tens of thousands have lost everything. Everything. Everything is too much.

Nevertheless, there is still good news out there. There is still hope.

The New Orleans Culinary Resurrection

In the September issue of *Bon Appetit* magazine, New Orleans was listed as one of America's top five restaurant cities

The ill-timed edition—which hit newsstands two weeks prior to Hurricane Katrina's landfall—serves as a tangible reminder of what the nation's restaurant customers have lost.

The other four cities—San Francisco, Chicago, Las Vegas, and, of course, New York—are worthy cohorts, but none hold the charm, culture, and history that the Crescent City offers. The citizens of New Orleans—and those of us who have been lucky enough to live around the periphery—worship food. It is a religion. It is a devotion that runs deeper than that of any other city's, including New York's.

The restaurant business in New Orleans has been temporarily eliminated, and one wonders if it will ever be able to return to the glory days of its past.

Watching the post-storm, post-flood news coverage on a battery-operated television in the days following the hurricane, I thought of the tens of thousands of restaurant employees who clocked out after a busy Saturday night on August 27 and haven't worked since. If one subtracts an entire city from the *Bon Appetit* thesis, 20 percent of the nation's top dining was wiped out in one windy day.

The road to restaurant revival on the banks of the Mississippi River will be long and arduous. The cleanup will take months. Perishable food is involved, so the job will be neither hygienic nor easy. We must remember that the restaurants, too, closed for business that Saturday night, and haven't been reopened since. Toxic floodwaters rose to as high as fifteen feet in certain sections of the city. Electricity has been off
for weeks and coolers and freezers are still full of abandoned and
rotting food.

In a recent Associated Press article, Donald Link, co-owner of restaurant Herbsaint (one of the properties featured in the *Bon Appetit* piece), said, "I looked at the lost food—the pig heads in brine were the worst—and I thought I can't do this. I can't take it."

Nevertheless, Link summoned the will and used a commercial gas mask borrowed from an oil refinery to empty Herbsaint's five coolers and freezers that were crammed with spoiling inventory. Before the job was finished he had filled seventy large trash bags.

Link plans to reopen sometime in October, but first the restaurant will have to be decontaminated and all new equipment will have to be purchased.

In New Orleans, millions of dollars of inventory—some of the world's best-tasting inventory—was wasted. It is hard to get a grip on the scale of this disaster as it relates to the New Orleans and Gulf Coast restaurant business. One can take Donald Link's story and multiply it by thousands. From the little po'boy shops to the convention hotels, the job of cleanup and decontamination will be grueling, problematic, and nauseating.

On the second day after the storm, I collected a few of my managers and cleaned the six coolers and two freezers at my Hattiesburg restaurants. Although the food had been held without electricity for two days, some had remained under forty degrees, and most was still cool to the touch. As I began to stack boxes of produce on the sidewalk, an amazing thing happened. Residents and evacuees, who had been wandering through the parking lot in a state of post-disaster shock, looking for food, water, batteries, or an opened drugstore, began forming a spontaneous line. We were able to give all of the safe and usable food to those in need.

The restaurateurs of New Orleans weren't able to give away their inventory, and a lot of them haven't even been able to return to their properties. Some will reopen; others are rumored to be closing permanently. My guess is that the city's thriving restaurant trade will return, and quicker than expected.

Before long, the French Quarter will be filled with tourists. The aroma of fried-seafood po'boys and gumbo will fill the air. The Uptown and River Bend eateries will open their doors and welcome the world with open arms. I'll be there with an empty stomach and a hearty appetite.

Tomorrow, if *Bon Appetit* were to compile an updated list of the nation's top five restaurants—even with all of its eating establishments closed—New Orleans would still make the list. The ranking wouldn't be for sentimental reasons, or for being the cause célèbre, but because New Orleans food is just that good.

Hurry back, guys. We're hungry.

The Loss of a Legend

Last week Austin Leslie, the creator of Creole soul food and a true New Orleans culinary journeyman, died in Atlanta. He was seventy-one.

Leslie, who most recently manned the stoves at Pampy's Creole Kitchen, was best known for his groundbreaking Creole soulfood restaurant Chez Helene and his world-class fried chicken.

I met Leslie while he was working the deep fryer at Jacques-Imo's on Oak Street in the Carrolton district of New Orleans. At that point in his life he had seen all of the highs and lows of the restaurant business over the course of a fifty-year career in which he began as a fried-chicken delivery boy, rising to the pinnacle of multi-restaurant proprietor—including one property that inspired a CBS television series.

While in high school, Leslie delivered chicken via bicycle from the kitchens of Portia's restaurant on Rampart Street. Years later, he would credit Portia owner Bill Turner as the man who taught him how to fry chicken. After a brief military stint, he began his lifelong culinary tour of duty with a job as an assistant chef in the kitchen of the D. H. Holmes department store on Canal Street.

In 1964 he joined his aunt Helen at her restaurant Chez Helene in the Seventh Ward. It was there that he perfected his version of the Portia's fried chicken recipe.

After he purchased the restaurant from his aunt in the mid-1970s, Leslie's fame and popularity grew. In short order, a string of fried chicken franchises opened and satellite Chez Helene restaurants opened in Chicago and the French Quarter. He was on top of the world and being touted as the next Prudhomme—the African-American Prudhomme. His Creole soul food was the hit of one of the nation's most prominent food cities and was on track to becoming a nationwide phenomenon.

In the mid-1980s CBS aired the television show *Frank's Place,* inspired by—and based loosely on—Leslie and his restaurant. The show tackled dramatic inner-city social issues in a sitcom format, but though critically acclaimed, it failed to reach an audience and was canceled after one season.

By the early 1990s urban decay, lack of management, and poor business decisions led to the closing of Leslie's restaurants, including the flagship on North Robertson Street. He spent the next few years picking up odd kitchen jobs in locales as far away as Copenhagen, Denmark.

In 1996 Leslie wound up back in New Orleans manning the fry station at Jacques-Imo's. It was there, one evening before a concert, that I met the man who first fused Creole and soul into what would become a much copied culinary style in a city known for its culinary style. He was humble and gracious and jovial. The restaurant business had beaten him down, but the scars weren't visible.

The Leslie signature on a perfectly cooked chicken thigh was a sprinkling of chopped parsley and garlic. Those simple ingredients, along with an evaporated milk marinade, are what took the man from neighborhood delivery boy, to the heights of Hollywood, to the fry station at a neighborhood joint.

Recently, Leslie was hired on as the new executive chef at Pampy's Creole Kitchen in the Seventh Ward. It would be his last stop.

Austin Leslie spent two days in the attic of his home after Hurricane Katrina. The septuagenarian was finally rescued from the sweltering ninety-eight-degree heat and stifling humidity and relocated to the chaos and horror of the New Orleans Convention Center. He remained there, lost in a sea of distress, until he was relocated to Atlanta. On September 28 he was admitted into an Atlanta hospital with a high fever. He died the next day.

New Orleans was Leslie's lifeline. Over a fifty-year period he had survived all of the blows that the brutal restaurant business could deliver and was still enduring. The man who helped put New Orleans cuisine on the map died homeless, in a city that had no clue of his culinary pedigree. In the end, the storm that continues to take lives even a month after its landfall, struck one of its most monumental blows in a city far removed from the one that care forgot.

There will be no shrines erected for Austin Leslie. No publisher will ever issue a tribute to his legacy. Two hard-to-find and out-of-print cookbooks are all that remain as a testament to his career—that and the memories of the hundreds of thousands who enjoyed his fried chicken, Creole-stuffed peppers, and étouffée.

Revival, Reopening, and Renewal

My last New Orleans meal prior to Hurricane Katrina was a lunch with my wife and children at K-Paul's restaurant. I have often revisited that memorable experience during the stress and rebuilding of these last four months. For my first dining experience back in the city I wanted to return to Paul Prudhomme's mainstay on Chartres Street.

After easily finding a prime parking space, my wife and I began our leisurely walk through the French Quarter. It was the Friday evening before New Year's Eve and the city was eerily still. We passed a bar, usually loud and packed with tourists, only to find a lone bartender behind the bar and a cocktail waitress—chin in her palms—sitting on the only occupied barstool.

All was quiet on the restaurant front. There seemed to be more police than pedestrians. I commented to my wife that I felt safer than I have ever felt walking the streets of the Crescent City.

We turned at the Saint Louis Cathedral, headed south on Chartres, and were surprised that everything looked the same, though cleaner. As we approached K-Paul's, the sounds of a zydeco band playing on the sidewalk echoed off of the centuries-old buildings. Chef Paul was greeting guests in front of the restaurant. A routine, I am told, he has been observing every evening since the reopening.

I have often stated that the shrimp creole, jambalaya, and étouffée produced daily in the K-Paul's kitchens are the finest examples of those dishes ever created...the gold standard. We began the meal with an appetizer portion of shrimp étouffée and a shrimp Rockefeller dish served on fried green tomatoes. The étouffée was dark, rich, and flavorful, and held up to all previous billing.

When a guy wants to know how the national monetary system works, he goes to Alan Greenspan, when he wants to learn how to throw a pass he calls Brett Favre, when he wants to eat the world's best gumbo, he looks no further than Paul Prudhomme. Our second course was a bowl of chicken and andouille gumbo, and I quickly reminded myself—for the 935th time—why I love living so close to New Orleans.

As we finished our soup, the members of the zydeco band, who had now made their way through the front door, began strolling from table to table. I have eaten many a jazz brunch; this was my first zydeco dinner. Midway through the song, Chef Paul entered the dining room waving a white napkin and leading a conga line of customers. It was a surreal experience. "Only in New Orleans," my wife commented.

The city felt alive again.

After entrees of expertly prepared blackened tuna and pan-fried drum, we skipped dessert, with hopes of visiting the newly reopened and virtually tourist-free Cafe Du Monde.

On the sidewalk outside the restaurant, I asked Prudhomme how his life had been impacted since the storm. "We have fed thirty-five thousand relief workers since the storm," he said. "We were the first tablecloth restaurant to [re]open in the Quarter."

When I told him that his étouffée and Creole dishes were the finest examples of those dishes I had ever tasted, he replied, "It's all in the stock." I then commented on how his stocks were so intense, rich, and deep with flavor. His response was, "They have to be," the food, like the man—no nonsense.

No one has impacted the nation's regional cooking scene more than Paul Prudhomme. He is the most underestimated chef in America. He is much more than blackened redfish. Make no mistake, he is still the king. He packs more flavor and boldness into a dish that anyone I know.

Julia Child and James Beard were two of this country's greatest culinary icons. Sadly, they are gone, which—in my mind—makes Paul Prudhomme America's greatest living culinary national treasure. He has won countless culinary awards and accolades, lectured around the world, fed heads of state, given tirelessly to charities, written eight cookbooks, and produced six instructional cooking videos, two of which topped the *Billboard* charts for fifty-three consecutive weeks.

In these days of image-conscious and cleavage-bearing TV chefs, designer foams, elaborate vertical presentations, and salads made with fiddlehead ferns, it is refreshing when a world-class chef sticks to the basics. Prudhomme has the knowledge to prepare any type food he wants. Lucky for us, he stays true to his roots.

While we were walking past the Saint Louis Cathedral, a military Humvee stopped in front of the church and six National Guardsmen stepped out. As we spoke to the soldiers, bells began chiming at the cathedral. Of all of the times I have been in that area, I have never heard a bell ring. I don't know if the carillon has always been there, or if the bells have been installed since the storm. Either way the sound was beautiful, signaling the end to a perfect night in the city, and heralding a fresh start with good things to come in the upcoming year.

Hurricane Food

As I sit and write this column, I am watching the television coverage of Hurricane Gustav as it makes landfall a few hundred miles west of my breakfast room.

My family hunkered down several days in advance this time, which beats the last-minute scramble we endured before Hurricane Katrina.

This morning I am ice rich. I am surrounded by ice chests, bottled water, and hurricane food.

Ice is the key.

Before Katrina, I encouraged my managers and friends to load up on ice from one of the three large ice machines located at our restaurant. They seemed skeptical, but filled their ice chests nonetheless. I was remembering the days after Hurricane Camille when, as an eight-year-old, I waited in line with my mother at the local ice house every afternoon for two weeks until electricity was restored.

Once my friends and managers loaded up on pre-Katrina ice, I filled a large ice chest with the cubes left at the bottom of the restaurant's bin. After securing my business, I lifted the ice chest into the back of my truck and headed home to ride out the storm with my family.

Three blocks from the restaurant, as I was pulling through an intersection, I heard a loud crash. I looked into my rearview mirror and watched, as the last available ice in Hattiesburg, Mississippi, spilled all over the hot August asphalt. I had forgotten to close the tailgate on my truck and the ice chest had flown out the back as I drove through the intersection.

This morning I am ice rich. I am surrounded by ice chests, bottled water, and hurricane food.

My first memory of hurricane food was as that eight-year-old in the aftermath of Camille. My mother, brother, and I cooked over Sterno leftover from my brother's Boy Scout days. Our neighborhood also banded together and gathered at the house of a man who had a natural-gas grill.

In 1969, at the exact time concertgoers were listening to Jimi Hendrix, Janis Joplin, and the Who make rock-and-roll history at the Woodstock concert in upstate New York, we were eating beanie weenies in the sweltering heat of my backyard. From what I've seen in the Woodstock movie, the conditions were similar.

Kids don't mind adverse conditions. I never remember complaining about the heat in the days after Camille. To me, it was like camping out in the backyard.

As a forty-something I was about as hot as I've ever been in the still, quiet days following Katrina. Several months after Katrina blew through town, my son asked my wife, "Momma, when do we get to sleep in the den and eat ham sandwiches again?"

No power, no water, no ice, no trees, and my son remembers ham sandwiches. I remember Sterno. Most attendees at Woodstock probably don't remember anything.

This morning I am ice rich. I am surrounded by ice chests, bottled water, and hurricane food. It appears that we dodged Mother Nature's 120-mph bullet. Let's all pray that it will be many years before we again have to worry about Sterno, ice, and hurricane food.

Shrimp Season 2008

Mississippi's shrimp season is open.

I was eating oatmeal in my breakfast room watching WLOX's morning show when the opening-day announcement was made. The television station cut to their on-location camera covering the waters of the Gulf of Mexico and there was one shrimp boat on the water. One boat.

I can remember sitting in the same spot ten years ago, watching that station's coverage of the opening day of shrimp season. There were hundreds of boats in the water. As the sun rose near Ocean Springs, boats were crisscrossing the Gulf, lines out, nets down, dragging the Gulf for the single most popular seafood offering in the world.

The history of Mississippi shrimping is rich and storied. Fourth-generation Biloxi fishing families, Croatian immigrants, and Vietnamese refugees have shouldered the load for us. Shrimping has always been a family business. In 1900 Biloxi was labeled "The Seafood Capital of the World." Today we have one shrimp boat making news on opening day.

With two thousand-gallon fuel tanks, $4-per-gallon gas, and processor's pricing challenges caught in the middle, we are headed into uncharted waters. The Mississippi Gulf Coast was built on the scarred and calloused fingers of its oyster shuckers and shrimp pickers, and on the backs of its shrimp boat captains. They all seem to be going the way of the buggy whip and moving inland.

Hurricane Katrina wiped out many of the local shrimpers, and it seems that Middle East oil prices are working on the rest. We have lost more than 50 percent of our working shrimp boats since Katrina. Something has to be done, but I'm afraid that I don't know the answer. I'm not sure if anyone does.

Shrimp is the number one seafood in America. Oysters are more controversial, complex, and complicated, and crabmeat is more delicate and formal, but shrimp are universal. Local shrimpers might be one of the most underappreciated working groups in the country.

Last May a photographer and I traveled to Biloxi to photograph the shrimp fleet. The boats were all docked. At the time gas was $3 per gallon. A few were selling shrimp off of the back of their boats, but most boats seemed abandoned.

A Vietnamese woman in a straw hat and her two daughters were icing down shrimp on the back of their boat. The woman seemed to be in her late fifties, her daughters in their mid twenties. The mother was unloading ice from her pickup truck, loading it into yellow plastic laundry baskets, and then filling large ice chests on the boat. She was lifting amounts that I would've had trouble handling. I offered to help, but she didn't speak English, her daughters said, "No thank you."

For the thirty to forty-five minutes we spent shooting in and around the dock, the woman was steadily shoveling ice and loading ice chests. She never stopped. She never looked up, and she never once complained, or even hinted at an expression that demonstrated complaint.

The daughters were smiling and joking with each other. Their mother's face was focused and determined on the task at hand. Here was a woman who had probably dealt with untold controversy before she came to this country, and was steadily enduring life's daily blows with her family in today's local seafood industry. The look in her eyes was pure determination and focus—a mother's mission to endure.

At the time, I talked to my photographer friend about the woman's work ethic and focus. It was remarkable.

A year has past. As I sit here today, I wonder if the woman and her family will survive today's economic challenges and the untold trials that lay ahead. If I were a betting man, my money would be on her. I've seen the look in her eyes.

What will become of the independent, family shrimper? I wish I had the answer.

The Sun Will Come Out Tomorrow

At a book signing on the Mississippi Gulf Coast last week, I was hit with a blinding jolt of reality.

I have been a victim of out-of-sight out-of-mind Katrina apathy. My hometown of Hattiesburg was hit hard. Yet we bounced back quickly.

At Pass Christian Books—a small, independent bookstore which used to overlook the Gulf of Mexico—business is not the same. As with most beachfront structures in Pass Christian—and all along the Gulf front in the post-Katrina world—only a slab of concrete remains.

Pass Christian Books has moved five miles north of the beach to Delisle, Mississippi, until the city's infrastructure is restored.

I am a huge fan of the old-line seafood restaurants of the Mississippi Gulf Coast. I have fond memories of eating at Baricev's, the Friendship House, McElroy's, and the like. I have always encouraged support of the independent restaurants of the Coast.

One restaurant that I must have passed a thousand times, but never once visited, was Annie's at Henderson Point. As with most of the independent restaurants within a few blocks of the Gulf, Annie's was a casualty of Katrina. They, too, moved to Delisle after the storm.

As Wyatt Waters and I signed books, we ordered a cup of gumbo from the newly relocated Annie's (now Cafe Annie, located next door to the bookstore). The gumbo was rich, the roux was dark, and it had the distinct taste of a well-made crab stock in the foreground.

As I finished my gumbo, I felt an overwhelming pang of guilt for not visiting Annie's in its original location.

Annie's restaurant opened on Henderson Point in 1928. The family-run operation withstood three hurricanes, two fires, and everything that Mother Nature could throw at it until Katrina blew through the Coast in 2005.

Annie Lutz—who recently celebrated her eighty-ninth birthday—has been working in the restaurant since she was a little girl and still mans the cash register out front. Her niece, Jackie Jex, says that Annie's been there "since she was able to reach the counter."

Annie lived her entire life in an apartment attached to the restaurant. It's gone, too.

In addition to excellent seafood gumbo, Cafe Annie serves a full array of old-line Coast favorites such as Trout Amandine, broiled fish, and Italian-inspired seafood dishes which have been the mainstay of independent Gulf Coast restaurants for over a century. As Jex gave me an oral history of the restaurant while pointing to photographs on the walls, I lamented the fact that I would never again know the restaurant in its original state.

The day before the Coast book signing, I was at a book event in New Orleans. During a conversation with a New Orleans customer, Hurricane Katrina came up. As the conversation moved to national attention and national media coverage of the event in the months following the storm, the New Orleans woman apologized to me for all of the coverage that they received and offered an "I'm sorry," saying Mississippians hadn't received enough of the attention.

I told her that everything is OK. We never wanted a lot of attention. We took care of ourselves, we took care of our neighbors, and our governor took care of the rest.

To a person, everyone who bought books at the Pass Christian book signing had lost all of their cookbooks—and their homes along with them—to the storm. No one complained. No one seemed resentful. They had gotten on with their daily lives and to the business of rebuilding the Coast. "It's only stuff," one woman commented.

It's people like Scott Naugle at Pass Christian Books, Annie Lutz at Cafe Annie, and the customers of those, and many other, businesses who have rolled up their sleeves and are back fighting the good fight—the daily fight, the hard fight—and doing business in what remains of a storm-ravaged community.

At Cafe Annie, eighty years of Gulf Coast restaurant history have been reduced to a small wall of black-and-white eight-by-ten photographs. There are hundreds of businesses with similar stories all along the Gulf. Let's throw apathy to the wind and keep them in sight, and in mind, during the holiday shopping season, and throughout the coming years.

Heroes

The world is filled with heroes; unfortunately we sometimes don't know where to find them.

Years ago I was closing a deal with a very successful businessperson. One of the principals involved in the negotiation ran a large national company that was responsible for inventing a certain product. I was given the lengthy details of his business success story immediately before the deal was negotiated, in the hopes that I would be awed and intimidated during the negotiation process. I wasn't.

I am not easily awed. Especially when basing someone's worth is being based on the size of his or her bank account.

Our society has misplaced the worth and value of its people. We are all valuable, each and every one of us. Basketball stars are put on a pedestal simply because they can jump high and throw a ball through a hoop. For this they receive millions and millions of dollars and the general public's admiration.

Actors make a living by pretending to be someone else while speaking dialogue written by someone else. For this they command salaries as high as $20 million per movie and become the subject of half of the magazine articles on the news rack. It's as if the more money they make, and the more "celebrity" they garner, the more we become enamored with their lives.

Those people are not heroes. True heroes are people such as Cookie and Bill Proubt, a couple who had successful professional careers and left it all to start a soup kitchen to feed those who couldn't afford to eat. Twenty years ago they formed Christian Services, Inc., in my hometown, where they feed, clothe, and counsel tens of thousands of people every year. I'll take Cookie and Bill Proubt over the roster of every NBA team, any day.

Heroes are people such as Tommy Griffin, who was forced to sell his family business and spend a year away from his wife and three children to honor his National Guard duty in Iraq. I'll take one Tommy Griffin over the entire audience at the Academy Awards and not think twice about it.

Cat Cora, a native of Jackson, Mississippi, is nowhere near the pinnacle of her career, yet on her way up she founded the Chefs for Humanity organization, which is the only group of its kind.

Chefs for Humanity was formed to be a first responder to food during crises and emergencies. In the immediate days after Hurricane Katrina, Cora and a group of notable volunteers mobilized to the Coast and set up mobile kitchens to feed those in need. Today, the organization continues to grow and expand its mission.

One idea, one thought, from one person is making a huge difference in the lives of those who need help the most.

Today there are people on the Gulf Coast who wake up every morning in tents and FEMA trailers not knowing what is in store for them, that day, or any day in the future. All across the country, people are in need. We've got plenty of stars; what we need are more heroes.

I am truly awed by the Proubts, Griffins, Coras of the world.

The true heroes aren't in the pages of *People* magazine or *Sports Illustrated* but right next door, down the street, and across town. Join them and be a true hero to someone in need.

Chapter 5
Food

Little Biscuits, Big Appetites

The fondest food memories of my youth are drawn from my grandmother's house.

For seventy-plus years my paternal grandmother lived in a large white house on an oak-lined, brick-paved street in my hometown of Hattiesburg, Mississippi. Her home had thirteen-foot ceilings, Oriental rugs, crystal chandeliers, European antiques, and a window-unit air conditioner in every room. I spent many days propped on a stool in the kitchen next to the window unit watching her fry chicken, roast lamb, or roll biscuit dough.

Summer lunches were eaten in the breakfast room. The formal dining room was reserved for special-occasion evening meals and Sunday lunches. I spent almost every Sunday lunch for the first eighteen years of my life in that dining room.

The Sunday lunch menu was on a revolving schedule. One Sunday we'd eat roast beef, the next week she would serve fried chicken. Turkey and dressing made a once-a-month appearance and were not reserved for Thanksgiving alone. My favorite meal in that house—roasted leg of lamb—was served at least once a month.

The vegetables changed weekly. The starch was usually rice and gravy though mashed potatoes made an appearance on fried chicken day. Iced tea was served in sterling silver goblets, and the one constant, week in-week out, were her biscuits. The woman could flat-out bake biscuits.

The biscuits were very small—about the size of a silver dollar—and light, and good. I could eat a dozen of them. Nothing sleeps as hard for a Sunday afternoon nap as a meal of a dozen biscuits, leg of lamb, and rice and gravy.

She served mint jelly on lamb day, but my brother and I always opted for grape jelly—not for the lamb, but for all for the biscuits we consumed. We called it "plain jelly," I am not sure why, unless we thought mint jelly was "fancy."

I have tried to replicate my grandmother's biscuits for years, to no avail. She never wrote down her recipe and, unfortunately, I never asked for it. Two cookbooks ago my sous-chef and I spent almost two weeks trying to recreate those biscuits but hit dead end after dead end.

In the almost twenty years since her death, I have not eaten a biscuit as good as my grandmother's. Until last week.

Last week I was a guest speaker at the Natchez Literary and Cinema Celebration. Included with the admission to my speech was a luncheon following the speech at Stanton Hall's Carriage House Restaurant. On the short drive to the restaurant, my host informed me that the restaurant's specialties were fried chicken and biscuits. I hear this often, and every time I do, I say to myself—*Good, sure, but not as good as Mam-Maw's.*

While I was eating and visiting with my hosts, someone passed a plate of little biscuits. Even though they were small, I was polite and took only one. I placed it on my plate, where I forgot about it until midway through the meal. When I finally took a bite, I was stunned. "That's it!" I said.

"What's it?" said one of my hosts.

"My grandmother's biscuit, this is just like hers. I haven't tasted anything like this in twenty years." My hosts asked the server for one more plate. The server brought two. I threw manners out the window and put three biscuits on my plate. Someone passed the butter and then the man next to me handed me a small bowl of grape preserves—plain jelly.

The rest of the meal's conversation went something like this:

"That was a great speech today, Robert."

(With mouth full.) "Would you please pass the biscuits?"

"Robert, how's that diet you've been writing about coming along?"

"Is there any butter left in that bowl? Where's that other plate of biscuits?"

"Robert, I just love when you wrote about the diet devil and the diet angel. That was clever."

"Y'all, I know I'm making a pig of myself, but I think I'll have a few more biscuits."

"Robert, would you like dessert?"

"No, but I'll take a few more of those biscuits. Do you think we could get some more plain jelly?"

Apparently, word of my substantial biscuit consumption made its way to the restaurant's manager, who handed me a recipe card on my way out the door and invited me for a return visit.

I haven't prepared the Carriage House Restaurant's biscuit recipe yet. But if the results are anywhere close to the ones I ate last week in Natchez, a two-decade search is over.

Benton's Bacon Is Best

I have discovered the world's best bacon.

Chef John Besh recently introduced me to Allan Benton's bacon. Besh was introduced to the product through Chef John Fleer of Blackberry Farm in the foothills of the Smoky Mountains, not too far from the smokehouse where Allan Benton does his magic.

Benton has been curing hams, bacon, and prosciutto for thirty-three years, though the business has been in operation in Madisonville, Tennessee, for almost sixty years. Madisonville is located a few miles off of I-75 between Chattanooga and Knoxville and from this day forward will be known to me as the center of the porcine universe.

In 1947, a dairy farmer named Albert Hicks began curing hams and making bacon for his neighbors. In 1973, Benton, a former high school guidance counselor, purchased the business, and luckily for us, he has been smoking and curing pork ever since; using the tried-and-true methods passed down from generations of Smoky Mountain farmers.

Benton's bacon is perfect. I am convinced that when God invented bacon, this is how He wanted it to taste. When I asked Benton why his bacon was so superior to the store-bought variety, he stated, "We do it like your grandparents would have done it. Like my grandfather did it, and like Albert Hicks did it."

The country's taste buds are waking up from a decade's long dry spell. The heirloom vegetable movement is taking hold, and the general public is beginning to recognize the impact of individual flavor on a dish. Today's mass-marketed tomatoes have been genetically altered over the years to have thicker skins so they will ship well, redder color so they will have more eye appeal, and they're grown to be picked early and ripened in a box on the way to the market, sacrificing taste at every alteration.

Bacon is the same. Mass-produced commercial pork bellies are injected with brine in the packing house, flash-smoked in a smoke room, and are being packaged and shipped—twenty-four hours later. It's quick, it's easy, it's profitable, and the result tastes nothing like bacon did years ago.

The Allan Benton process for curing and smoking bacon takes time—a minimum of five weeks. First Benton mixes together a dry-rub blend of salt and brown sugar, rubs the pork bellies, and stacks them in a thirty-eight-degree cooler for two weeks. Next he transfers the bellies to another cooler where they hang in a forty-five-degree environment for a week-and-a-half. They are then moved to an aging room for two more weeks before they are taken to Benton's smokehouse, where they spend forty-eight hours in an intense billowing fog of thick hickory smoke.

"You wouldn't believe how much smoke you can generate out of an old wood-burning stove," Benton says. I believe it because I have eaten the end result.

In the past few years Benton's bacon has found a home in some of the finest restaurant kitchens from New York to Napa. "For years I thought I would starve," Benton says, as he gives credit to Chef Fleer for introducing his product to top chefs around the country.

The operation is still small by most standards. Benton cures approximately 12,000 hams per year, smokes around 3,500 pounds of bacon each week, and produces a prosciutto that will rival any produced in Parma, Italy. The prosciutto is cured for fourteen to sixteen months and on occasion eighteen to twenty-two months. "I like to cut the prosciutto into one-eighth-inch strips and eat it on a sandwich," Benton says.

He makes sausage, but doesn't ship it retail like the bacon, ham, and prosciutto. I ordered bacon and ham last week and am going to have to place another order soon; it's so good that I keep giving it away to my friends. Benton ships anywhere in the U.S., and the bacon keeps for up to four months in the refrigerator. Benton's Smoky Mountain Country Hams: 423-442-5003, www.bentonshams.com.

Breakfast

Recently I realized that I can look back over the course of my life and track my age by what I was eating for breakfast.

Some people associate songs with certain periods of their lives (I do that, too), but these days I tend to lean more toward food, especially breakfast food.

When I was a small child, I ate kids' cereal for breakfast. Anything with a ton of sugar and a toy in the box was good enough for me. I lived at home and watched Captain Kangaroo and the Three Stooges every morning.

When we were out of kids' cereal, I ate my mom's Corn Flakes. At first glance, they would seem to be the healthier alternative, except that I dumped loads of sugar on them. Left to my preparation, Corn Flakes were ten times as sugar-laden as Fruit Loops.

At the end of a substitute Corn Flakes breakfast, all that was left in the bottom of the bowl was a one-inch layer of white sludge. I, of course, was bouncing off of the walls on a sugar high that wouldn't wear off until noon. I have a feeling that my elementary school teachers did everything within their means to make sure that the St. John household never ran out of Fruit Loops or Count Chocula.

In junior high school I was into sweet rolls and Pop-Tarts, still sugary but quick. By the time I reached high school and had purchased my first automobile, I'd gotten into the habit of stopping by the doughnut shop on my way to school.

In my college years I rarely ate breakfast, either because I was not feeling up-to-snuff in the morning, or had yet to roll out of the bed before noon. Due to the fact that I couldn't wake up before midday, my first attempt at a college career ended abruptly when the university I was attending informed me that they no longer needed my services.

I went through a phase in my twenties where I ate lunch food for breakfast. A local fast-food joint prepared hamburgers as early as 7 a.m. I lived rent-free in a garage apartment behind my grandmother's house and rarely cooked anything, especially early in the morning.

At twenty-six-years old I opened my first restaurant. I was working ninety hours per week and pulling early morning shifts in the restaurant. I had a thirty-two-inch waist and more energy than a rabid hummingbird. I lived on cinnamon rolls and drive-through fast food in the mornings.

Over the next several years my breakfast eating grew worse and my waist grew exponentially. As I look back to the early days of my breakfast career, it seems that I made one bad choice after another. I spent forty years eating junk in the morning. It's strange because breakfast is my favorite meal.

These days, if I am home, I eat oatmeal with protein powder and Splenda. When I eat breakfast out, I usually eat a bagel, or a croissant, and scrambled eggs.

Breakfast is said to be the most important meal of the day. Yet people claim to be too busy to eat breakfast. We keep inventing gadgets to make life easier—cell phones, computerized vacuum cleaners, and heated toilet seats—yet we allege that we are busier than ever.

Maybe we are spending too much time trying to figure out how to operate all of the time-saving gadgets in our lives and not taking time to sit down and share a meal together.

My great-grandmother ate one scrambled egg, two pieces of bacon, and a slice of toast every morning. She lived to be one hundred-years old. I had a grandmother who ate toast and fresh fruit every morning. She lived to be ninety-six years old.

Less Stress + More Breakfast = Long Life. Neither of those ladies gave a hoot about time-saving technology. My grandmother once asked me, while pointing to a multicolored Wurlitzer jukebox in the corner of a nursing home public space, "Robert, is that one of those new computers I keep hearing about?"

Maybe it's time we slowed down and enjoyed breakfast. Put the cell phone in a drawer, unplug the toilet seat, and pass the orange juice.

I spent four decades eating sugar-laden junk in the morning. Maybe it's time I grew up. Then again, maybe I've got just a few more cinnamon-roll mornings left in me.

Catfish

In Sunday's *New York Times Magazine* there was an extensive article on catfish. In the article I learned that the Catfish Institute, located in Jackson, Mississippi, has chosen a new name for the catfish—Delacata.

As new made-up names for fish go, I guess "Delacata" is as good as any, though I would like to see the list of names that were eliminated. The story claimed that the Catfish Institute had "market-tested" the new name. Market-tested or not, I will still call it catfish.

The most troubling part of the story was a sentence about local catfish farmers which read, "About a third of the region's [catfish] growers have quit, and those remaining increasingly see their ponds as liabilities. If attrition continues apace, very little catfish will be farmed in the United States before long."

This is a major loss for farmers throughout the South. I have toured several catfish farms and processing plants and have been amazed by the scientific approach and world-class efficiency with which these Mississippi farmers and processors operate their businesses. And I continue to be impressed with the high-quality fish that they produce.

The problem stems from imported freshwater fish which a few unscrupulous suppliers and restaurant owners dishonestly market as catfish. There is a Vietnamese variety called Basa which is harvested in the Mekong Delta and is still marketed and sold in some establishments as "catfish." In addition to having a terrible name, Basa is an inferior-tasting fish and can't—even on its best day—compare to Mississippi farm-raised catfish.

That same day I read a story in *The Sun* about a "mutant catfish" that was killing people in India. The Goonch fish has been feeding for so long on corpses that have been thrown in the river that it has now developed a taste for human flesh. Folks, this is not the plot for an upcoming Halloween movie, it's real.

A man once caught a 161 pound Goonch. That's a big mutant catfish. *The Sun* also reported that, "the first live victim of a Goonch was thought to have been a 17-year-old Nepalese boy in April 1988," and "an 18-year-old Nepali [boy] disappeared in the river, dragged down by something described as an 'elongated pig.'"

A "flesh-eating river monster" that looks like a pig? Muddy-tasting Vietnamese Basa putting Mississippi farmers out of work? I prefer to eat my catfish, not the other way around. Make mine Mississippi-raised catfish, every time.

There is a sport practiced in rivers and lakes throughout the South called "grappling," in which people reach into logs and stumps and pull out giant catfish (or Delacata) by sticking their hands in the fish's mouth. I have seen pictures of this and the catfish they bring out of the water are huge.

To my knowledge, grappling is exclusively an American sport. One thing is for certain: If anyone is grappling for fish in India, they aren't around later that night to hang out at the campfire and tell the fish tale.

Had I sat on the Catfish Institute's what's-our-new-name-gonna-be committee, I might have gone along with the name change, but I certainly would have suggested a new tagline: "Delacata: It might not be a great name, but at least it doesn't eat you."

If you are like me and enjoy one of Mississippi's best crops—catfish— ask the owner of your favorite fish house if he or she is using American (preferably Mississippi-raised) catfish. And if that restaurant isn't, take your business elsewhere, and if the owner says, "Actually, we're serving 'Delacata,'" let 'em slide, and take solace in the fact that the place isn't serving Basa or Goonch.

Deer Sausage

I am not a deer hunter, yet I have a freezer full of deer sausage.

A few weeks ago I wrote a column about the so-called Obese Bill (HB 282). In it I offered several pieces of alternative legislation to the Mississippi House of Representatives bill that proposes to ban fat people from eating in restaurants.

In my haste to meet an editor's deadline, I forgot an alternative bill that should placed in the hopper with the rest: the Deer Sausage Law.

The Deer Sausage Law, HB 282G, states: Licensed Mississippi deer hunters, or any of their relatives or assigns, are not allowed to give away any deer meat to anyone, ever, period.

I have a theory: I believe that most people don't like to eat deer meat. Proof: I have a freezer full of deer sausage and I'm not a deer hunter. People shoot deer because they like to shoot deer. I'm OK with that. I have no objection to people shooting animals for food or for sport.

That said, the point still remains, deer meat is not good. If deer sausage was good—if it tasted like a filet mignon or a rib-eye steak, or a hamburger, even—deer hunters would hoard it in their own freezers. Even if deer sausage tasted like pork sausage, they wouldn't be trying to pawn it off on me.

My deer-hunting friends—and I have many—purchase secondary freezers to store the deer sausage that accumulates each deer season. Most of them empty these freezers at the beginning of deer season, throwing out all of the leftover deer sausage from the previous hunting season (read: 90 percent), and prepare to fill them with a new batch of deer sausage that, again, won't be eaten.

As I write, I have just thought of an amendment to HB 282G: All of the leftover deer sausage from the previous deer season must be donated to the state penal system. You say you want to crack down on crime? Make inmates eat deer sausage in our state prisons. The crime rate will drop immediately.

I like steak. My friends never try to fill my freezer with steak.

Therefore, I also propose a statewide cow-hunting season. During cow-hunting season, my friends who like to shoot things can go out and hunt a few steer. Then they can bring all of the ribeyes, strips, prime ribs, and even hamburger that won't fit into their freezers to me. I will welcome them with open arms, and a baked potato.

Cow hunting will save money, too. No one would need camouflage or long-distance rifles. Tree stands will be rendered useless, high-powered scopes won't be needed, and there'll be no need to soak one's clothes in urine. Just park the truck by the side of a field, walk out into the field. Shoot a cow. Presto! Roast beef for everyone!

And what about pig season? Pork sausage tastes a lot better than deer sausage. I would love to see one of my hunting friends arrive at my front door with a few slabs of ribs and bacon after a successful week hunting at the deer, oops make that, pig camp. I'll even purchase a supplemental deep freeze for that hunting season.

Chicken season might be a good idea, too. We can release the chickens from all of the state's chicken houses and let them assimilate into the wild. The countryside will smell a lot better and you'll never get stuck behind one of those big chicken-hauling trucks ever again.

The problem of wildlife walking out in front of your car won't be so bad during chicken season. A full-sized deer can total an automobile. What harm can be done by a rooster?

My friend Marshall Ramsey says that being on the Natchez Trace after dark is like driving through a petting zoo at night. Actually it might be fun to drive down the Trace at night while chickens are crossing the road. We could implement a statewide points system: 10 points for a Bantam Rooster, 15 points for a Rhode Island Red, and for a Black Breasted Red Cubalaya, 25 points and a new upright freezer.

Question: Why did the chicken cross the road?

Answer: Because everyone was sick of deer sausage.

Donald Duck Orange Juice

As I sat at the breakfast table this morning, I stared at my glass of orange juice and contemplated the beverage's evolution.

When I was a child, orange juice was kept in a small can in the freezer. One opened the can, dumped the syrupy, icy, orange clump into a pitcher, filled the empty can with tap water, added it to the pitcher, stirred, and orange juice was born.

I was born in an era just before major changes in food packaging were implemented. I am sandwiched between milk delivered in glass bottles on the back doorsteps and milk purchased in half-gallon paper cartons in a store. In those days all orange juice came in a can, just like chicken came on a bone.

For centuries—before freezers and concentrate cans—one had to squeeze one's own orange juice, if there were fresh oranges available. That is still an option today, though I don't imagine many people do it.

Upscale grocery stores have machines that mechanically squeeze fresh oranges while you wait. The quality, as always, depends on the quality of the oranges used. Occasionally the orange juice squeezed from one of those grocery store robot juicers tastes a little like orange rind. Bitter.

Today orange juice mostly comes in half-gallon cartons. There are many options available. As a kid I had two options in the morning—orange juice concentrate or no orange juice at all—today I can have orange juice with no pulp, orange juice with a small amount of pulp, orange juice with a lot of pulp, orange juice with calcium added, orange juice with less sugar, with fiber, low acid, heart healthy…you get the point.

Actually there were three orange juice options back in the day: orange juice, no orange juice, or Donald Duck orange juice. Option three— Donald Duck orange juice—was an option that was actually worse than not drinking orange juice at all. It was bad.

Donald Duck orange juice tasted like grapefruit juice. I hate grapefruit juice. For some reason, back in the 1940s, the Walt Disney Company gave a license to an orange juice manufacturer to use the likeness of one of their top cartoon characters, Donald Duck, in selling a new beverage. The company then proceeded to put bitter-tasting grapefruit juice in a can and market it as orange juice. Disney has licensed everything imaginable, and this is their oldest surviving license.

The cans of Donald Duck orange juice always looked rusted on the outside and the product inside always had a faint taste of the metallic can.

Question: If Donald Duck orange juice tastes like grapefruit juice, how awful does Donald Duck grapefruit juice taste?

My mom bought Donald Duck orange juice every once in a while. I am not sure why. The Sunflower grocery store always had plenty of frozen concentrate on hand.

As I sat staring at my orange juice this morning—orange juice, by the way, that had been poured from a paper carton (medium pulp)—I reflected back on my first experience with Donald Duck orange juice. I was around eight years old. I was eating sweet rolls prepared by my across-the-street neighbor. I had asked for milk (the perfect sweet roll accompaniment). My mother poured orange juice, and not just any orange juice, Donald Duck orange juice.

It was the first case of taste-bud shock I had ever encountered. Taste-bud shock is when one thinks one is drinking a particular beverage, and there is an entirely different beverage in the glass. For example, your taste buds are ready to taste milk, your brain is sending signals all over your body— here comes some cold, delicious milk. Except it's not milk, it is orange juice. Immediately your taste buds panic and your brain goes into sensory overload.

In my inaugural bout with taste-bud shock, my taste buds were bombarded with Donald Duck orange juice when they were expecting milk. That is a third-degree taste-bud shock, skipping two steps altogether and going from milk expectancy to something that tastes like canned grapefruit juice.

We switched to Tang after that. I hate Tang, too, but next to Donald Duck orange juice, Tang is nectar of the gods.

Before long, we switched back to frozen canned orange juice concentrate, and that is where we stayed until I moved away from home.

In my twenties I drifted away from orange juice, and by the time I returned to the fold, orange juice was being sold in cartons.

Sometimes we get caught up in romanticizing the "good old days." Folks, there are no "good old days" when it comes to orange juice. It's better than ever.

Today I drink orange juice that comes from a carton. And I don't even have to open the carton and make a paper pour spout out of the corners of the top. The good folks at the orange juice manufacturing plant have seen fit to put a small plastic screw top on the side of my orange juice carton. I shake and pour. No can, no grapefruits, no rust, and no taste-bud shock—just sweet, slightly pulpy, Florida orange juice.

Fall Peaches?

Is it fall yet?

I don't know when the first official day of fall arrives, but around here, it doesn't feel like "fall" until mid-December. The first day of autumnal equinox is September 23. But on September 23 in South Mississippi it doesn't feel much different than August 23, or July 23 for that matter.

"Autumn" is a term reserved for people who live in a part of the country where leaves turn brilliant shades of red, yellow, and orange. They wear wool sweaters in October; start worrying about when the first frost will arrive, and whether the snow blower needs a pre-season tune-up.

We have no leaves. We have green pine needles which turn a dull and ugly brown. We use our lawnmowers into November, have no idea what frost looks like, and—with the exception of those attending an Ole Miss football game—our wool sweaters, skirts, and jackets stay packed in mothballs until they are ready to be pulled out for the two-week period in late January we call winter.

Autumn is a season that sounds cool and brisk. It was ninety-two degrees yesterday. It has been said that South Mississippi has four seasons: almost summer, summer, still summer, and Christmas. I have friends who measure the seasons as: dove, deer, duck, and turkey. We badly want to have a fall in South Mississippi, though all we can really do is keep raking pine straw and reading *Southern Living* to find out when the leaves are at their peak in every other zone but ours.

Our weather does have its advantages. I was traveling down U.S. 49 last week and noticed a sign at a fruit stand that advertised fresh "tree-ripened peaches." I wheeled in and checked out the newly arrived crop. When I asked the lady where they were picked, she said, "South Carolina." I was expecting the typical off-season answer of California, Mexico, or South America.

To my knowledge, I had never eaten South Carolina peaches. As far as I was concerned, the summer peach season started with Chilton

County, Alabama, and later moved to Georgia, where it ended. I guess it makes sense that the late season would keep the crop moving farther east, into South Carolina.

I bought two baskets and dreamed of sliced peaches for breakfast.

I went to the South Carolina Department of Agriculture's website to research South Carolina peaches, and learned more than I ever needed to know. They seem to resent Georgia's peach popularity and don't hide their discontent with statements such as: "South Carolina ranks #3 nationally in fresh production. At one time, one county in South Carolina could produce more commercially grown fresh peaches than the entire state of Georgia." They have also adopted the motto "Tastier Peach State." Talk about a chip on your shoulder.

Ultimately what I learned from this entire experience is that no matter where the peaches come from, unless you are buying them in late June, July, or early August, they just don't taste like summer, no matter how hot it is outside.

Give Me Some Skin, Big Ganny

During the first twenty years of my life I never encountered a boneless, skinless chicken breast.

When I was a child, all chicken came under cellophane with bone and skin attached. The drumstick, the breast, the thigh, and even the wing, all had skin and bones. That's the way God intended chicken to be sold and fried. Read it, it's in the Bible somewhere. I think in one of those obscure Old Testament chapters like Amos or Obadiah.

True story: The first time I ever saw a boneless skinless chicken offering, I was at a restaurant on a date. The girl I was with asked, "How do they walk around without any bones, and don't they get cold without any skin?" For the record, she wasn't blond, but she was very, very pretty.

I was having dinner with a group last week when a friend posed the question: "Where do you suppose they are hiding all of that chicken skin?"

It was a good question. There's so much boneless, skinless chicken being sold, they've got to be storing all of that skin somewhere. The skin is the best-tasting part. It truly is—crunchy, crispy, salt-and-pepper-laden, tasty chicken skin. It's the greatest component of fried chicken.

In the poultry section at my local grocery store, I conducted an extremely scientific survey which proved that 47.62 percent of chicken available for sale is sold without bones and skin. Which means almost half of the world's chicken skin is just hanging around the butcher department in limbo, lonely, and without a mission.

Restaurants whose primary offering is fried boneless, skinless chicken breast strips are popping up all over the place. They're the "in" thing with teenagers and twentysomethings. I don't want to eat a chicken's fingers and I certainly don't want to eat his nuggets. I demand skin on my chicken and I want dark meat, too. Where has all of the dark meat gone? I want dark meat. I want it to have skin and bones, and I want it now.

Save me the but-all-of-the-fat-is-in-the-skin argument. Most people who are eating fast food don't give a rooster's beak about fat. How does one explain fifteen years of chicken strip-only restaurants and sixty years of Baskin-Robbins? The Baskin Robbins Heath Bar Shake has 2,300 calories and 108 grams of fat! Trust me, fat is not an issue in that segment of the restaurant biz.

I want to open a restaurant that serves only fried chicken skin. Of course there will have to be some type of sauce to dip the fried chicken skin into—comeback sauce (the ultimate condiment)—and two side orders. No fries or coleslaw like the traditional chicken strip places. How about tater tots and applesauce? Granted, applesauce isn't very popular and doesn't fit in with the concept, but I like applesauce, and, after all, it's my fried chicken-skin restaurant, isn't it?

I once knew a lady whose grandchildren called her "Big Ganny," no "r," just Ganny. She made excellent fried chicken, yet the only part of the chicken her grandchildren would eat was the skin. Smart kids. "Give me some skin, Big Ganny," they would say. I think I'll call my fried chicken-skin concept Big Ganny's Chicken Skin Palace.

And after I open Big Ganny's Chicken Skin Palace, I'm going after Hooters. I will open a chain of restaurants that serve only spicy buffalo chicken thighs with the skin on. I'll call the place Buffalo Thighs. Or maybe I'll purchase land across the street from Hooters and hire a lot of diminutively chested waitresses and call it Peepers. Equal time for all, I say.

Either way, I'll be serving my bird with the skin on. It's the best-tasting part. The rest just tastes like chicken.

Is That a Piece of Cornbread in Your Pocket...

My grandmother made the world's best biscuits.

She passed away twenty years ago and I have been trying to replicate them ever since. Her biscuits were small, light, and slightly salty, with a hint buttermilk. She never followed a recipe, yet they were consistent every time she made them. I could eat a dozen over the course of a Sunday afternoon meal.

A few years ago I gave a speech in Natchez. Afterward my hosts invited me to lunch at the Carriage House Restaurant. At the Carriage House, they served my grandmother's biscuits, or at least a recipe that tasted exactly like my grandmother's biscuits. They were great. I ate a dozen of them.

Yesterday, I was invited to be a part of an after-church luncheon to celebrate a friend's book release. The meal was of the standard Deep-South-after-church-Sunday-meal variety—roast beef, gravy, corn, beans, fried okra, and iced tea—right up my alley, and all good.

There was a basket of cornbread—sticks and muffins—at the end of the sideboard. I opted for a stick. I took one bite and was instantly transformed to my grandmother's table. My grandmother served biscuits with formal Sunday lunches, but cornbread with casual Saturday afternoon meals. This cornbread tasted just like my grandmother's.

The cornbread at my friend Chalie's house was crisp on the bottom from baking in hot cast-iron and dusted with a light sprinkling of cornmeal. It wasn't sweet, crumbly, cake-like, or dense. It was everything I require from a stick of cornbread. Beautiful.

I threw manners out the window and placed a second and third piece of cornbread on my plate. I ate a few pieces of okra and pushed some roast beef around and then grabbed my fourth piece of cornbread.

The table conversation was rapid-fire and graciously raucous. I spoke a little, but held back because my mother always told me not to speak with my mouth full, and at this meal my mouth always seemed to be crammed with cornbread.

Every once in a while I would add to the conversation with something like, "Did someone steal my cornbread?" Or "I could have sworn that there were two pieces of cornbread on my plate just a few seconds ago."

There was no subtle way of gorging myself with cornbread, because the basket was located across the room and I had to get up and walk over to it every time I wanted another piece. Had the basket been on the table, I could have placed it in front of me and then pointed to an imaginary something out the window. "Is that a woolly mammoth in the front yard?" And while everyone's head was turned, I could have grabbed a few pieces of cornbread and hidden them in my lap.

I was debating on slipping a few cornbread sticks in my pocket and taking them into the bathroom to eat in private, when I noticed that all of the sticks were gone—only muffins remained. But I wasn't finished. I wanted more. I was desperate, but not so desperate as to walk around the house with cornbread muffins poking out of my front pockets—sticks, maybe…muffins—no way.

The lunch was being served during a thunderstorm. By the time the electricity went out, I was on my seventh piece of cornbread. In the dark, I snuck over to the sideboard to nab number eight. I don't think anyone saw me. They might have heard some contented moaning and smacking coming from my end of the table, but there was no visual evidence of my gluttony.

"No dessert, thank you. Is there any more cornbread?"

Just for one brief moment I was back at my grandmother's table, and for that I will be forever grateful.

Leftovers

I know a man who never has to eat leftovers.

I grew up across the street from him. When he woke up in the morning, breakfast was waiting for his arrival to the table. In the middle of the day, he left work and drove home to enjoy a freshly prepared lunch. When he got home from work, dinner was on the table. Day in, day out, this was the routine, still is. He doesn't eat leftovers.

He is a lucky man, indeed.

His wife is an excellent cook. Her leftovers are better than what a lot of us eat as first-round offerings.

I am not a very good leftover eater, either. It's not that I have an aversion or dislike for leftovers, but I am so passionate about food that I am usually thinking about what I am going to eat for the next meal while I am eating the current meal.

One of my favorite leftover foods is turkey. During Thanksgiving I usually prepare an extra turkey just in case all of the primary turkey is gone after the main meal. The pure simplicity of a turkey sandwich on good-quality whole-grain bread with homemade mayonnaise, salt, pepper, and lettuce is one of my holiday treats.

Meatloaf might be the universal—and best—leftover food of them all. Mashed potatoes, too.

Necessity might be the mother of invention, but a growling stomach is the father. I imagine there are many foods that started out as leftovers and became featured entrees later—shepherd's pie comes to mind.

In the Purple Parrot Cafe, we occasionally develop a "keeper" recipe while using leftovers. Recently, Chef Linda Nance created a fried potato salad. It's like a potato cake except one uses the standard picnic-style, yellow-mustard potato salad, forms it into patty, rolls it in bread crumbs, and fries it in a skillet. I have a friend in Jackson who has been raving for two months about the Purple Parrot's Fried Potato Salad.

Some foods actually taste better as leftovers the next day—red beans and rice, chili, and gumbo are all better the second or third day.

Here are my Top 10 Leftover Foods:

10. Fried Rice—it's a fence rider. Fried rice almost fits into the better-the-next-day-than-the-first-day category
9. Split Pea/White Bean Soup—using stock made from leftover/scrap smoked ham bones
8. Cold Pizza for breakfast—my son's favorite leftover food (and one his mom almost never lets him eat)
7. Chicken Salad—made using last night's roasted chicken or fried chicken (throw the skin in, too)
6. Cornbread dressing and gravy—who needs turkey if you make a great dressing?
5. Bread Pudding—made using yesterday's croissants instead of stale French bread
4. Bacon, Lettuce, and Tomato Sandwiches—using leftover bacon from breakfast and homemade mayonnaise
3. Meat loaf—the quintessential leftover. As a child I hated meat loaf. Today, I am one of its biggest proponents. I am ready for meat loaf to make a comeback in a big way.
2. Turkey Sandwiches—again, not only for the holidays
1. Steak and Biscuits—wrap leftover steak-dinner scraps in aluminum foil and refrigerate overnight. The next morning, slice the steak into strips, reheat in the oven, and serve inside buttered biscuits sprinkled with a little steak seasoning (this one's worth cooking an extra steak the night before so you'll have plenty the next morning). Rib eyes work best. Serve with scrambled eggs on the side and fresh fruit.

Honorable mention leftovers: Spaghetti, pot roast, and lasagna

The worst leftover of all time: Tuna Casserole. Hands down, no question. It's as bad the second time around as it was the first.

Be careful with leftovers and always use proper food handling techniques. It's a good idea to label and date leftovers. A good rule of thumb: If you can't remember when you made the dish the first time, it's too old to eat.

Peaches

One of the unexpected benefits of writing a weekly column that is centered mostly around food is that people always give me food. I love my job.

At a book signing earlier this year a man walked up with a flat of blackberries and blueberries. "Here, check these out," he said. An entire flat! That's twelve pints. Did I mention that I love my job?

Over a breakfast earlier in the summer my friend Chris brought me a bag of peaches. I love my friends, too.

Peaches are a great gift. I used to go to a local peach orchard near my hometown and buy several bushels of peaches at the height of the summer and deliver them to my friends.

A few weeks ago a reader from Clarksdale sent me a case of South Carolina peaches. They were great. South Carolina peaches usually show up later in the year.

I write often of the difference between Alabama and Georgia peaches. When I write one of these columns, I end up with several emails touting the qualities of South Carolina peaches over Georgia peaches. There is a constant battle between Georgia and South Carolina as to which state has the best peaches.

Trust me, there is no love lost between Georgia and South Carolina when it comes to peach production.

Each state is trying to top the other. Years ago Georgia named itself "The Peach State." After hearing this, South Carolina adopted the moniker "The Tastier Peach State."

These interstate battles of one-upsmanship can turn nasty if left unchecked. Be on the lookout for Georgia to rework their "The Peach State" motto and name themselves "The Really, Really, Really Good Peach State."

Then watch for South Carolina's counterpunch when they adopt the motto "The Tastier Peach State with Slightly More Coastline Than Georgia on the Atlantic Ocean."

Realizing this, the Georgia Peach Board will go to their state legislature and petition for their slogan to be changed to "The Really, Really, Really Good Peach State with a Professional Baseball AND Football Franchise."

South Carolina will then counterpunch with "The Tastier Peach State with Slightly More Coastline Than Georgia on the Atlantic Ocean That Doesn't Want a Perennial Losing Professional Football Franchise (and Besides, The Carolina Panthers are Half Ours)."

Georgia will then elongate its name to "The Really, Really, Really Good Peach State with a Professional Baseball AND Football Franchise That Doesn't Have a Compass Point in Our State Name."

After petitioning for a larger state seal to hold the entire new motto, South Carolina will propose to change their moniker to "The Tastier Peach State with Slightly More Coastline Than Georgia on the Atlantic Ocean That Doesn't Want a Perennial Losing Professional Football Franchise (and Besides, the Carolina Panthers are Half Ours) Which Doesn't Have Bad Traffic Like Atlanta."

It will finally take a steel-cage wrestling match between Ted Turner and Steve Spurrier to resolve the issue. Turner's mean as hell, but my money's on the visor-wearing Spurrier in the third round.

Georgia and South Carolina aside, I am a fan of Chilton County, Alabama peaches. They seem to be the redheaded stepchild of the Southern peach world.

Peaches taste like summer no matter where they're grown or what's stated in their home state's motto.

Salads

The weather is warming and salad sales in the restaurant are booming.

I like salads, but I am not an entree-salad eater. I like a salad as a small course or as a component in or accompaniment to a main course.

When I am entertaining friends at home, I rarely serve a salad. Sometimes at lunch, I might throw together something quick and uncomplicated, but mostly I opt for soup in lieu of salad.

My grandmother always served a salad when she hosted a formal meal, though her salads were not of the tossed variety. She never served a bean salad or a pasta salad. She occasionally served a fruit salad. Mostly what she served were little-old-lady congealed salads.

I loved my grandmother more than I have column inches to describe, but I hate congealed salads.

Congealed salads are evil. They are the greatest trick ever played on children. They looked like Jell-O, they shook like Jell-O, but they tasted like V-8 juice. She would even put a dollop of mayonnaise on top, which, of course, looked like some type of sweet whipped cream, shook like some type of whipped cream, but tasted like Miracle Whip.

My grandmother, may she rest in peace, was the queen of the congealed salad. She had hundreds of small metal molds in dozens of shapes and designs—seashells for congealed salads made with clam juice and V-8 juice, tiny wreath molds for a green jiggly concoction with vegetables in it, and small, scalloped dome-shaped molds for congealed fruit salads that didn't taste like fruit and still had a dollop of mayonnaise on the top.

I love shrimp salad. My grandmother made the world's best chicken salad. We serve a salad named Sensation Salad at the restaurants that I could eat to accompany most meals. What do those salads have in common? None of them use Jell-O. None of them try to deceive little kids into thinking that they are dessert when they are actually cloudy, bitter, and vegetable-laden tomato juice.

When one eats a shrimp salad, one knows one is eating a shrimp before one even takes the first bite. The same goes for chicken salad and tuna salad. That is what I require from my salads—honesty.

While we're on the topic of salads that I hate, add that nasty carrot-and-raisin salad to the list, and also that salad that is made with English peas, sour cream, and green onions. Ambrosia? No sir.

I like fruit salad as long as there's no grapefruit in the general vicinity. There is a comedian—I have forgotten his name—who does a hilarious ten-minute bit on why grapefruit is bad and why it destroys a fruit salad. I am in full agreement.

The best salad I have ever eaten was at the Gotham Bar and Grill in New York. I order it (or its current incarnation) every time I go to the city. It is a simple creation of frisée lettuce, bacon lardoons, roasted shiitake mushrooms, and goat cheese, tossed in a light dressing made from extra-virgin olive oil, red wine vinegar, Dijon mustard, and shallots. Beautiful.

It's amazing how something so simple can taste so complex when left in the hands of one of that city's best chefs—Alfred Portale. Then again, it's startling how something so fun-looking—the congealed salad—can taste so awful, even in the hands of a sweet, well-meaning and gracious Southern lady.

Chapter 6

Diets

2007

New York has banned trans fats, Chicago has banned foie gras, and my hometown of Hattiesburg has just banned cigarettes.

That is how I intended to start this week's column. Typically, I would use the next several paragraphs to make fun of the overzealous food police, vegetarians, and New Yorkers in general—some of whom fit all three categories—easy targets, all. Next I would use a few paragraphs to humorously point out what would happen if the trans-fat food police came down to Mississippi and tried to shut down our catfish shacks and barbeque joints.

I would then use the closing paragraphs to take a few final jabs at vegetarians, diet junkies, and members of PETA, before finally delivering a humorous knockout blow to those who are trying to regulate every aspect of our lives.

Unfortunately, I am writing this column on New Year's Day and I have resolved to lose twenty-five pounds in the next four months. A trans-fat ban is actually looking pretty good right about now.

Full speed ahead, Captain, straight into dieting hell.

I have been on an eating spree since June of 2006. I once read an article that stated one's taste buds change every seven years. At forty-five years old, I must be on the cusp of another one of those changes as I have developed an abnormal and obsessive love of onion rings. Like a pregnant woman's craving for asparagus cupcakes, it has come from nowhere. Three years ago I endured the same phenomenon—that time with turnip greens—though turnip greens are much healthier than onion rings.

Recently, I have felt like a teenager on a growing spurt, though the only way I have been growing over the last six months is—out.

The catalyst for this most recent food-inspired resolution is pure vanity. My publisher is sending a photographer down from New York for a two-week food and lifestyle photo shoot in May, and I don't want to end up looking like the Mississippi version of Paul Prudhomme circa

1982 in my next book. Up until now my published works have featured beautiful watercolor paintings, self-deprecating cartoons, or vintage photography. Now the subject matter has taken a definite turn for the worse: Me.

A published book is as close to permanent as almost anything in life. Once it goes to the printer, it's as final as final gets. Scary, yes. Motivating, double yes.

So I have resolved to dust off the old diet books, remove the stacks of cookbooks that are piled up on the treadmill, stop using the exercise equipment as an alternate clothes-hanging closet, and throw out all of the chips and sugary kids' cereal in my pantry.

I am not quite sure which route I will take to drop this excess poundage. In the past I have counted calories, eliminated fat, used Sugar Busters, and spent a few months with Dr. Atkins and his sadistic slow-torture method of carbohydrate deprivation. No matter what I end up doing, I know cardio persecution will be a major part of it. I hate cardio.

I now join the millions of other slugs who waited until New Year's Day to make the decision to drop excess poundage, and will now be eating healthier. Even still, I am comforted by the fact that I made the choice on my own. New Yorkers have to rely on their local government.

For the immediate future, the catfish houses, barbeque joints, and meat-and-three cafes of South Mississippi will be serving one less customer—no onion rings, less bread, and bland chicken breasts are on the horizon. Sayonara, trans fat. I'll miss you (at least until June).

Diet Dilemma

I was walking from the restaurant to my office the other day and, out of the corner of my eye, caught a glimpse of C'est La Vie, the French bakery across the street.

The morning sun fell gently on the face of the bakery and a golden glow shone all about the building. Through the glimmering radiance I could have sworn I heard a heavenly choir of angels singing "Gloria" (not Van Morrison's G-L-O-R-I-A *Gloria*, but the glory-hallelujah-type ditty usually sung by a choir). The bakery was calling to me. My thoughts turned to pastry.

The custard-raisin croissant is a thing of simple beauty—butter, flour, milk, egg, and yeast. A touch of custard in the dough and the addition of raisins and cinnamon make it one of my favorite breakfast treats.

I continued to walk toward my office, ignoring the siren song of the heavenly choir. Approximately halfway across the parking lot, the diet angel and the diet devil instantly appeared—one on each shoulder—as they have many times before.

The diet devil spoke first. "Go over and get one of those custard-raisin croissants. You deserve it. Those scales in your bathroom are broken. There's no way you weigh that much. Eat. Enjoy. Live."

The diet angel chimed in saying, "Robert, you know those scales aren't broken. If anything they are seven pounds off, giving you a false sense of security. Croissants are loaded with butter and…"

"Don't listen to him," the diet devil interrupted. "He'd have you eating sunflower seeds and rice cakes all day. You're a chef. Chefs aren't supposed to be skinny. Eat one. Heck, eat two."

"Skinny? Ha! You haven't seen skinny since the Reagan administration," the diet angel replied. "Just go into your office and eat a protein bar."

"A protein bar? You've got a world-class bakery across the street and you're going to eat a protein bar?" said the diet devil. "I'll bet they just pulled the custard-raisin croissants out of the oven. They're probably warm enough to melt in your mouth."

"Just think of how many extra miles you'll have to walk to burn off those calories," said the diet angel. "You're gonna have to start shopping at the Big and Tall store again, and everyone knows you're not tall."

The diet angel won that battle, but the diet devil will live to fight another day (a potential rematch might be convened on my shoulders as early as this afternoon).

Light-headed from a lack of substantive food, I sat at my desk and wondered how fate had dealt me such a terrible blow.

Why couldn't a Frenchman have opened a bakery ninety-seven steps (yes, I've counted them) away from my office when I was in my twenties? Back then, I could eat anything in site and not gain an ounce. When I opened my first restaurant, the people at the pizza delivery joint down the street from my house knew my name. I had a standing order when I got off work at midnight: a large pepperoni pizza and a two-liter Coke—all that and a thirty-two-inch waist, too.

In those days I had the metabolism of a hummingbird.

In my early thirties, I could eat a seven-course meal at a fine-dining restaurant and three hours later eat a late-night breakfast at an all-night diner—all that and a thirty-four-inch waist, too.

In those days I had the metabolism of a mountain goat.

By the time I reached forty years old, my waist had expanded to an all-time high of forty-two inches and my metabolism was like that of a potbellied pig.

Today, at forty-five, I purchase jeans with a thirty-eight-inch waist and am currently on my way back to 36's (as long as the diet angel can keep me away from French pastries). My metabolism is like that of an average forty-five-year old mammal and I am learning to live with it.

National Geographic Adventure magazine just published a list of America's Top 10 cities. Along with Nashville, Austin, and Chicago, my hometown of Hattiesburg made the Top 10 list. These lists have been around for years, but this is the first time that Hattiesburg has shown up on a list that didn't feature retirement communities.

I don't think that it's a coincidence that the same year a French bakery opens in town, we land on a Top 10 list. The quality of life is going up. My waist size is going down, and through it all, the heavenly choir of angels is still singing.

Angels, and Devils, and Diets, Oh My!

I picked the wrong month to go on a diet.

Like a million other slugs out there, I started dieting the day after New Year's. Since then, business travels have taken me on several waistline-expanding trips.

For the first several days I walked around with a diet angel one shoulder and a diet devil on the other. The diet devil kicked back and told me that onion rings would be OK. Then the diet angel would whip out a picture of me at the swimming pool last summer.

Around two weeks in, the diet devil spread a map on my desk, pinpointed all of the locations that would tempt my palate, and handed over the airline tickets.

During this period the diet angel was not on my shoulder encouraging me to "do right and eat well" because—as all angels know—it's not polite to speak with your mouth full of cheesecake.

The diet-busting journey began in New Orleans at Restaurant August. It continued to Las Vegas, where I sampled several of that town's finest. The diet devil made it easy to get reservations at all of the restaurants I wanted to visit. The diet angel was nowhere to be found—probably playing blackjack in the casino.

The next week, business took me to Columbus, Mississippi to tour the Jubilations Cheesecake factory (details in a future column). I don't know if you've ever toured a cheesecake factory, but the diet devil and I suggest you do so, sometime soon.

The next week I found myself in San Francisco—again on business— yet this time only in town for forty-eight hours. At the request of one of my associates, I called the French Laundry in Yountville to see if I could secure a table with only thirty-six hours notice. "You're dreaming," I told him. "I have people calling me for help two months out. There's no way we'll get in."

Obviously the diet devil has access to the French Laundry's reservation book. Two nights later I was seated among a six-top in the French

Laundry that included three business associates, the diet devil, the diet angel, and me. The six of us participated in the kind of fourteen-course bacchanalia that one rarely ever experiences. Actually, our web guy from New Orleans—the pickiest eater on the planet—mostly ate bread. Therefore the diet devil and I, not wanting to waste any of Thomas Keller's brilliant offerings, picked up his slack and ate at least twelve courses off of his plate(we didn't share any with the diet angel).

Safe at home, but not for long, I discovered that a Frenchman has opened a bakery directly across the street from my office. How much can one man take? There are several bakeries in my hometown, but most are miles from my office. Out of sight and out of mind equal out of stomach.

The new bakery, C'est La Vie, is exactly ninety-seven steps from the front door of my office, and on top of that, everything there is good. As a matter of fact, everything is fantastic.

The bakery is owned by a French-Polish man named Janusz. That is what his business card states, just "Janusz," like Elvis, Bono, or Sting, one word: Janusz. And folks, Janusz is a rock star when it comes to baking pastries and cakes.

He and his wife are from France and Poland respectively, but he is a bread-baking, cake-making journeyman who has pulled many stints as a pastry chef in multi-starred kitchens all over the world. As a matter of fact, I found out that he trained the pastry chef that is currently working at the French Laundry.

The new bakery has a true European sensibility. The pastries are light and not too sweet. The cakes are world-class, and the man makes the lightest and best-tasting quiche I have ever eaten. My entire family eats there, often. The diet devil is usually somewhere near the pastry case pushing the chocolate croissants.

During my first visit to C'est La Vie, the diet angel was sitting on my right shoulder and constantly ranting about bread and carbs. By the second visit I made him wait outside while the diet devil and I enjoyed a custard- and raisin-filled croissant.

Now I'm back to square one. Willpower was along for the ride during the first few weeks, safe and warm in a secure spot in my back pocket. Then the diet devil found him, shivved him like a jail-yard stooge, and sent him packing.

They say that life is all about timing. It appears that dieting is about timing, too. So now the question: Lose twenty pounds or eat freshly baked pastries and quiche from an extremely talented French baker's kitchen? Well, I wasn't ready to buy a bunch of new smaller-waisted pants, anyway.

As for the diet angel, in the words of Don McLean, "He caught the last train for the coast."

I have to go now. My friend the diet devil is saving a table across the street for our mid-morning pastry.

Diet Diary Week II

Welcome to week two of dieting hell.

I hesitated to write about this subject two weeks in a row for fear that new readers to this column might think that the only topics ever discussed within these paragraphs are my eating habits (or lack thereof). The hesitation only lasted a few seconds though, as the hunger pangs emanating from my stomach broke my train of thought and I began typing fortuitously.

I am in the early stages of a three-month diet and all I can think about is food. Not all foods, just unhealthy foods. I was walking through the grocery store yesterday looking for healthy alternatives that I could incorporate into my diet plan, when a strange phenomenon occurred. I call it a diet mirage. It struck me as I was reading the nutritional information on a Pop-Tarts box.

Innocently enough, I had started in the oatmeal section, and before I knew it, I had inched my way past the breakfast bars and wound up at W.K. Kellogg's prepackaged, toaster-ready answer to French breakfast pastry—the Pop-Tart (according to the label there is nothing nutritious, healthy, or dietetic in a Pop-Tart, but I already knew that—that's the point).

The diet mirage had kicked in as soon as I walked through the automatic doors. Like a parched man in a barren dessert, at every turn of every aisle I envisioned a cool, palm-laden, water-filled oasis—though these oases took the form of junk food. Fact: Foods that are bad for you have much better packaging. They jump off of the shelves and beg to be purchased. Healthy foods, on the other hand, are wrapped in dull, boring, and unappetizing containers.

Case in point: the gosh-almighty Pop-Tart. I haven't eaten—or wanted to eat—a Pop-Tart since I was in elementary school. Yesterday I was debating whether I should rip the box open and eat a few on the way to the cash register, or rub them all over my body. I did neither. I kept walking down the aisle looking for whole grains, fiber, and sugar substitutes.

The diet I have chosen this time around is one of my own making: a low-sugar, low-fat, nothing-fried, high-fiber hybrid diet I will hereafter now call the

St. John Plan. I lost six pounds last week, so something must be working.

The St. John Plan is a method I have developed over 10 years of failing at Sugar Busters, South Beach, The Zone Diet, calorie counting, no-fat diets, and Atkins.

I once tried Dr. Atkins' torturous method of carbohydrate deprivation, and three weeks into the diet wrote this paragraph in my journal: "Everyday I get an afternoon craving for a Milky Way bar. 'Just eat some pork rinds or beef jerky' they say. I tried that. Pork rinds are smelly and greasy, and it takes approximately 37 hours to chew one single piece of beef jerky. Note to future Atkins dieters: 50 pounds of dried beef or fried pig skins can't come close to one tiny bite of a chocolaty, silky, heavenly, wonderfully delicious Milky Way bar—Pure joy in a brown wrapper."

An obvious side-effect of the St. John Plan is the grocery-store mirage phenomenon. Sweet rolls never looked as good as they did yesterday in my local market. At one time during the visit I actually wondered what a chocolate-covered doughnut filled with Fritos would taste like. Note to reader: Don't sign any wills, loans, or other important legal documents while you are on a diet.

Another side effect of my dieting is that everyone who reads your column knows you're on a diet. Three times in the course of my grocery store visit I was asked how the diet is "coming along." One lady asked that question while I was holding the Pop-Tart box. "How's the diet coming along, Robert?"

"Take a guess," I said, as I picked up a box of Strawberry Milkshake Pop-Tarts.

As of this writing I have been dieting exactly 198 hours. That's 11,882 minutes without a french fry, 7,132,920 seconds without an onion ring. No chips, dips, candy bars, cake, pie, or fried fish—many of the things that make life worthwhile. Keep me in your prayers and—come April—pass the Pop-Tarts.

Doughnuts and Age

I am in my forty-sixth year. Some days I feel every minute of those four-and-a-half decades, others I feel as I did in my teens. My wife would say that, maturity-wise, I am still in my teens... early teens.

I ate breakfast this past Saturday and felt older than I have ever felt before. Sadly, I have reached an age where I can't eat doughnuts and feel good afterward. It was 7:30 a.m. and I was instantly tired, listless, bloated, and ready for a nap. Et tu, doughnut?

Doughnuts are the universal breakfast treat. Sure, eggs and bacon might rule the roost, but doughnuts were the first handheld, drive-through breakfast item out there. Long before egg-filled burritos, French toast sticks, and pancake sandwiches with the syrup built into the bread, there were doughnuts. They were simple and they were good.

I have a long and storied history with doughnuts. As a kid, I stopped by the doughnut shop on my way to school. My church always had doughnuts on Sunday morning, and at Sunday-night church, we ate the leftover doughnuts cold. While working at a radio station during high school, I finished my air shift at midnight and stopped by the doughnut shop for a couple of custard-filled doughnuts and a pint of milk. As a bachelor living in Destin, Florida, I often visited the Doughnut Hole in the wee hours of the morning—all this and a thirty-two-inch waist, too.

When my daughter was born, I used to take her to the doughnut shop every Saturday morning to watch the men make the doughnuts. She loved it.

Recently, I have used the doughnut shop as a rare, surprise treat for the kids, as I occasionally stop by on the way home from church or another activity. The first time I did it the kids went wild. "Doughnuts at eight-thirty at night? Dad, you're the best! Mom is gonna kill you!" Those surprises have become less common as the no-more-doughnuts-for-Robert realization has begun to sink in.

Granted, doughnuts might be one of the most unhealthy foods out there—bread, deep-fried in grease, and then topped with sugar and chocolate—but I used to have an iron constitution. I could eat anything and it didn't affect me.

I used to be able to drink highly caffeinated beverages at bedtime and sleep all night, not anymore. Last year I learned that I can no longer enjoy a roller coaster ride. Somewhere in my late thirties, my thrill-ride equilibrium flew out the window. Today I have more hair on my back than I do on my head. And where did this hair in my ears come from?

I see old men hanging out in doughnut shops all of the time. Their mornings are filled with newspapers, gossip, cigarettes, gallons of coffee, and doughnuts. They have hair in their ears, too. How do they walk away from the doughnut shop not feeling poorly?

As a kid I could eat anything. I ate a lot and I ate often. When I reached my mid-thirties, my metabolism took a nap—a long nap—and has yet to wake up.

I am past middle-aged. Some say that sixty years old is middle-aged. Sure, it's middle-aged if you are going to live to be 120. I figure I hit middle age around my forty-third birthday. I'll take eighty-six years on the planet—men die young in my family.

I wonder if there are any other foods that I will have to stop eating. If so, I will gladly give up Brussels sprouts right now if I can have my once-a-month doughnut fix returned. I would give up cauliflower and kiwi for a few more years of roller-coaster riding. Apricots for chocolate cake, that's an easy trade. What if rib-eye steak starts making me feel poorly, or bacon? I don't know if a life without bacon is worth the effort.

Before long I'll be wearing goofy pajamas, reading the obituary column, and reeking of Bengay, while surviving on a steady diet of Cream of Wheat, and Ensure. But I'm not going down without a fight, so pass the doughnuts (and the Mylanta, and the aspirin).

Baby Boomer Body Piercings

I have a staple in my ear.

Actually, I have a staple in each of my ears.

I understand that for most food writers the preceding two sentences might be a strange way to begin a column. However, if you ever spent a week lumbering a mile in my shoes, you would realize that, in the scheme of things, this is no strange occurrence.

My wife heard from a friend of a friend of a coworker's friend that an acupuncturist specializing in weight loss was coming to town. Being the type that believes anything she hears, she signed us up to attend a seminar with the needlemaster.

My wife would tell you that she doesn't believe everything that she hears. Exhibit one, Your Honor: the drawer full of Tae Bo tapes (still in their wrapper). Exhibits two through twelve, may it please the court: the "amazingly easy" Ronco rotisserie oven (currently residing at a friend's house), the box of kitchen knives that "never need sharpening" (rendered useless after a few weeks' use, and currently being used as butter spreaders), gospel CDs for her grandmother who didn't own a CD player (still in the wrapper, still in the drawer), and countless other cooking gadgets, and household instruments du jour.

So, being the faithful husband (read: spineless, henpecked, whimpering specimen) that I am, I went with her to the hotel where the acupuncture diet specialist had set up shop in a small conference room.

In an admittedly blatant case of reverse-cultural discrimination, I was expecting an older Oriental gentleman, probably someone along the lines of Mr. Miyagi from *The Karate Kid,* who would stick a few needles in my back and tell me to "wax on, wax off" while the pounds melted away.

When I walked into the room, a Texan in his mid-forties was standing at the front. *This must be the guy that sets everything up, I thought. He probably does the paperwork and Miyagi the Middle-Eastern Mystic comes in to do all of the complicated sticking-needles-into-all-parts-of-your-body procedure.*

When the meeting started, I found out that the wise Zen-master weight-loss expert was not a martial-arts, new-age, old-as-dirt Oriental gentleman named Miyagi, nor was he a young female Oriental person, or even a part-Asian slightly Polynesian-looking person. He was a guy from Texas named Dennis.

Through the lecture we learned that from now until the end of our lives, we were to eat only enough food that would fit on the inner surface of a six-inch plastic plate. "Just enough food to fit in the palm of your hand," Dennis said. In addition to that shocking revelation, the only foods we were allowed to eat on that tiny six-inch plate were oatmeal, eggs, meat (except pork), one Granny Smith apple per week, and vegetables (except corn, potatoes, and carrots).

We would also have to take four fruit and vegetable pills every day because Dennis wasn't going to let us eat actual fruits and vegetables.
We were now to pay for our fruit and vegetable pills by mail order.

The good news was that we could eat once every hour; the bad news was that we couldn't eat bread, potatoes, or diet soft drinks every hour.

Back to the staples, it turns out that the acupuncture-aided weight loss has nothing to do with lying on a table while incense burns and Enya music plays softly in the background. There were no young, nubile assistants aiding Mr. Miyagi as he carefully inserted needles with mystical precision.

In the world of traveling weight-loss-through-acupuncture programs, Dennis takes you to the back of the room at the end of the lecture—staple gun in hand—and staples a small metal ring into the knobby portion of your inner ear, which was intended for nothing stronger than a Q-tip. Thank you very much, that will be $99 please, and remember, nothing larger than the palm of your hand and nothing that tastes really, really good.

Dennis said that the staples will send a signal to my stomach telling it that it's not hungry. Actually, the only signals the staples sent were to my brain, and they said: OUCH!

As of this writing, it's been just over twenty-four hours since Dennis stuck his magical weight-loss staples into my ear. They are still there, and amazingly enough, I'm less hungry than usual. More on the ongoing weight-loss saga of the henpecked husband and the gullible spouse in a later column.

Just When You Thought It Was Safe to Go on a Diet…

It's cookbook testing time, again.

Last week I started a new diet. This week I started the recipe-testing phase for a new cookbook. Testing recipes and watching calories go together like the New Orleans Saints and the Super Bowl—never the twain shall meet.

Last spring I signed a three-book deal with Hyperion Books in New York. In addition to the Hyperion contract, Wyatt Waters, the noted watercolorist, and I are publishing another book, *Southern Seasons*, which will be released next fall. Over the next ten months I will conceptualize, develop, write, and recipe-test three new cookbooks, and re-release another cookbook in the backlog. Sure, that's a lot of writing, but mostly that's a lot of eating.

Recipe testing for cookbooks is a blast. In the heat of the development phase, four to six recipes are created and tested every day. The finished recipes are tasted, critiqued, and rated. The next day, changes are made to the written recipes, and the process starts all over again, until the final products are the perfect result of what was envisioned at the recipe's conception. Sometimes one specific recipe can be prepared and tested every day for two weeks before the final recipe has been perfected. Occasionally, we nail it on the first try.

The three deciding factors of a winning recipe are: First and foremost, does it taste good? Secondly, can it be easily replicated at home with everyday ingredients found at the local grocery store? And finally, does it fit the theme of the book? The savvy reader will notice that the terms low-fat, low-carb, and low-calorie are not listed anywhere in the preceding sentence.

Recipe testing is fun, but it wreaks havoc on a diet.

Actually, I am writing this column in between bites of Lamb Kabobs with Mediterranean Spice Rub and Raspberry-Mint Dipping Sauce; Cheddar-Rice Crackers; Corn, Crab, and Avocado Dip; Mushroom-Stuffed Pastry Purses; Smoked Beef Tenderloin with Chive and Tarragon

Sauce, and Horseradish Mustard; and Chicken and Andouille Empanadas. Note: It is 6:24 a.m. and these items make for an unusual breakfast.

I have thirty pounds to lose and three book deadlines to meet in the next ten months—January 15, April 15, and September 1. Seeing as none of the books are diet manuals and most of my recipes are *not* developed with health-conscious calorie counters in mind, I am going to have to develop a system. I don't yet know what that system is going to be, but, unfortunately, a gym and a treadmill will probably be major components in the final plan.

And in case you were wondering, the Lamb Kabobs were nailed on the first try, although the sauce is a little too sweet. The Cheddar-Rice Crackers need more cheddar. The Corn, Crab, and Avocado dip needs something; I'm just not quite sure what that something is. Maybe sour cream. The Smoked Beef Tenderloin is perfect, but I have doubts that it can be easily replicated at home. The Mushroom-Stuffed Pastry Purses had been in the freezer for two days to see if they could be made in advance, frozen, and then baked. They can be. And the Chicken and Andouille Empanadas might need a name change.

Gotta go, the treadmill is calling.

Too Short, or Too Demented?

"You're too short for your weight," said my doctor.

"Pardon me," I said.

"I'm looking at this chart, and it says right here that you're way too short for your weight. You're supposed to be between six feet five inches and six feet seven inches tall," he said.

"But I'm five-ten."

"I know," he said, and turned back to the chart to scribble more notes.

I got the point.

I suggested that he might have a future in politics, closed the door on my annual check up, and headed home to eat breakfast before going to work.

As I walked into my kitchen, two ladies on the *Today* show were talking about obesity.

"People in their forties with belly fat are more likely to have dementia in their seventies," said one of the ladies.

I've got enough belly fat to fill the cargo hold of a whaling vessel. *I'm gonna be full-goose bozo by the time I reach seventy-five*, I thought to myself.

As I sat down to eat my oatmeal, I opened *USA Today* and there was the aforementioned study on the bottom of page 4D, "Belly fat linked to an increased risk of dementia." Someone or something was trying to tell me something, and it was more than just the growling in my stomach. I wondered if my doctor thinks I'm too short to be a demented septuagenarian, too.

The lady on television moved on to something she called the waist-hip test. She was measuring her waist and then her hips. She then divided the waist measurement by the hip measurement, or something like that. I started to go to the junk drawer for the measuring tape, but quickly realized that doing so would be futile. I can't even see my hips because my waist is too big. Why take a test that is doomed from the start?

The signs are everywhere. My waist is expanding; my chins are multiplying faster than feed-store rabbits, summer is quickly approaching, and I'm still shopping at the Big and Tall store (and I'm only five-ten). I need to lose weight, if for no other reason than to make sure I'm not a drooling, babbling, demented buffoon by the time I turn seventy.

I had a crazy uncle who used to sit on his front porch, shout obscenities at his across-the-street neighbors, and shoot at passersby with his BB gun. The genetics are there, but he was bone-thin. How much worse will it be for a fat guy if this lady's theory is true?

I once heard someone explain the difference between the North and the South: In the North, they put their crazy uncle in an asylum. In the South, we put our crazy uncles on the front porch. It's true. My uncle, Garland St. John, was crazy as...well, as crazy as an uncle who shoots people with a BB gun, and he spent most of his waking hours on the front porch of the old St. John home in Brooksville, Mississippi.

Loyal readers of this column have followed my dieting ups and downs for eight years. The cumulative result (750 words per week for 416 consecutive weeks = 312,000 words) is that if one charted my dieting successes and failures over that time period, the chart would look like a Colorado mountain range.

There will be no diet this time, just a common sense lifestyle food/living plan. Hopefully my weight will catch up to my height and I won't spend my later years shooting BBs at my neighbors from my front porch swing.

Viral Victuals

I've got a virus.

My particular virus is not influenza, a common cold, or a computer virus. I don't have chicken pox, mumps, Ebola, or rabies.

There are many viruses with exotic and interesting names, such as: cereal yellow dwarf virus, Leaky virus, and Four Corners hantavirus. There are viruses named after plants and vegetables, such as: squash mosaic virus, tobacco viruses, tomato bushy stunt virus, and rice dwarf virus. There are also viruses named after animals, such as: squirrel monkey retrovirus, Swiss mouse virus, European elk papillomavirus, wooley monkey sarcoma virus, turkeypox, camelpox, sealpox, and gay elephant tycomabanucleoid virus. I don't have any of those either.

Yesterday I read an *Associated Press* story with a headline that stated: "Obesity linked to virus, new experiments suggest." It appears that I have contracted the fat virus and that is the reason that I do all of my shopping in the big and tall section.

I've been trying to lose thirty pounds since January. At the moment I'm fifteen pounds lighter than I was on New Year's Day, but a few weeks ago I hit a plateau and the scales aren't budging. I must have contracted a bad case of this fat virus while I was on Spring Break.

Whew! At least it's a virus. I thought all of those barbeque ribs and late-night refrigerator raids were to blame for my flabby midsection.

When I told a doctor friend of mine that I thought I had come down with the fat virus, he asked if the article mentioned a vaccine. "I don't think so. But if there were a vaccine, where would I get one?" I asked. He then told me that vaccines are small doses of the actual virus that one is trying to defend against. So I asked him if loading up on gravy-cheese fries, cornbread, and jelly doughnuts would help kick-start the vaccination process and assist in my fight against the fat virus. He didn't have an answer.

Then it hit me—maybe I can battle the fat virus with an antibiotic. As everyone knows, antibiotics are made from mold. It just so happens that mold comes from bread. I love bread. Around the time I started my diet, a new French bakery opened across the street from my office. At the time, I thought that might make dieting harder, as they have many beautiful and tasty pastries. Now that I know about this fat virus and its dangers, I am going to do my best to find an antibiotic. I think I'll start my search for a fat cure in the C'est La Vie bakery's pastry case.

As a matter of fact, as I write this I am eating a custard-raisin-filled pastry from C'est La Vie and I feel better already.

The fat-virus study was conducted at the University of Wisconsin, which proves that when it's snowing up north, those people truly have nothing to do. It seems that they could have spent some of their snowed-in time coming up with a name for the fat virus.

My home state, Mississippi, is statistically the fattest state in the nation. Who better to name the virus?

Here are my suggestions for fat virus names: Double Chinfluenza, Dimpled Thigh Disease, Chunky Gut Syndrome, Chronic Lap-Over Flabbyitis, NASCAR Barley Bug, Mississippi Blubber Flu, or Pudgypox.

So it turns out that I am fat-virus positive. It could be worse; I could have come down with that yellow dwarf stuff.

Roll Out the Vertical Stripes

The diet is over.

On January 8 I started dieting in preparation for a photographer flying in from New York to shoot my next book. My goal was to lose thirty pounds in four months.

The time has come. The photographer is here. I hit just above 50 percent of my goal. I lost sixteen pounds.

Looking back, it might have been the visit to the cheesecake factory in the first week of my diet that led to a bad start. Though, if you have never toured a cheesecake factory, I suggest you do so immediately.

The Jubilations Cheesecake facility in Columbus, Mississippi is a wonderful place to spend the better part of a morning. From the second I walked in the door and smelled the aroma of freshly baked cheesecakes in the air, I knew that the diet was in trouble. There is not much in this world that smells better than a cheesecake factory after one has been surviving on chicken breasts, broccoli, and oatmeal for an entire week.

It's almost as if they piped in the aroma to tempt me.

Here's a million-dollar idea: Someone should make an air freshener or candle that smells like a cheesecake manufacturing plant.

It could have been the twelve-course meal at the French Laundry in Yountville, California, when I was in San Francisco in February. Or it could have been the new rib place I discovered later that month. Either way, I gave in to temptation more times than not.

Cookbook recipe testing is in no way conducive to dieting. I have developed, tested, and tasted over two hundred new recipes for two new cookbooks over the course of the last three months. Some recipes had to be prepared again and again until we got them right. Some had to be prepared again and again because we got them right and we wanted second helpings.

I was on a roll for a few weeks, and then I hit a plateau. I have been stuck at this weight for the last two months.

More than likely it was the French Bakery that opened across the street from my office in my hometown of Hattiesburg, Mississippi that did me in. It's not the bakery's fault. It's my love of food mixed with my fondness for bread that keeps me going back. I can do without sweets, but freshly baked breads and pastries in the hands of an experienced French baker are a temptation that is too tough for me to resist.

Janusz, the French/Polish baker, is said to love Polish techno music, and if one gets to the bakery before it opens, one might catch him dancing around the small shop with music blaring.

A friend of mine walked in the bakery early the other day and reported that Janusz did, indeed, have Polish techno music blaring from the small stereo and was dancing with abandon throughout the store. I love that. That is exactly what I want in a baker: innate skill, a yeoman's work ethic, and a well-formed sense of rhythm.

I have yet to catch Janusz dancing through the bakery, but I always look through the windows at 6 a.m. when I am on my way to the gym.

Maybe I should go across the street before I go to the gym and dance around the bakery while holding one of those custard-raisin croissant things to burn off a few calories. It would be the world's first—and only—French-Polish Cardio-Bakery.

I never read the book *French Women Don't Get Fat,* but maybe the reason they don't get fat is because they dance more than we do. I quit dancing around the time I stopped drinking. When I sobered up—almost twenty-four years ago—I realized that my dancing didn't look quite as cool as I thought it looked while I was drinking. Maybe I should start dancing again.

French women might not get fat, but Southern men sure do. So crank up the Polish techno music and say, "cheese."

Chapter 7

Holidays

The Great Christmas Compromise

Christmas is full of compromises.

When couples wed, they bring many things into the union. I'm not talking about bachelor-apartment wire-bale coffee tables, milk-carton two-by-four college-dorm shelving, or Great-Grandmother's tacky faux-antique tea set. I'm talking about family traditions and ideas about how things are done within the family unit.

Nowhere are family traditions and long-standing practices more evident—or volatile—than during the holidays.

Christmas has such fond memories attached to it from our youth. We like to celebrate the holidays exactly how we used to do it, and that is the way we want to keep celebrating forever, and ever, and ever, ad nauseam, ad infinitum, and a partridge in a pear tree, or a partridge on a wire-bale coffee table, depending on who wins the argument.

The granddaddy of all Christmas quandaries is whether to open presents on Christmas Eve or Christmas morning. My wife would open presents on September 28 if they were available. She came from a family that opened presents on Christmas Eve. Actually, she came from a family that had to take drastic measures in hiding presents from her so she wouldn't break into them as soon as they were placed under the tree. My wife can open and rewrap a present with the stealth and precision of an international secret agent.

The dilemma of living with a Christmas-present peeker is that all gifts must be locked down in a bank vault until Christmas morning. Either that, or all presents must be completely bound by layers of duct tape before being stashed under the tree.

The first Christmas compromise that took place in our marriage was the icicles–no icicles debate. I am a direct descendant of a long line of icicles-on-the-tree Yuletide decorators. We take our tinsel seriously. We throw icicles on the tree in heavy clumps. As a matter of fact, children from all over the neighborhood used to come to my house to throw tinsel with abandon.

My wife's family views icicles with a contempt normally reserved for dog beaters. In the St. John house, the weeks leading to Christmas are filled with the constant placing and removing of icicles from the tree.

The children are on my side and will thankfully carry on the long-standing St. John icicle tradition. When tree-decorating time rolls around, the three of us hurl tinsel on the finished product with the agility and accuracy of an Olympic discus thrower. For the next three weeks, my wife comes behind us and removes most of the icicles from the tree, which, in turn, leads me to wake up at 3 a.m. to add more tinsel to it. I have spare boxes stashed all over the house.

White lights vs. colored lights is another predicament. We used to alternate years. My year we would use colored lights on the tree and during her year we used white. Finally we compromised eight years ago and place both white and colored lights on the tree. Our children each have a small Christmas tree in their respective bedrooms. Amazingly enough, the tree-light debate has fallen along gender lines—my son likes colored lights and my daughter sides with her momma.

Some families eat their "big meal" on Christmas Eve, others opt for Christmas day. My family always ate a formal dinner on Christmas Eve. We still do. Chalk up one for my team.

Luckily, the other typical Christmas food compromises have not had to be made within our union. When it comes to the ham vs. turkey quandary, we both prefer poultry over pork. When adorning the aforementioned bird, we both prefer dressing baked separately instead of giving the bird a celery- and breading-spiked enema. No stuffing in the St. John house. Stuffing is for Yankees.

And when it comes to dressing, we both came into the marriage with a strong appreciation for cornbread dressing. My soon-to-be brother-in-law once brought an oyster dressing to our Christmas Eve dinner. It was shaded in a freaky green hue and had a puddinglike consistency that could curl your toes backward after one bite. No thank you. My family eats cornbread dressing; it is yellowish tan, it doesn't jiggle, and that's that.

Our marriage has seen a few disagreements through the years, but

I will be eternally grateful to my Creator for placing a woman in my life who hates marshmallows on her sweet potatoes as much as I do. Marshmallows do not—I repeat—do not belong anywhere in the vicinity of a sweet potato.

My holiday advice to newlyweds is: Hide the marshmallows; keep oysters out of the dressing; install tamperproof security features on all under-the-tree gifts; no matter how tacky her grandmother's tea set looks—don't comment on it; colored lights or white—it doesn't really matter as long as you decorate the tree together; and finally, throw icicles with your children, throw them hard, throw them long, and throw them with abandon.

Eggnog

I am not a fan of eggnog.

I quit drinking alcohol over two decades ago, but that has nothing to do with my dislike of eggnog. I could drink the non-alcoholic variety if I wanted to; I just never developed a taste for it.

Earlier today, while I was watching a football game, my eleven-year-old daughter came to me and said, "Daddy, I don't like eggnog."

"I don't either, sweetie," I said. I thought her statement seemed somewhat random, but I assumed her mother had bought a carton of non-alcoholic eggnog at the store earlier in the day and she drank some.

"Your mother loves eggnog," I said.

"It's pretty bad. How does she drink it?"

"I don't know. She's just always liked it," I said. Then I began to worry that one of our friends might have delivered a bottle full of spiked eggnog as a Christmas happy for my wife, and my daughter drank some of it while her mother was taking a nap. "What kind of eggnog did you drink, sweetie?"

"The carton said Egg Beaters," she said.

"What?"

"Egg Beaters. It's awful."

I quickly told her that she had not, in fact, drank eggnog, but a carton of an egg substitute product that I sometimes use on my current diet.

"How do you drink that stuff?" she asked.

"Well, sweetie, I don't drink it, I cook it." She looked relieved.

Believe it or not, she's a very intelligent girl. Though I am not sure why she thought Egg Beaters were eggnog. The words "beaters" and "nog" have nothing in common. The Egg Beaters carton doesn't have a poinsettia on it. I don't even know what a "nog" is.

As long as she keeps making good grades in school, I'll let this one slide and write it off to holiday enthusiasm.

Eggnog is made with milk, sugar, cinnamon, nutmeg, some type of alcohol—bourbon, whiskey, brandy, or rum—and eggs. It's the egg part that gets me. There is something about drinking raw eggs and milk that doesn't appeal to me. I can eat a soft-boiled egg, but I do so with toast or biscuits, not milk. Like Egg Beaters, the combination of eggs, sugar, and milk should always be cooked. Custard = good. Eggnog = Bad.

For those who want whiskey, it seems much easier to just pour some in a glass over ice and dispense with the milk and egg.

In the first *Rocky* movie, the title character woke up every morning and drank a few raw eggs before he went out on his morning jog through the streets of Philadelphia. Maybe my daughter has seen the movie. Maybe she was inspired by the drive and determination of Rocky Balboa. Maybe it was the Bill Conti score, who knows? Maybe she's opting for a twenty-first century sixth-grade version of *Rocky* and drinking a healthier alternative—Egg Beaters—before she jogs through the streets of Hattiesburg.

One thing's for certain: In the future, I'll bet she starts paying closer attention to product labels.

Christmas Morning Excitement

Christmas morning excitement is an emotion unmatched by any other.

Adult excitement pales in comparison to the holiday-exhilaration recipe of two parts anticipation, mixed with one part delight, a dab of enchantment, and a pinch of joy that is experienced every Christmas Eve until our pre-teen years sweep the thrills away.

The excitement reaches its fever pitch just before sleep. Lying in bed—blankets and sheets pulled to the chin—listening to every bump and creak in the attic and on the roof. Occasionally daring to get out of the bed to run across the room and peek through the curtains to see if reindeer might have landed in the front yard.

I miss that thrill. Granted, it is a materialistic feeling at its core, and pales in comparison to the adult excitement of babies being born and offspring accomplishments, but it is a memory that is too strong to be denied. It is a singular emotion that is unlike any other we experience for the rest of our lives.

The anticipation begins at dusk on Christmas Eve. Children realize that the greatest kid day of the year has almost arrived. It's the day they have been waiting for since December 26 of the previous year. It's the one day that is unlike any other—the day when children all over the world wake up and open gifts that have magically appeared from nowhere. It happens on only one morning and it is the crux of kiddom.

As Christmas Eve night progresses, kids realize that they are only hours away from waking up to the frenzy of flying wrapping paper, shiny toys, and colorful presents. Excitement mixes with exhaustion and anticipation—it's almost time.

What a great concept. Waking up to stuff. New stuff. Stuff you have been dreaming about for months. Everyone is happy. What a great feeling.

Remember that Christmas morning feeling this holiday season. Remember the excitement and the elation. Let's do what we can to revive that feeling in ourselves and in our neighbors throughout the year. Most of all let's pass it on.

Some children won't wake up to flying paper and shiny toys. For them, it's not about colorful presents and new stuff. It's about survival and getting by on a daily basis.

This holiday season make sure that the joy you experienced happens for everyone.

The man who learns how to put Christmas morning excitement into pill form will be a rich man, indeed. Meanwhile, many of us have the power to make it happen for the under-resourced children in our communities. This Christmas Eve, let's pull the sheets to our chin knowing that we did everything we could to create Christmas morning memories and excitement for everyone.

We Wish You a Figgy Christmas

A group of Christmas carolers stopped by my house last night.

I like the whole caroling thing, but I often worry about the family of unsuspecting foreigners who might have just moved into the neighborhood from a faraway land with divergent customs. I wonder what they must think when they open their front door and two dozen happy people, dressed in wool sweaters in seventy-two-degree weather, begin belting out random songs with no preliminary forewarning.

Last night's carolers ended their five-song set with the obligatory Christmas carol encore of "Free Bird." Actually it was "We Wish You a Merry Christmas." And as I sit here trying to write this column, I find it hard to focus on my topic. I can't get the words "figgy pudding" out of my head.

I looked up the lyrics this morning:

> *Oh bring us a figgy pudding;*
> *Oh bring us a figgy pudding;*
> *Oh bring us a figgy pudding and a cup of good cheer.*

Last night I thought they were singing, "Oh bring us a figgy pudding and bring it right here." I was a little offended. It's not every day that a group of strangers show up at your house during *Sunday Night Football* demanding fruit dessert.

Though after looking up the lyrics, I am more troubled. I found out what they were really looking for was "a cup of good cheer," which led me to believe that this group of carolers were most likely Episcopalian. I didn't have enough booze in my liquor cabinet for twenty-four thirsty Episcopalians so—in the end—it's good that I misheard the lyric. Had my mom been there, she would have given them a dollar and told them to make sure and spend it on food.

Nevertheless, a melodious demand for fruit pudding and booze while someone's watching football is overtly rude.

The problem is that I don't know anything about figgy pudding. I eat for a living. I'm good at it. Eating is going to put my kids through college, but I don't believe that I have ever eaten anything that was figgy.

The name itself is silly. "Figgy" is not really a word, is it? "Figlike" seems better, maybe even "fig-style," but figgy sounds like a cruel nickname given to an introverted fat kid by the fourth-grade bully.

No one has ever given me a figgy pudding, and I'm not sure I would eat it if they did. My friend Gene Saucier makes the best fig preserves I have ever tasted. He brought me some last week. He didn't sing a song, or ask for a cup of hooch, he just said, "Here's some fig preserves," and I said, "Thank you."

Correction, it *is* a word. I just looked it up: figgy [fig-ee]—adjective, containing figs: a figgy cake (origin 1540–1550).

Actually, I think "figgy" comes from the Latin word *figgusius*, meaning, "I want some damn pudding, and I want it now, bring it at this instant—with some whiskey—or I will continue to sing on your front porch."

The most awkward moment in the Christmas carol/home-owner routine is always at the end. Last night—once they finished singing—they just looked at me. I looked back at them and thanked them, they said "Merry Christmas," I returned the sentiment, they looked back at me, and I said "Merry Christmas" again. They kept looking and I didn't know what to do. I wasn't sure if they wanted to come in, or if they wanted me to join them at their next stop. I just said, "Thank you," once again and closed the door.

Sitting here, it occurs to me that they might have been serious. Maybe their demand for figgy pudding was genuine and resolute. Maybe they did, in fact, want a sixteenth century figlike dessert.

Note: To those carolers who stopped by my house during the Cowboys-Giants game, please come back. I don't have any figgy pudding, but I will certainly share a few of my son's Fig Newtons with all of you (as long as there's no football game on).

Christmas 2005

Christmas is a season for reflection. As I look back over forty-four years, I am humbled by the joys and blessings that I have received, and I am in awe of all of the warm Christmas memories that have been created.

It took me almost forty years to realize the aspects of life that matter the most. For me, they are: faith, family, friends, food, and fun. I call them the Five Fs and they are listed in that precise order for a reason.

Faith is the foundation. It is first. It is foremost, and it is the basis for the following four Fs. Without a strong foundation, it's hard to build a fulfilling life. Faith comes in many forms and many denominations; you know best what "faith" means to you, and so I'll leave it at that.

No other time throughout the year offers as much opportunity as Christmas does to appreciate and enjoy family. Even when we think we've had all of the "family" we can stand, the holidays keep giving us more. My fondest Christmas memories have strong ties to family: my daughter's first Christmas, my son's first Christmas, the first Christmas in a new home with my newlywed wife, my crazy aunt Virginia—three sheets to the wind on Christmas

Eve—singing "Mele Kalikimaka" on top of the coffee table.

The things—the toys and junk—aren't what make a memorable Christmas. Sure, I remember the Christmas I received my first bike and the morning I unwrapped the Easy-Bake Oven Santa brought, but I don't remember many other material gifts. I do remember the last Christmas afternoon I spent with my grandfather. I remember the last Thanksgiving meal I ate with my grandmother. I remember the stupid-looking matching pajamas my mother made my brother and me wear every Christmas Eve.

Today's quirky Christmas event is tomorrow's fond Christmas memory.

Friends are vital at Christmas. Being a friend during this first Christmas following Hurricane Katrina might be more important than ever. Everyone in our area was affected. Most of us lost something; many lost too much, some lost everything. Friends came to the rescue—friends next door, friends from other towns, friends from other states. New friendships were created and lasting relationships were cemented. Never in my lifetime have friends—new and old—been more important.

Christmas is synonymous with food, and food has such strong connections with our memories. Christmas is the only time of year that friends stop by the house throughout the day bearing gifts of food. For generations my family has eaten a huge formal meal on Christmas Eve, and I can remember each and every one that I have attended or hosted. Christmas morning wouldn't be complete without a batch of my neighbor Mary Virginia McKenzie's sweet rolls and my mother's garlic-cheese grits.

For many years I chased fun. I looked under every nook and cranny in search of fun, I tried to create fun. In retrospect, my fondest memories have occurred when I wasn't trying to make fond memories, and certainly when I wasn't trying to create fun. Most of my fondest remembrances were unintentional memories that were created by accident or happenstance; most happened when the other Fs were in play.

When three or more of the Five Fs are present, fun happens. It doesn't have to be created. Relatively late in life I have found that true fun and sheer joy come from the unintentional implementation of the Five Fs.

This Christmas enjoy all of the joys the season unintentionally offers, for they will surely become fond memories in years to come. Pray for those who need help and guidance. Give to those in need like you've never given before. Give food, give clothing, give time, and give your friendship. Spend time with your family, spend time with your friends, make new friends, and make sure to do everything you can to assure that everyone who needs to eat is able to eat.

In the meantime, my children will be wearing matching pajamas and I'll be singing "Mele Kalikimaka."

Move Over, Ralph Lauren, the Burger King's in Town

When I was a young boy, a neighbor asked if Santa was going to bring me everything on my Christmas wish list. I told her, "Yes."

My mother jumped in and said, "Don't be so sure, Robert. You know Santa keeps a naughty and nice list."

To which I replied, "Well, I acted worse than this last year and still got everything I wanted."

In 2008 I received everything I wanted for Christmas except a bottle of Burger King's meat-scented cologne, Flame.

I was hoping there would be a bottle of Flame in my stocking Christmas morning, but I must have been on the naughty list. That's right, Burger King, the fast-food giant, has gotten into the fragrance business.

Flame, Burger King's cologne for men, was released this fall and carries the tagline: "The scent of seduction with the hint of flame-broiled meat." It's the truth, it's actual, Burger King makes cologne. I am not joking. We have now reached a point in this Fast Food Nation where we are purchasing toiletries with a side of fries and an apple pie.

Who was the food-service executive that thought this would be a good idea? I haven't visited a Burger King restaurant in a long time, but I wonder if they have gone the department store route and started posting a nicely dressed young woman at the end of the order counter with a tester bottle. "Double Whopper, hold the pickles, hold the lettuce, and would you like to try our new meat-scented cologne?"

"No thank you. I think I'll just order some meat-scented meat, and eat it between two pieces of bread with mustard."

I am not a cologne wearer. I mostly smell like soap. I have reached a point in my life where I don't even need to purchase shampoo. Soap and a washcloth work just fine on both my hair and body. But if I did wear cologne, I wouldn't wear one that smelled like meat, or fish, or any food product. I'd say, "Give me some of whatever Brad Pitt is wearing. That seems to work pretty well for him."

What kind of woman is attracted to the smell of charred meat? I like beef. I eat a lot of it. A medium-rare prime New York Strip is one of the greatest culinary joys in my life. Though I'm afraid that if I sprayed some of Burger King's cologne on me, I'd have Rottweilers chasing me down the street thinking I was an oversized T-bone.

What's next? Underarm deodorant that smells like a fish sandwich? Mountain Dew–flavored mouthwash? Maybe other fast-food restaurants will get in on the act. Will we see Big Mac special-sauce shampoo?

Actually, if this marketing gimmick works, maybe I can pick a few items off of my menu for sale as personal grooming products. How about a Corn and Crab Bisque–scented cologne, or speckled trout aftershave?

Will Burger King now get into the clothing business? Will cardboard crowns, polyester pants, and plastic name tags be the new black, or the new pink, or the new whatever is new?

For the purposes of this column, I went to the pharmacy next door to my office to see if I could purchase a bottle of Flame cologne. I wanted to give it a field test. I would spray some on, walk around my restaurant, and see if the ladies treated me differently. Unfortunately, my pharmacy only carries English Leather and Old Spice, so I'll never know if the women of the world would have viewed me as the standard bearer of seduction with a hint of flame-broiled meat, or just another item on the lunch menu—hold the onions.

Butterball Turkey Talk-Line

True story: A woman once called the Butterball Turkey Talk-Line to find out how long it would take to roast her turkey. The hotline worker asked how much the bird weighed. The woman responded, "I don't know, it's still running around outside."

The holidays offer no respite from idiots.

The following are actual questions asked of Butterball Turkey Talk-Line personnel:

"I lost a bet on a football game and now I have to fix Thanksgiving dinner for twenty people. How does a guy do that?"

"I know you're all about turkeys, but can you help me make cookies?"

"How do you prepare a turkey for people who don't eat meat?"

"The doorbell is ringing, everybody's here, but the turkey is still frozen solid. Can I serve it anyway?"

"I buried my turkey in a snowbank and now I can't find it. What should I do?"

"I'm calling from a cell phone and I'm walking up and down the aisles in the grocery store. I don't know what to get for Thanksgiving dinner. Will you walk with me and tell me what to buy?"

"What are you wearing?"

I have never called the Butterball Turkey Talk-Line. I have no problem cooking turkeys. I cook my turkey at an extremely high heat, never stuff, and never baste, and it comes out flawless every time. However, I do have a few questions I would like to ask the experts at the Butterball Talk-Line:

Does anyone eat mincemeat anymore?

Why in the world would anyone place a marshmallow on top of a sweet-potato casserole?

Who was braver—the first man to milk a cow or the first man to eat an egg?

Why do Yankees insist on calling dressing "stuffing?"

Can you explain the offside rule in soccer?

Is the hokey pokey truly "what it's all about?"
Why don't psychics ever win the lottery?
Giblets...come on, what's the real story?
How did Chuck Norris ever get into the movie business?
Why doesn't glue stick to the inside of the bottle?
Do you know anyone that actually eats fruitcake?
Why are hot dogs sold in packages of ten and buns only come in packages of eight?
Why does everyone fight over the white meat, when we all know dark meat tastes best?

Holiday Disasters

During the holidays we reflect on the kindnesses that have been shown to us over the years. We give. We receive. And we remember.

Memories are clearer around this time of year. We remember the Christmas we received our first bicycle and a few others when we received milestone presents. We remember bits and pieces of various Thanksgiving dinners through the years, but what we remember most are the holiday disasters. It's the bonehead mistakes that we all make that create the most lasting holiday memories.

My grandmother prepared dozens of flawless Thanksgiving dinners, yet the Thanksgiving meal that is Gorilla Glued to the forefront of my brain is the first Thanksgiving my newlywed wife cooked a turkey to the point of carbon dust with the giblets, liver, and neck still inside the turkey. The resulting odor remained in the house until after Christmas.

Of course, this is the same woman who, after being told she must "season" her new cast-iron skillet, asked, "Do I use salt and pepper?"

The holidays are rife with opportunities for cooking disasters. Anytime someone gives a turkey a cornbread enema, calamity is always waiting around the corner.

I once spent a Thanksgiving in the apartment of my recently divorced father-in-law on which he decided to prepare what is now legendarily referred to as Rick's Mexican Thanksgiving Dinner. Not caring that the citizens of Mexico have no use for Thanksgiving—and being a newcomer to the culinary arts—he dumped a can of every product that Old El Paso sells into a casserole dish and baked it for a couple of hours, dubbing it "Chili-Enchilada Surprise." It was not enchilada-like, but it was very surprising. Later we learned that it was a dish he had invented while being cooped up in a small, cramped sailboat for months—not the usual prerequisite for adding a Thanksgiving entree to the repertoire.

My brother-in-law once prepared an oyster dressing that looked more like lime Jell-O than a savory side dish. While getting ready for a

Christmas party, my brother's wife touched the tip of her tongue to an iron to see if it was hot enough to press her dress. It was.

I get some of my best material during the holidays. Last week my daughter did something that we all thought was funny. She even thought it was funny, yet before we could finish laughing, she said, "Daddy, you're not going to write about that, are you?" I told her that I wouldn't, but I'm hoping that the statute of limitations will run out by next Thanksgiving.

Actually I might have a personal holiday disaster in the making. At a recent book signing a woman told me about a cranberry recipe she serves at Thanksgiving: a bag of cranberries cooked down with one box of Red Hot's candies. I'm going to give it a shot. I figure it's a win-win. If it works, I've got a new recipe to add to the file. If not, I'll have a story to tell for years to come.

Déjà vu

I was driving to Tupelo for a book signing last week and was struck with the strong sense of déjà vu. It was late November and I was traveling north on U.S. 45. It is a route I traveled often as a child, usually around this time of year.

My earliest Thanksgiving memories are set in Brooksville, Mississippi. My grandfather's family, or at least what was left of them, lived there. Early on Thanksgiving morning my family would drive from Hattiesburg to Brooksville.

What struck me most in those early trips out of town was the leaves of North Mississippi. Somewhere around Electric Mills and Shuqualak the pines gave way to hardwoods. When I was a kid, growing up in the Piney Woods, my life was filled with pine straw. In Brooksville there were thousands of leaves of all shapes, sizes, and colors. I spent most of my time outside on those Thanksgiving trips crunching in the fallen leaves and playing football with my cousins, only journeying inside to eat lunch or to catch the score of the Mississippi State–Ole Miss game on the radio.

Thanksgiving 1968, I was seven years old. Charlie Shira's Bulldogs were playing Johnny Vaught's Manning-led Rebels in Starkville, just a few miles up the road from Brooksville. We listened to the static-filled AM-radio transmission as Jack Cristal called the game. Avenging a 17–17 tie in Oxford the previous year, the Rebels beat the Bullies 48–22.

Déjà vu, part two.

As my Brooksville relatives died off, we began spending Thanksgiving at my grandmother's house in Hattiesburg. It is the house in which most of my early food memories are located. My grandmother served a very formal Thanksgiving dinner. She also made the best rolls I have ever eaten. In twenty-two years of professional cooking I have not been able to duplicate those rolls.

To this day, when I walk through the Purple Parrot Cafe kitchen and smell the aroma of a roux being made, it takes me back to my grandmother's kitchen and her turkey gravy. The toasty smell of oil and flour being combined in a cast-iron skillet has strong connections to my youth and those early Thanksgivings.

My grandmother was big on congealed salads. The biggest collective Wet Willie ever given to the nation of kiddom was the dreaded congealed-salad hoax. It was a dreadful scam. It looked like Jell-O, it shook like Jell-O, but it had vegetables inside. Great aunts and grandmothers all over the world spent years devising this deception. They disguised their creations with names like "aspic" and "molds," but we knew them for what they really were: tomato-flavored gelatin with carrots inside, a lettuce leaf on the bottom, and a dollop of mayonnaise on top.

In those days, my grandmother's post-church Sunday lunch rotation always included a turkey and dressing dinner. One Sunday a month we ate turkey. Her Sunday turkey lunch was exactly like her Thanksgiving meal. It was not until this moment that I realized how lucky I was that, as a kid, I had an entire Thanksgiving meal once a month.

I think of crunching leaves, heated rivalries, and turkey and gravy. I think next year I'll go back to my grandmother's rotation and eat a Thanksgiving meal once a month. I might even make a congealed salad.

Where Have All of the Lamb Eaters Gone?

I have fond memories of childhood Easter lunches spent at my grandmother's house.

Each year she set a formal table with the finest china, sterling silver, crystal, and linen. Placed in the center of the large table was a simple arrangement of fragrant narcissus and paper whites.

The china and flowers were nice details, and ones I can appreciate today as I host dinners and luncheons. But as a child, I could have cared less about the frills and flowers; I was interested in the food. I still am.

My grandmother cooked the world's greatest leg of lamb.

She always served lamb on Easter, with rice, gravy, green beans, another vegetable that varied from year to year, small, lighter-than-air biscuits made with lard, and a congealed salad topped with a dollop of mayonnaise.

I was not a fan of congealed salads. Mayonnaise atop Jell-O with fruit tucked inside never appealed to me. It still doesn't.

I am, however, a huge fan of lamb, and the slightly thick, brown gravy made from its pan drippings. It wasn't until years later that I began to appreciate mint jelly, or some other variation of mint, served alongside lamb.

Some families are potato families, some are rice families. I came from a split household. My father's side was composed of rice eaters, my mother's side preferred potatoes.

Today my wife's family (potato eaters on both sides) has merged with my family (half rice, half potatoes) to raise our kids as one-quarter rice eaters, three-quarters potato. Luckily, my wife and I are both non–congealed salad eaters. Therefore our children will not have to worry about the percentage breakdown, or culinary lineage, of mayo-laden Jell-O.

Over the years I have tried to serve lamb to my family to less than stellar results. Six years ago I cooked a Sunday afternoon lamb lunch for my family, and only half of those in attendance were fans of lamb. My brother's children brought chicken strips from a fast-food restaurant, and my daughter had to be told it was roast beef before she would take a bite of lamb.

This year's Easter was an unorthodox one. I had planned a large-scale, multifamily event with over thirty-five friends and relatives. Due to a couple of illnesses, plans were scaled back at the last minute, and the extensive lunch for thirty-five became an intimate setting for eight.

Since only five of the eight were lamb eaters, I scrapped the plans for a roasted leg of lamb and cooked steak and chicken fajitas with Mexican rice.

Fajitas for Easter…how did this happen? I don't think my grandmother even knew what a fajita was. Where have all of the lamb eaters gone?

My fondest food memories are set at my grandmother's table. It is ground zero for my lifelong love of food. She was an excellent cook, an exceptional hostess, and she imparted that love—and possibly a little of her cooking talent—to me.

What will my children's memories of Easter be? They won't have recollections of linen and crystal, rice and gravy, lamb and mint. They will remember Southwestern spiced chicken and beef, rice and beans, cilantro and cumin.

On second thought, maybe it's not the table setting or the fineries, maybe it's not even the food or flowers. It's definitely not the congealed salad. Maybe the best memories are created just because one is with one's family. Family just being together no matter what the circumstance—that is the basis for a great memory.

My children will remember the quirky-but-cute way my three-year-old son says the blessing. They will remember the strange, funny, and sometimes out-of-the-blue statements their grandfather makes. They will remember Daddy cooking an Easterized version of Southwestern food for some strange reason. They will remember one relative recovering from illness, another staying the same. Most of all, they will remember lingering at the table long after the last person took the last bite, and just visiting, just laughing, just being "family."

After all, it's not about food, it's about family. That is what makes sharing a meal together so special, whether it's Easter dinner or a casual Saturday afternoon lunch.

So long, adios (for all of you fajita lovers), and will the last lamb eater in South Mississippi please turn out the lights.

Chapter 8
The Column and Other Stuff

Convention Diary
Day One

NEW YORK—Greetings from the once-every-four-years meeting of Hillary Clinton's Vast Right Wing Conspiracy.

We arrived in New York two days ago and spent the first thirty-six hours of our visit going through security checkpoints. When we finally left the airport, I nervously traveled through my first Hudson River Tunnel since 9/11. Any security concerns I might have had about traveling through an underground passageway, in the world's most politically charged city, during its most divisive event since Donald Trump fired Omarosa, were quickly quelled thanks to our taxi driver. As he sped down the highway at a meandering and lazy 125 miles per hour, I was on the floor of the cab praying that God spare my life, causing me to miss the event entirely.

Never once have I arrived in New York and not been struck by the lingering question: Where does all of the sewage go? Twelve million people, an average of 4.5 bathroom visits per day. That's 54 million flushes per day (and that's only counting one flushers, my guess is that in the borough of Brooklyn, alone, every other bathroom visit is a two flusher).

Being a food writer and not a political correspondent, I didn't know where to start this new journalism journey. I assumed that I would need to develop a set of questions to ask the delegates, politicians, and celebrities when I encountered them. Unfortunately the most pressing question on my mind was about the city's sewage treatment plant, and after a few minutes of mulling it over, I began thinking about which New York restaurant I would visit.

I couldn't very well go to a major political convention and ask the attendees about the final destination of New York's waste products, so the first order of business was to develop a question, or a set of questions, that would fool my newspaper editors into thinking that I knew what I was doing.

This all-important question would be my ticket out of the food section and onto the opinion page. Instant credibility and column inches next to George Will would be the prize. The question would need to be international in scope, possibly something terror-related, and definitely involving the political issues of the day. Nothing came to mind. I tried and tried to come up with a timely political query, to no avail. So I went to lunch.

Over dessert, I remembered a *New York Times* piece about the lackadaisical attitude of the Canadian Border Patrol. Aha! Canada! That's international, and if I remember my geography, it's close by, too.

I began to form my question. Let's see...Canada, Canada, who is the president of Canada? Don't know. Quick...everything you know about Canada...It's cold, it's big, they like hockey, their pro football sucks, half of them speak French, Anne Murray, and Celine Dion come from there (note to self: don't ask any musical questions), it borders some of the Great Lakes, they say "eh" a lot...still nothing.

Maybe some of the products that come from Canada would trigger a thought: timber, the aforementioned crappy music (with the exception of Neil Young), hockey players, Mike Myers, ginger ale...stop the presses! I've got it! Canada Dry ginger ale. That's it. That is the question that I will pose to the delegates and celebrities—why is it called Canada Dry if it is a liquid? It's probing, it's international, it's slightly food-related (you can take the food writer out of the food section, but you can't...well, you can't do something that would sound good if I ended that axiom with something politically clever and snappy).

The first night in town placed us on the Upper East Side, in my friend Julia Reed's apartment. Julia is a senior writer at *Vogue*; she contributes to *Newsweek*, and contributes to the *New York Times Magazine*. It was my first taste of the New York social life. By the way, the New York social life is not like one sees on *Sex in the City*. It's hot and crammed into a small, but tastefully decorated, third-floor apartment where it is hard to get to the food table.

Robert Novak, longtime political columnist and the star of CNN's *Capital Gang*, was there. I gathered up all of the courage I could muster, walked over to Mr. Novak, tapped him on the shoulder, introduced myself, and asked, "Why do the call it Canada Dry if it is a wet liquid?" He looked at me like I had just shot his dog, turned around, and continued the conversation he was having (another note to self: when asking cutting-edge political questions, make sure to back the subject into the corner so as to give them no escape). Obviously, this was too tough a question for Novak to comprehend in a light, social setting, so I gave him a pass and began looking for the smoked salmon.

As the evening progressed, other members of the media arrived, until finally, the coup de grâce, the Holy Grail of political subjects, NBC anchor Tom Brokaw walked in. This was truly my shot at big-time political journalism. I waited patiently until Brokaw was in between breaths, tapped him on the shoulder, and asked, "Why do they call it Canada Dry if it is a liquid?" He looked puzzled, squinted his eyes, and said, "Excuse me," and then turned around to finish his sentence.

Realizing that this question might be too tough for even the most veteran of reporters, I tapped him on the shoulder again and asked, "Where does all of the New York sewage go?" He ignored me.

Day Two: Protests on Seventh Avenue, the Bush twins' party, and Lynyrd Skynyrd sings Free Bird to Marsha and Haley Barbour.

Convention Diary
Day Two (and three) (and a little bit of day one)

NEW YORK—If I were an actual (read: competent) political journalist and not a food writer, this column would be timely and not dragging two days behind the political events of the day. But the newspaper couldn't afford to send a "real reporter" to New York, so this is what you get.

The following are notes, general observations, and random thoughts (along with some stuff that was entirely made up) from the second and third days of the Republican Convention in New York:

Sunday was the big protest day at the convention. Only in New York, a city with a population four times the size of Mississippi, can 250,000 people march down the street, while other people (namely me) located two blocks away, have no idea anything is going on.

Police made a few arrests at the protest; the most noteworthy was eighty-six-year-old *60 Minutes* correspondent Mike Wallace (who was arrested a few weeks ago for harassing a New York City taxi commission official while trying to pick up an order of meat loaf from Luke's Bar and Grill on the Upper East Side). Sunday, Wallace was arrested once again, this time for trying to wrestle an order of meat loaf from filmmaker Michael Moore's fork. Moore won the battle.

Not to be outdone, Republicans staged a few protests of their own. A group of delegates from Montana, in an attempt to one-up John Kerry's 1971 act of throwing a borrowed set of war medals over the White House fence, threw their convention credentials, Dole '96 campaign buttons, and ticket stubs from the Staten Island Ferry over the wall of Gracie Mansion in protest of the protesters. When told that the mayor of New York was, in fact, a Republican, they demanded, "Where's Barbra Streisand's apartment?"

Later in the day, a group of senior citizen Republican women from Kansas dressed in coconut bras and grass skirts and hung a likeness of Michael Moore from a telephone pole in the middle of Times Square.

Then they burned him in effigy while chanting, "Death to the infidel!"

At the last Republican convention the only celebrities the party planners could dig up were Bo Derek and Wayne Newton (of course there was Lee Greenwood, who they bring out of retirement every four years, dust off, and make sing the proud-to-be-an-American song). Now the party can add Don King and 25 percent of the Baldwin brothers to the list.

I attended the Bush twins' party at the Roseland Ballroom on Sunday night. However, my shameless attempt to hobnob with the first twins ended in vein. All I saw of the girls was the back of Jenna's head and a portion of Barbara's ear, which I was able to spot while looking through a side view of Don King's spiked hair. The twins arrived at the Roseland Ballroom followed by their posse—379 sorority girls and frat boys from the University of Texas and Yale—and hundreds of paparazzi.

Yes, Don King is here, and has apparently accidentally Super Glued an American flag to each hand.

A fashion note: As a rule, Republicans wear more expensive shoes than Democrats. However, Republicans do tend to starch and press their blue jeans, a true fashion faux pas.

Later in the evening, at Crobar, Haley and Marsha Barbour took the stage and introduced Lynyrd Skynyrd to a packed house. The Barbour box, a private booth on the second floor of the bar, typically reserved for ten chic New Yorkers, contained no less than 938 members of the Barbour family. I stood on a banquet and screamed "Free Bird" with a member of the Barbour clan who will remain nameless.

Located next to the Barbour box was the Bush twins' box (the girls get around). They were hanging over the balcony along with the 379 members of the first-twins' posse. (Surprising factoid of the day: Jenna Bush knew all of the words to "Sweet Home Alabama" and sang them loudly.)

An inside note: I am told that the confetti that will be dropped along with balloons on the final night is made entirely from hanging chads leftover from the 2000 election.

The financial impact of the Republican onslaught in New York is being debated daily in the local media and in every one of the city's 228,673 Starbucks coffee houses. New York's number one industry—knockoff watches and purses—has recorded record sales over the last three days. Erma Watkins, an alternate delegate from Waco, Texas said, "Ain't nothing better than a ten-dollar Rolex and a twelve-dollar Prada bag, honey!"

Last night in the convention hall, Michael Moore was surrounded by a large group of taunting Republicans. They were holding up four fingers and chanting, "Four more years!" However, certain members of the New Jersey delegation opted for one finger and an entirely different chant altogether.

That's it for today's report.

Oops, I almost forgot, Monday, the convention officially opened and a dozen or so people spoke to the crowd at Madison Square Garden.

You Be the Judge... I'm Full!

Rarely have I been so full that I could eat no more.

Last week I was asked to judge a food competition for the University of Mississippi Medical Center's A Taste of UMC event. Well before the event was over, I reached one of those rare occasions.

For the last fifteen years, the Taste of UMC fund-raiser has been held to raise money to help needy family members of patients cover expenses during hospital visits and to help build a new chapel at the hospital. Good causes, each.

Ask not what your hospital can do for your stomach; ask what your stomach can do for your hospital.

Those who know me, and regular readers of this column, would conclude that a situation such as this would be just what the doctor ordered (pun intended). Free food, all one can consume, live music, thirty-six booths, three to four different food items at each booth, Cajun food, Japanese food, country cooking, Thai food, did I mention free food? Throw me into the briar patch.

I am a world-class eater. This event would be a cakewalk.

The booths lined the large hallway of the Jackson Medical Mall. Behind each booth were mountains of food and dedicated hospital employees, doctors, nurses, and crew all with one goal in life: to shovel as much food as possible onto the judges' plates, with hopes of winning the grand prize, which was... I have no idea what the grand prize was, as I was in the bathroom trying to purge (unsuccessfully) while they were handing out awards.

By the end of the event I felt that if I had to eat one more tiny, minuscule, infinitesimal bite of any crumb that fell off of a piece of another crumb that fell onto the plate of something that used to be a crumb, I would explode. I was so full that I felt if I took a deep breath of air, I would burst.

To top it all off I had made dinner reservations for later that evening.

At the halfway point, I was ready to throw in the towel. I looked at my fellow judges—former first lady of Mississippi Melanie Musgrove and watercolorist extraordinaire and Renaissance man about town Wyatt Waters—and neither looked anywhere near the bursting point. I suspect Mrs. Musgrove was slipping her tasting portions into the trash can while no one was looking. Waters, that sneaky, ponytailed scoundrel, was probably stuffing food into his shoe.

How else could one explain how I, the man with a professionally trained and battle-worn stomach—one twice the size of the other two judges' combined—could not hang with a couple of tasting-event neophytes? Lightweights by mass-feeding standards.

Around the time we reached the gastroenterology booth (chili, by the way…cruel are the procto warriors), I was feeling overly bloated. Unfortunately, it was only the twentieth of thirty-six booths. Musgrove and Waters, for their parts, still looked hungry.

Could it have been the Keefer's gyro I had eaten six hours earlier? No way. I have been known to eat a full, six-course dinner at Commander's Palace and then camp out on a stool in the Camellia Grill for a chili-cheese omelet, fries, and a chocolate freeze with ice cream just two hours later.

Could it have been the hotter-than-Hades Thai pizza, the two sneaky entrants at booth 16 served us? Without warning, I might add. Possibly. The so-called "pizza" turned my taste buds into putty before we made the turn.

Somewhere around booth 28, I was served a Middle-Eastern Indian-type foodstuff that, in comparison, made the Thai pizza taste like bland oatmeal. I don't remember the formal name of the dish that we judges later referred to as "chewable flames of hell wrapped in something squishy."

I kept telling myself, *Eat. Do your duty. It's for charity.* My stomach kept telling me, *NO!*

Several booths had prepared dishes from my cookbooks. Bribery and flattery go a long way at events such as these. These contestants were given extra consideration for "excellent taste in source material" and extra points for helping to put even more shoes on my wife and daughter's feet.

I ate myself stupid. Not IQ stupid, but stupid like a guy who, earlier in the day, would make dinner reservations to host a four-course, pris-fixe dinner immediately after judging a thirty-six-booth, hundred-plus-item cooking competition.

Next year, when the University Medical Center calls, I will go into heavy training at least six weeks in advance of the event. I will stretch my already-expanded stomach and not eat on the day of the event. Or maybe I'll just take the easy way out and stuff the tasting portions into my shoe.

The Mac Attack

The holy grail of kid cuisine is macaroni and cheese.

When I wrote my second cookbook, *Deep South Staples or How to Survive in a Southern Kitchen Without a Can of Cream of Mushroom Soup*, I needed to include a macaroni and cheese recipe to complete the theme for updated home cooking. I had never eaten mac and cheese, so I turned over the recipe development of that dish to my chief recipe tester, and Purple Parrot Cafe chef, Linda Nance.

Linda created a great mac and cheese recipe for the book. I named it Linda's Macaroni and Cheese. When testing the recipe, I ate mac and cheese for the first time. It was good, and I imagine much better than the boxed varieties on local grocery store shelves. Unfortunately, there was a problem.

Deep South Staples, before it was purchased by Hyperion, was a self-published book. All of the work on the book—the recipe testing, the photographic research, the layout and design, the recipe data entry, and the proofreading—was done in house. That's where today's story begins.

There was a slight miscue between the person who helped me do the recipe data entry and the four people (one of which was me) who proofread the manuscript; slight in scope, but monumental in the life of the finished book. In Linda's macaroni and cheese recipe there was a typographical error.

The recipe calls for one twelve-ounce can of evaporated milk. The data entry person accidentally entered "1 12-ounce can condensed milk." Yes, that milk. The canned milk normally known as sweetened condensed milk.

Folks, I don't need to tell you the difference between evaporated milk and sweetened condensed milk, but trust me when I tell you that if you ever prepare macaroni and cheese using sweetened condensed milk instead of evaporated milk, you will end up with one of the worst-tasting dishes you have ever eaten.

Trust me, too, when I tell you that if someone spends a lot of time measuring, preparing, and cooking mac and cheese with sweetened milk, they will not be happy. Actually they will be mad enough to call the cookbook's author on the telephone and write him nasty emails calling him all sorts of names and wishing harm on the author, his forebearers, and all of his heirs.

This would not have been a problem had I published the recipe in the newspaper and been able to print a correction in a subsequent column. Unfortunately, there were ten-thousand copies of the book printed, and within a matter of weeks, all of them were in people's homes or, more specifically, in their kitchens. Nothing feels as "permanent" as having one's words in a published book.

A correction was made in subsequent editions, and the problem soon went away, or so I thought.

Last spring, my wife and I hosted a dinner for one of our church groups. The adults were bringing their young children to our home, and while the grown-ups were meeting over dinner in one room, the children would be having dinner and playing in another room.

Don't get ahead of me, here.

I asked the chefs in my restaurant to prepare a few recipes for both groups. Unfortunately, the mac and cheese from *Deep South Staples* was one of them. Even more unfortunately, the copy of the book being used in the restaurant was an uncorrected first edition.

To compound matters, the adults had spent a lot of time giving their kids the hard sell and getting them excited about "eating at a real chef's house"; expectations were high, the outcome was terrifying.

In the course of my twenty-eight-year restaurant career, I have never had food thrown at me, especially one of my recipes, but if it ever were to happen that would have been the night. Halfway through dinner I walked through the breakfast room to check on the kids; they were in full culinary revolt. They looked at me with hate, disdain, and disappointment all at once.

Do you remember the food fight scene in the movie *Animal House*? We were that close. Only after bribing them with extra ice cream did they settle down.

Lessons learned: Never trust a typist, always load up on ice cream when children are coming over, and never—I repeat never—mess with a kid's favorite food.

Lent

The Lenten Season has begun.

In most Christian denominations, Lent is the forty-day period of fasting and prayer before Easter.

Growing up, I attended church, religiously. If the doors were unlocked at Main Street United Methodist Church in my hometown of Hattiesburg, I was usually there—Sunday mornings, Sunday evenings, Wednesday evenings, Thursday night youth group, and skating in the Fellowship Hall on Saturdays.

My favorite time to attend church was Wednesday nights during the summer for covered-dish suppers. My church was filled with great cooks. Ladies would line the Fellowship Hall with casseroles, fired chicken, and homemade cakes and pies. In addition to my grandmother's house, my love of Southern food was formed in church.

At my church we loved to eat. That might be why I don't remember anyone fasting during Lent. Actually, I was in my forties before I learned that fasting during Lent wasn't an practice exclusive to Catholics.

As a kid I always heard the term "Lent," but it was never followed by the word "fast," other than, "It's the twelfth day of Lent. How 'fast' can we get to the Fellowship Hall to eat some green-bean casserole?"

Maybe I wasn't paying attention, though I don't remember anyone in my family ever fasting, either. None of my relatives fasted and none of my neighbors fasted. As far as I was concerned, fasts and fish-on-Fridays were for the Catholics.

I never knew any Baptists who fasted. I knew a few Episcopalians who gave up drinking for Lent, but I don't know any who made it all the way until Easter.

It might have been a communication problem. Maybe the word just didn't circulate in my church. I have Baptist friends who tell me about how fast news travels in their church. They call it "gossip." In the Methodist church, we don't gossip, we just put your name on the prayer list. "Betty, did you hear what Erma's husband did? We better add his name to the prayer list."

I am so ignorant when it comes to fasting that the first conversation I ever had with anyone about the subject was last year. My friend Kevin (a Methodist, by the way) fasted for twenty-eight days drinking water only, he went another seven days with no solid food, and then spent fourteen days eating just vegetables. Because he's a Methodist, odds are high that a green-bean casserole was the first vegetable dish he consumed after thirty-five days without food.

"Verily I say unto you, Pyrex is the dish that pulls us through"—Book of Robert, Chapter 2, verse 34.

Maybe it's not ignorance. Maybe it's selective listening. My wife says I have a chronic case of that particular malady. Maybe people were talking about fasting all of the time while I was growing up. Maybe I was too busy eating to pay attention to what they were saying. It could have been that they were talking with their mouths full and I couldn't understand all of the important details that pertained to fasting. All I remember is that we always ate before church, at church, and after church.

Nevertheless, I am not fasting this year. Actually, the only thing that I am giving up during this the Lenten season is fasting. Though that's actually nothing different than I do during the rest of the year, so it probably doesn't count.

I don't mean to be disrespectful to people who fast. I have nothing against it. I am probably as devout as the next guy. It's just that eating is in my church DNA. I am Methodist, therefore I eat (casseroles). For the rest of you—hurry Easter!

The Denomination of Punch

I am a Methodist because my grandfather owned a pair of shoes.

My great-grandmother was a Baptist. My great-grandfather was a Methodist. My grandfather was the oldest of seven boys. His family was poor and could only afford Sunday shoes for the two oldest boys. The five younger boys stayed barefoot in the warmer months.

In Brooksville, Mississippi, in the early 1900s, the Methodist church was located a mile from their home. The two oldest boys walked to church with their father. The five youngest boys attended the Baptist church—which was located a few houses away and an easy walk on the grass—with their mother.

A tattered pair of Sunday shoes has provided me with a lifetime of covered-dish suppers.

It's sometimes hard to pick a Methodist out of the crowd. A Muslim might have a prayer rug, a Jewish man might wear a Star of David, and the Catholics have the rosary. We Methodists can't walk around with a casserole dish hanging from our necks.

My friend Bill explains the denominations this way: The Baptists pick you up out of the gutter, the Methodists clothe and feed you, the Presbyterians educate you, and the Episcopalians introduce you to all of the right people, which sends you back into the gutter so the Baptists can pick you up again.

I know a better way to define the Protestant denominations—through their punch. Not their boxing punch, mind you, but their ladle-it-out-of-your-grandmother's-cut-glass-bowl, fruit-juice-and-ginger-ale-with-a-floating-ice-ring-in-the-middle church punch.

Three cookbooks ago, I released *Deep South Parties*. In the chapter that included various celebratory beverages, I published several actual punch recipes from local small-town church cookbooks. The procedural instructions for the various church punches were basically the same among the denominations. The yields were similar, as each recipe made enough punch for about thirty thirsty churchgoers. Where the rubber meets the road, or better still, where the ring mold meets the fruit juice, is in the ingredients.

The ingredients of the church-punch recipes I found are a telling factor. When I was a boy, a lady named Mrs. Lampkin was the hostess at my church. Here is the recipe for her punch: one forty-eight ounce can pineapple juice, one three-ounce package instant lime gelatin, two cups sugar, one cup lemon juice, one small bottle of almond extract. Simple, easy, green.

Methodist punch follows the liturgical calendar. During Advent, the liturgical color is purple, so we substitute grape Jell-O. During Christmastide, when the liturgical color is gold, we use pineapple.

Here is a punch recipe found in a Baptist cookbook in my hometown: two cups cranberry juice, two cups apple cider, one cup pineapple juice, one cup orange juice, half cup lemon juice, two cups ginger ale. We know it well, and have drunk it often at Baptist weddings. Some might have even snuck into the back room at Baptist weddings and added something a little stronger.

Speaking of stronger, the Catholic punch recipe I found is made using half gallon burgundy wine, one pint gin, two quarts ginger ale, half cup sugar, and quarter cup lemon juice. With my Catholic friends, it's all about the wine.

My uncle is an Episcopal priest in the Northern Neck of Virginia. This is an actual recipe for church punch that I pulled from of one of his church's cookbooks: one fifth bourbon (100 proof), one fifth brandy, one fifth sherry, one fifth sparkling red wine, juice of twelve lemons, two cups sugar, one fifth soda water. Which is proof that one will always need a designated driver when attending a Whiskeypalian wedding.

My grandfather owned a pair of Sunday shoes, and that's why I'm forever destined to drink green punch.

Punch and Friday Night Lights

In twenty-first century life, there aren't too many settings in which punch is served. Today, punch is strictly a church party offering.

Years ago my grandmother and her friends owned elaborately decorated sterling silver and crystal punch bowls. They were brought out at bridge clubs and sewing circles and loaned out for weddings and receptions.

Those days have gone. Most punch bowls in use today are made of glass and come from the party rental store.

At weddings, the punch bowl has given way to the champagne fountain. I am not a fan of the champagne fountain. The champagne fountain is a health-inspector's nightmare. Stand around the champagne fountain at the next wedding you attend. Within five to seven minutes, someone is going to sneeze or cough in the direction of the fountain. Moments later someone will stick their glass under the fountain— champagne splashing on their unwashed hands and falling into the bottom of the fountain to be recirculated.

The cascading chocolate fountain is just as bad, if not worse. The first time I attended a party with a liquid chocolate fountain, I stood and watched as guests stuck strawberries into the cascading chocolate. The chocolate oozed over the berries and their fingers and then back into the bowl to be recirculated, and no one knew where those fingers had been.

Today, punch is usually reserved for weddings and religious socials. Usually, both are church events. There are many forms of church punch. I have always felt that one could determine one's denomination just by keeping a close eye on the punch bowl.

Baptists dunk the entire cup into the bowl when serving it. Methodists only sprinkle a little bit of punch at a time. Catholics add a lot of wine to their punch. Lutherans will only drink punch if the recipe has been nailed to the door. Jehovah's Witnesses believe in drinking punch, but only if they can do it two at a time. Mormons, on the other hand, can drink as many glasses as they want.

My high school had a punch that was served after football games, at the post-game dance in the gym. Named for the school, it was called Beeson Punch.

Beeson punch was a non-alcoholic variety most of the time. Occasionally, if a chaperone was asleep at the wheel, it was given a little spike by one of the students. But I have no idea who would have done anything like that, and if I did, hopefully the statute of limitations has run out.

Beeson Academy was located on the edge of town, situated directly behind the area's landmark drive-in theater, the Beverly Drive-in. On Friday nights, the screen at the Beverly Drive-In was in full view of the Beeson Academy football field.

Beeson wasn't big enough to have a marching band, so in lieu of drum majors, majorettes, and tubas, our halftime entertainment featured the Beverly's huge screen filled with Burt Reynolds, Sally Field, and Clint Eastwood, without sound.

In the latter days of the Beverly Drive-in, and in the waning days of the drive-in movie craze, new management at the drive-in resorted to cheesy soft-core skin flicks to help jump-start their dwindling business. This posed quite a dilemma under the Friday night lights of the Beeson Academy football field.

I can remember looking up from the huddle and seeing all manner of depravity shining forth on the Beverly Drive-in screen. Our team had grown accustomed to the momentary flashes of flesh (or as accustomed as any seventeen-year-old boy can become to a sight such as that). However, it served as a great strategic distraction for the visiting team. Nothing created a better home-field advantage than Swedish stewardesses on a gigantic screen in front of eleven testosterone-filled high-school football players from out of town.

Blond stewardesses in the distance will thwart any opposing teams play calling. To this day I think that it was the ten-thousand square feet of exposed and jiggling flesh, rather than the mighty Beeson Trojans' awe-inspiring football prowess, that helped our tiny school win as many football games as we did.

In a state where breast-feeding in public is punishable by six months in jail and/or a $500 fine, the ultimate home-field advantage was the sight of a seventy-five-foot-tall bosom bouncing up and down in the distance, and it was always worth 7 to10 points on the home team's scoreboard.

After the game, punch for everyone!

Keep Those Cards and Letters Coming

I love receiving emails from readers of this column.

The positive correspondence is flattering, and always appreciated, but nothing tickles my funny bone more than someone who has taken offense to something I have written. I love it.

It's so strange. In every other aspect of my life I would cringe to think I had offended someone. In my non-column life, I go to great pains to make better a situation in which someone disagrees with me. In the newspaper, for some strange reason, it's different. Most of the time, the madder the author is, the better—and more entertaining—the email.

I once wrote a column about my daughter and the scam she ran on me when trying to sell her Girl Scout Cookies. I never criticized the cookies. No way. I love the cookies. It was they way my daughter decided to sell the cookies by getting all of the money from me up front.

The emails began pouring in. I was awed by the Girl Scouts' ability to mobilize their troops (maybe we need to send a battalion of cookie-wielding Girl Scouts over to Iraq). They telephoned my daughter's den mother, they called the house. It was a blast. In the end, I was stuck with a few dozen cases of cookies and an inbox full of hilarious emails.

PETA members, vegetarians, and fans of Barbra Streisand are the most vocal and rabid of my regular emailers. But now I have added a new group who are in the process of pushing Streisand fans out of third place—people who love to eat deer sausage.

A few weeks ago I wrote a column about my dislike of deer sausage, and how my friends are always trying to dump their excess deer sausage onto me. My point was: If it's so good, why not eat it yourself? No one ever brings steak or pork chops to my house, etc...yada, yada, yada. You know the drill. I jokingly proposed a cow, chicken, and pig season so that my hunter friends might be able to feed me more tasteful hunting leftovers.

A lady named Debra began her email with the sentence "This is the most disgusting article I have ever read." I surmise from Debra's correspondence that she is not up to snuff on the plight of the citizens of Rwanda or—as my mother used to say—"the starving Armenians."

Donna in Savannah, Georgia, opined, "You apparently don't know how to prepare it in your high and mighty upscale restaurant." Actually, we occasionally serve venison in one of my restaurants. Unfortunately, as I have stated before, I am not a fan of deer meat, so I always order the fish.

Several people offered to take the excess deer sausage in my freezer off of my hands. Thank you, but I don't think my deer-hunting friends will be bringing their hunting bounty to my house anymore. I have a strong feeling that my supply has forever run dry.

My favorite email came from a fellow named Calvin in Madison, Mississippi, who wrote, "Because, in your opinion, deer sausage is not good, does not mean to say that it is not good to others…You might not like the taste of venison, but do not write negative articles about a food that thousands of people around the world do in fact enjoy consuming." I wrote Calvin and told him that his sentence baffled me. I think he is under the erroneous assumption that I have some type of mysterious power over newspaper readers, and can magically make thousands of people around the world who "love" eating a certain food immediately discard their love of said food just because I don't like it. That's just not the case. Thousands?

There were a few who thought I was serious when I proposed a cow-hunting season. I don't know how to respond to those concerns.

In the end, I did learn that there are several charitable organizations who feed excess deer sausage (and there's probably a lot of it) to those in need. If you have freezers full of unwanted deer meat, I suggest that you donate it to charity.

Maybe I'll talk to my publisher and publish some of the email correspondence I have received over the past nine years. It will probably be more interesting than the actual columns themselves. In the meantime, keep those cards and letters coming.

Big Trouble on Sandwich Day

I used to serve as a lunch volunteer at my daughter's school.

My assigned day was Wednesday. Wednesday is sandwich day, ham or turkey. Simple enough, right? Not so fast.

The lunchroom volunteer placed me at the condiment table. It was explained that after the children (kindergarten through sixth grade) picked up a plate with their sandwich selection, they would stop by the potato chip box, and then progress to my condiment table.

I began my prep work getting ready for the lunch rush. I brought out a big bowl of mustard and a big bowl of mayonnaise, each with a spreading knife. Next, I sliced a few tomatoes and fanned them over a small plate of chopped lettuce. I showed the other volunteers how everything on my table had been strategically arranged for maximum efficiency, while simultaneously taking into account eye appeal. I was ready for the rush.

At the last minute, a cafeteria volunteer brought out two extra-large squeeze bottles of ketchup. "Oh, they get French fries, too," I said.

"No," she said, "we don't serve French fries."

"Well what's the ketchup for?" I said

"The sandwiches and chips," she replied.

"You've got to be kidding," I said.

"Nope."

I immediately began delivering a fifteen-minute rant on how crazy and out of touch this woman was if she thought kids were going to eat ketchup on a ham or turkey sandwich, not to mention potato chips.

"You'll see," she said.

"I'm a professional food person," I said. "I know what people want to eat and how they want to eat it. I've been in the restaurant business for twenty-three years. I have two small children at home."

"Yeah right, you'll see."

The bell rang and, class by class, the children began filing into the lunchroom. The first two stopped by the condiment table, one for mustard, one for plain. I gave the lunch lady the see-I-told-you-so look. She smiled confidently. The third child walked up and I said, "Mayonnaise or mustard?"

"Ketchup," the little boy replied.

"No, I'm talking about for your sandwich, son. Do you want mayonnaise or mustard?"

"Ketchup," said the little boy, this time looking a little perturbed.

"Are you sure you want ketchup on a turkey sandwich? Typically people like mayonnaise and a little..."

"I want ketchup!" he shouted.

In quick order I squirted some ketchup on his turkey and looked toward the next child. "Hi there. Would you like mayonnaise or mustard on that sandwich?"

"Ketchup, please," the little girl said.

"No, trust me. You really want mustard and lettuce; you just don't know it yet. You see, the thing about mustard and ham is that the tartness of the mustard..."

"Ketchup."

"Maybe if you just tried the mustard once you would..."

"Mrs. Smith, the fat man in the Hawaiian shirt is scaring me!" said the girl.

"Yeah, he's holding up the line!" said another.

"Well, how about a little lettuce and tomato on that sandwich, you know dietary fiber is..."

"Ketchup."

"When I eat a ham sandwich, I like to mix the mayonnaise and mustard together..."

"KETCHUP!"

"We're out of ketchup," I said.

"But I see that bottle behind your back and it looks full to me. I'm going to tell the teacher."

"All right kid, here's your ketchup."

"I want some for my chips, too."

As soon as the shift was over, I took the half-used bowls of mayonnaise and mustard, the full plate of lettuce and tomatoes, and two empty bottles of ketchup off of my artfully arranged condiment table and back to the kitchen. Defeated, I turned in my apron and rubber gloves, threw in the towel, and walked away from sandwich day forever.

The next semester I signed up for pizza day. They placed me in the kitchen, behind a stack of pizza boxes. The lunchroom volunteer explained the process. "It's very easy," she said. "All you do is hand them either pepperoni or cheese. They'll let you know which one they prefer."

"But what about sausage or mushroom?" I said.

"Just cheese and pepperoni," said the lunchroom volunteer.

"Don't you think it would be nice to offer a selection..."

"Listen, mister, its cheese and pepperoni, period. That's what they want,"

"But what about..."

"I've heard about you, bucko. You're the troublemaker who made all of the ruckus last year. I'm keeping my eye on you."

"But what about extra cheese to sprinkle on top?" I said. "Or crushed red pepper flakes, or French dressing for dipping."

Walking away, she turned her head, grimaced, and shouted, "Just give them some ketchup!"

The Morning Beverage Minority

I do not drink coffee.

I wish that I drank coffee. I would love to be referred to as a coffee drinker. "There goes Robert," they would say. "He's a coffee drinker."

I think it would be cool to sit in a coffee shop and sip some type of mocha concoction and read the *New York Times.* On occasion I would order an exotic frappe-something-or-other. At Christmas I would order the Holiday Blend, at Valentine's the White-Chocolate Blend, and on Millard Fillmore's birthday, I would order the Millard Blend—a Fillmorchino.

Maybe I would order a "tall coffee," even though "tall" is the smallest size. In my mind's eye, I see myself saying, "I would like a *tall* mocha-frappe something." And I look cool saying it.

"Grande" is a medium-sized coffee. Saying "grande" is not as hip as saying "tall." It seems that a word such as "grande" should refer to the largest size available. Not so. "Venti" is the largest-sized coffee available.

Venti sounds like a foreign car, not a beverage size. If I was a coffee drinker, and I drank a lot of coffee, I would not order a venti or a grande. I would order a tall and go back for refills, often.

On second thought, if I was a coffee drinker, I don't think I would want my coffee to be mocha'ed or frappe'd or Millard'ed. I wouldn't want any flavoring in my coffee. No caramel or vanilla or pumpkin— just coffee-flavored coffee.

If I were not in a coffee shop, I would order black coffee. There is something manly about ordering a "black coffee." No sugar, no cream, no foamy stuff, just a cup of three-hours-hold, sitting-on-the-hot-plate, hot-as-a-McDonald's-lawsuit, sitting-next-to-the-microwave-at-the-convenience-store, pours-like-maple-syrup black coffee.

I want to be that guy—the black-coffee-drinking guy—the one who holds a small (or tall) non-eco-friendly, un-biodegradable Styrofoam cup of bitter, burn-your-tongue-while-it-warms-your-buns black coffee.

I am not that guy. I drink Coke Zero. Coke Zero is not as manly as a cup of black coffee, though the can is black. I like that. I used to drink a lot of Diet Coke. The Diet Coke can is silver. Silver is not as manly as black.

I drink from a black can. I drink it cold. No cream, no sugar, just Coke Zero, black, straight out of the can. I am not hip or cool.

In our society, non–coffee drinkers are discriminated against. I am a member of the morning-beverage minority. It's true. It's brutal, and it's not fair. The next time you attend a breakfast meeting, check out the beverage offerings—black coffee, decaffeinated coffee (both stored in very cool spaceage–designed air pots), and a pitcher of ice water. No soft drinks. Ever.

Try asking for a soft drink at the average morning business meeting and then watch the all-out scramble to find a beverage. After twenty frantic minutes, they'll return to the table with a leftover Tab that has been sitting in the back of the break-room fridge from the days when cigarettes were still being advertised on television.

Most coffee shops don't even sell soft drinks. They offer crazy mango-papaya concoctions, and overpriced water, but no soft drinks. The baristas look down their noses at any poor slob who would not drink coffee.

Coffee servers even get cool names: baristas. Who serves the members of the morning-beverage minority? Soda jerks.

I want to be a coffee drinker when I grow up. I want to sit in the coffee shop and drink a steaming tall cup of un-mocha'ed, non-frappe'd, black coffee. Until then, I'll be a card-carrying member of the morning-beverage minority.

Greasy Spoon Tenure with a Side Order of Attitude

I recently enjoyed two meals at one of the South's greatest breakfast joints.

The Silver Skillet in Atlanta has been dishing out breakfast for almost fifty years. It is on my top 10 list of the South's greatest independent restaurant joints. The others—with the exception of the Camellia Grill in New Orleans—all have one thing in common: apathetic service.

One aspect that makes eating in a true diner/breakfast joint an authentic experience is an indifferent, if not rude, waitress. I love rude diner waitresses; they are one of our nation's greatest treasures.

I'm not talking about someone serving a $200 meal at Commander's Palace. I'm referring to the place where they specialize in coffee and eggs, a get-in-and-get-out and don't-read-the-paper-too-long-so-somebody-else-can-have-a-seat type place. There is something about a grumpy, unconcerned septuagenarian wearing comfortable shoes and a smock that makes me smile.

In my hometown of Hattiesburg, I usually eat breakfast away from home about once a week. I frequent two restaurants. Both are national chains and both have extremely nice, well-trained, and over-accommodating waitresses. I am grateful for the service I receive when I eat at those restaurants. However, when I am out of town, the restaurant masochist in me wants an old, gum-smacking, rude waitress.

Scrambled eggs, bacon, and toast are just about the same wherever you go. To have them served with a side order of attitude while not overly offending the customer is not an easy feat to accomplish.

My restaurants spend weeks training servers to be over-accommodating. We teach them how to anticipate the customer's every need. We stress the finer points of service and encourage them to go the extra mile for their customers.

Independently owned small breakfast joints and diners don't worry with terms such as "the finer points of service." Most have employed waitresses for over twenty years who probably know more about running the front of the house than the manager does.

Richard Melman, one of the country's most creative and successful restaurateurs, developed an entire concept around rude waitresses. In the early 1980s Melman single-handedly created the short-lived fifties-themed diner craze. Ed Debevic's in Chicago is Melman's tribute to cheeseburgers, chilidogs, and customer abuse. The atmosphere at Ed Debevic's is authentic, the attitude is manufactured. The servers are taught how to abuse customers in the style of the classic diner waitress.

I can see through the theme-restaurant charade at Ed Debevic's. What the servers don't have there is greasy-spoon tenure. It takes years, decades even, to develop an I-could-care-less-what-you-want-just-tell-me-and-let-me-get-it-out-to-you-as-quick-as-I-can attitude while not offending the customer.

In my opinion, the real diner veterans have earned the right to be indifferent. From countless mornings waking up at 4 a.m., no benefits, no vacation days, making just a little over two bucks an hour, and paying for their children's college tuition, and their ex-husband's excesses, from nothing more than customers' tips. They field complaints and special requests with the grace of Attila the Hun, but they show up every day, rain or shine, keep the coffee cup full, and eventually warm up to you if you come in often enough.

My friend Bill Kirby (the man who originally told me about the Silver Skillet) and I are going to spend part of this summer on a culinary quest to find the South's rudest diner waitress. It will take a lot of pancakes, bacon, and eggs to find the rudest, most abusive, grumpiest waitress in the South, but our stomachs are up to the task.

We will most definitely visit Atlanta on our culinary quest. However, on my last two visits, the waitresses at the Silver Skillet—home to the best pancakes and rudest waitresses in the state of Georgia—were accommodating and polite. The pancakes lived up to the billing, but the waitresses let us down a bit. They were nice on both visits. If they don't tighten up and get ornery again, they're going to lose their well-earned reputation.

The character of a small town can be summed up within the walls of its local breakfast joints. Every morning throughout the South, the news of the town and the news of the world is recounted and debated at Formica-coated tables, over strong coffee, newsprint, tobacco smoke, fried eggs, pancakes, and rude waitresses.

Support your local breakfast joint…overtip a rude diner waitress today.

It's A Wrap… or a Box, or a Plastic Thingy

Food packaging has come a long way from the days of Grandma canning fruits and vegetables and selling them to the downtown cafe.

Today, ketchup, milk, and mayonnaise are shipped in bags, boxes, cans, packets, bottles (glass or plastic), and cartons. Potato chips, which used to be packed in clear bags, now come in non-see-through bags filled mostly with air.

When I was a child, one had to use a can opener to open a canned soft drink. The pop top was invented, and after the zillionth person cut his heel on a discarded pop top, the permanent, in-the-top-of-the-can pop top was invented. Nowadays my children just stick a straw into a plastic pouch and sip away.

Overnight delivery has changed the way we ship and pack many items. Live lobsters arrive at the restaurant in packaging that looks like a case of wine, with twelve subcompartments, ice packs, and seaweed everywhere.

Question: Whose job it is to put rubber bands on lobsters claws, and how many fingers does he have left?

We purchase baby lettuce, foie gras, truffles, and heirloom vegetables that are sent overnight from locales as far away as California and upstate New York. These foodstuffs sometimes arrive in climate-controlled boxes packed in peanuts and tucked inside another box. I hate Styrofoam peanuts. They conduct static electricity and, within seconds, scatter all over the place. I am not a violent man. However, I believe that if I ever met the scoundrel who invented the Styrofoam peanut, I would punch him square in the nose.

As continual improvements are made in food preservation, packaging, and shipping, the toy industry is taking backward steps in packaging.

As the father of a seven-year-old daughter, I speak from experience when I say that the most impossible package to open is the twenty-first-century Barbie doll. I don't know what they were packed in back in the sixties and seventies (I was playing with GI Joes that were crammed inside a basic cardboard box with a cellophane window), but today it's easier to bust into a vault at Fort Knox than it is to open a Barbie package.

Having opened several dozen Barbie dolls over the last seven years, I have found that I actually spend more time opening the package (an average of fifteen minutes) than my daughter spends playing with the doll.

A Barbie doll has a packaging system so detailed that I believe the Mattel company wants to make sure that each of their dolls could survive being dropped ten-thousand feet from a jumbo jet during a nuclear holocaust. The three-step, packaging-reinforcement plan is an evil scheme devised by someone in the home office who has a major vendetta against fathers.

Step One: the clear, hard-plastic, molded outer protection made from a polymer material so strong that it could take on the weight of an oversized steamroller, a half dozen Sumo wrestlers, and every customer at an all-you-can-eat seafood buffet and still keep its shape. The outer package must be cut with a very sharp, and very strong, pair of scissors and then pried away from the doll using both hands, all ten toes, and at least half of your teeth. I have ruined two pair of scissors and three bicuspids opening Barbie dolls.

Step Two: the twist ties. I don't know where Barbie dolls are manufactured, but whichever foreign country manufactures them must have—as their country's leading export—twist ties. The Barbie doll comes bound with at least 2,451,968 twist ties that secure every nanometer of her hourglass body to the pink cardboard packaging tucked inside the hard-plastic outer shell.

Step Three: the plastic hair thingy. To make sure that every strand of Barbie's hair stays in place during her long journey from the Republic of Twisttieland, Mattel Inc. has developed an evil, mind-wrenching piece of plastic that is part glue, part comb, part Rubik's Cube, which fastens to the cardboard packaging and keeps her hair secure. Trust me; there is no way to remove the hair thingy without turning Barbie into an instant spokesmodel candidate for a Rogaine commercial. My wife and I never had to worry about our daughter cutting her Barbie doll's hair, because Daddy removed most of it when he was trying to remove her flowing blond mane from the plastic hair thingy.

My three-year-old son is always more interested with the box or packaging than the actual toy itself. He could spend hours popping a sheet of Bubble Wrap. (If I ever met him, I might kiss the man who invented Bubble Wrap.)

It's all in the name of progress. We keep inventing ways to get it there faster, to make it open easier, to keep it fresh longer, if for no other reason than to keep the GDP of Twistieland in the black.

So You Want to Be a Rock-and-Roll Star

When I was six years old, I wanted to be Darrin Stephens when I grew up. Not only was I attracted to the idea of being married to a smoking hot woman who could make problems disappear with a twitch of her nose, I liked the idea of working for an advertising agency. The pitching of an idea to a client seemed creative and appealing. I was also enamored with the concept of entertaining clients. I didn't want to be a policeman, a fireman, or a cowboy. I wanted to be an advertising agency executive.

After my advertising phase, I decided to become an astronaut. The United States had just landed on the moon. It was the ultimate adventure. By then, my crush had moved from Samantha Stephens on *Bewitched* to Barbara Eden on *I Dream of Jeanie*. Larry Hagman was an astronaut, and once again, the beautiful woman in his life could make problems disappear, this time with a nod of the head. I stayed in my space-traveling phase until I found out how astronauts have to use the bathroom in outer space. I also never developed a fondness for Tang.

The career ambition that took me into my preteen and early teen years was rock star. I started playing the guitar and planned to be a member of Led Zeppelin or the Rolling Stones. I wasn't sure how one got to that point, but I loved the music, and life on the road performing in front of thousands of screaming girls was extremely appealing.

As we all know, I ended up in the food/food-writing business, though food is a major component of rock and roll. That's right. Not booze, drugs, or women—food.

Occasionally I visit a website entitled the Smoking Gun (www.thesmokinggun.com). In addition to celebrity mug shots (Glen Campbell and Nick Nolte alone are worth the visit), it lists musicians' riders.

An artist's rider is an attachment to a performance contract that lists specific sound and light requirements, but also specifies the specific food and beverage necessities of the performer.

Paul McCartney's rider demands, "There will be no meat, or meat by-products allowed to be served in the dressing rooms, production offices, or areas within the 'backstage area.'" He also specifies no leather furniture or furniture made from animal skins.

The artist formerly known as "the Artist" but once again known as Prince requires "Yogi cocoa tea" and "jasmine and lavender candles."

The four members of Van Halen demand one-half case "regular local beer" in cans, one-half case premium beer, one pint Jack Daniel's, one pint Absolut vodka, one 750 ml. bottle rum, two bottles white wine, one bottle red wine, one 750 ml. bottle top-shelf tequila, Cointreau, Grand Marnier, and ingredients to prepare bloody marys. At this point I should note that Eddie Van Halen didn't attend his induction ceremony to the Rock and Roll Hall of Fame a few weeks ago. He was in rehab.

The band Aerosmith asks for "NO alcoholic beverages" backstage and specifies "no pressed meats." Bon Jovi wants sushi after the show, Sting says that he is "adventurous enough to try local fare," and Metallica's catering needs are carefully detailed in three pages of a twenty-four-page document.

Eminem wants turkey burgers, Kansas needs prune juice, and Willie Nelson likes free-range pork chops.

Clarence Clemmons, Bruce Springsteen's longtime saxophone player, asks that a whole roasted chicken be delivered to his dressing room halfway through the performance and also demands beluga caviar, while The Boss, Springsteen, requires nothing more than energy bars, green tea, soft drinks, and coffee.

Some artists ask for only green M&M's, while others require bottled water flown in from Europe.

ZZ Top asks for "a medium serving bowl of cocktail franks in special sauce (consult with production assistant for the recipe and preparation instructions)." Johnny Cash wanted an American flag "in full view of the audience" while performing.

At sixteen years old I realized that my rock-star career would never materialize into anything more than my being a garage-band wannabe. I made the decision that if I couldn't be a rock star, I would write about the rock stars and set my sights to be a contributing writer for *Rolling Stone*. I haven't written for *Rolling Stone,* yet. But I've got a few years left in me.

So Long, Julia

Kitchens across America have gone dark. Spontaneous moments of silence are being observed, pilot lights are being extinguished, whisks are still, and chef's side towels are hanging at half mast. The grande dame of cooking has died.

On Friday the 13th last week Julia Child, the godmother of American cooking, died, just two days shy of her ninety-second birthday.

Child brought French cooking to the American mainstream, and then she brought American cooking to that same mainstream. Food TV and other cooking shows are here today because she invented the format in 1962.

In the introduction to the anniversary edition of *Mastering the Art of French Cooking*, the book that started it all, Julia simply states, "If you can read you can cook." That book, though French in theme, was the beginning of American cooking as we know it. It made such an impact when it was introduced in 1961 that Craig Claiborne, food editor for the *New York Times*, said in his review, "Probably the most comprehensive, laudable, and monumental work on French cuisine was published this week, and it will probably remain as the definitive work for nonprofessionals...It is a masterpiece."

After receiving formal training at Le Cordon Bleu in Paris, Mrs. Child opened a cooking school, L'Ecole des Trois Gourmandes, to teach American wives whose husbands were stationed in France the intricacies of French cooking. In 1961 she published *Mastering the Art of French Cooking*, the first of her eleven books. It is still in print and remains one of the definitive works on the subject.

She began her Emmy-award-winning television cooking career in Boston with *The French Chef.* That was 1962, and she didn't slow down until last year.

I had the privilege of spending two separate breakfasts with Mrs. Child. Upon meeting her, I was struck by three things—she was very tall (over six feet), she was very humble, and she was very funny. Julia Child possessed a razor wit.

I sat in awe of her knowledge, passion, and modesty. I learned volumes in the short time we visited. On the first occasion, we talked about cooking. Her favorite ingredient: "butter." Her cooking advice: "Know the basics and everything else will fall into place." She spoke of the simple beauty of a perfectly scrambled egg or an expertly prepared omelet.

During our second breakfast she shared tips on how to maintain a healthy lifestyle while cooking with classic French ingredients. When I asked how she was able to stay fit and trim after years of cooking with heavy cream and butter, she said, "Eat small portions. Don't deny yourself good food. Have three or four bites and leave the rest on the plate." Simple, practical, common-sense advice, from a woman who practiced the same principles in her cooking.

Julia Child was America's most significant culinary icon. Child was breaking through barriers before barrier breaking was *en vogue*. She was the first woman in a man's world. Due to an archaic and outdated French kitchen system, female chefs were not allowed in the back of the house. Some of our nation's best chefs were stuck in home kitchens. Even in American restaurants, women were considered cafe waitresses not chefs. Thanks in large part to Mrs. Child, the professional kitchen, formally an exclusive all-male club, was liberated. She did more for women in the workplace than she will ever be given credit for.

Before the 1970s, the nation's finest restaurants employed only French chefs. American food was considered substandard and American chefs were thought of as second-class citizens. Thanks to Julia, and her friend and American culinary pioneer James Beard, we now lead the world.

In preparation of this column I pulled the fortieth anniversary of *Mastering the Art of French Cooking* from the shelf. In the new introduction to the anniversary edition, Child gave her secrets to a full and healthy life: "Small helpings, no seconds, no snacking, and a little bit of everything. Above all—have a good time. The pleasures of the table are infinite." Well said, and well done, thy good and faithful servant.

What does one say about the person who did more for American cooking than anyone? What does one say about the person who helped pave the way for women in the professional kitchen? How does one honor the person whose impact on the culinary arts was so great that her home kitchen is on display at the Smithsonian? One says, simply, what she would say… *Bon appetit.*

The food in heaven tastes a lot better today.

Chapter 9
Strange

Fireworks and Food Foibles

One of the benefits of being a writer is that I am always on the receiving end of humorous and informative stories reported to me by the people I meet.

Last week I heard one of the best yet. A friend of a friend was recounting a recent Fourth of July meal with his family. His grandmother, a spry ninety-three-year-old, picked up a small box of bang snaps—the small firecrackers that are wrapped in paper and explode when thrown on the ground—and popped a few them into her mouth thinking that they were candy.

I am not sure if they exploded when she bit down on them or not, but the young man recalling the story told of a puzzled look on her face as smoke drifted out of her mouth while she sat at the dinner table. Luckily, she wasn't harmed and apparently laughed it off. Others in attendance were witness to a story that will certainly be told, retold, and added to the file of ancestral remembrances that are recounted every time the family gets together, and certainly every Fourth of July.

The story reminded me of my brother's wedding, twenty-eight years ago this month. At the time, the practice of throwing rice at weddings was beginning to go out of style. Apparently the wedding rice was being eaten by birds, creating intestinal problems. This was the first wedding I attended that offered birdseed to throw at the bride and groom as they made their escape.

The wedding reception was held at the bride's home. Small bowls of birdseed were placed around the front door so guests could grab a handful when the newlyweds made their exit.

At one point during the reception, I rounded a corner to find my grandmother, a very prim and proper Southern lady, popping handfuls of birdseed into her mouth. Well into her eighties at the time, and possessing all of her teeth, she smiled politely as she crunched and chomped the birdseed. When I told her that the bowls were not filled with nutlike hors d'oeuvres for eating, but a rice substitute to hurl at the newlyweds, she looked confused and relieved all at once.

I could tell that she had been wondering why the people in that town ate such strange food. Minutes later, I found my uncle doing the same thing.

Families are full of these stories. They happen all of the time, most of the time when a group is gathered together and sharing food and/or drink. Through the years, we relive them often.

One Christmas Eve, my inebriated septuagenarian aunt did the jitterbug on my mother's coffee table. It embarrassed all of the grown-ups in the family, but we kids have been repeating the story ever since.

As a child, my wife tried to reheat pizza in a pop-up toaster, which, as a story, is not quite as popular as the time she put her entire hand in the toaster. Her father reminds us of these childhood blunders often, and we remind him of the tamale surprise he once cooked for a Thanksgiving meal.

Fortunately, these types of family-food legends are being told less and less in my family through the years. Not because people have tired of telling them, but because as my children grow older, they create new stories with each passing day. Stories that we will certainly tell and retell, embarrassing them often, especially in front of company, as our parents did before us and their parents did before them.

What have we learned today?

1. Be careful what you do at family gatherings unless you want your foibles to be relived and retold ad infinitum.
2. Throwing rice at weddings is for the birds.
3. Old people will put almost anything into their mouths
4. Fireworks and grandparents don't mix.

Beefamato

A physician once ordered my ninety-year-old grandmother to drink Beefamato.

Beefamato is tomato juice with beef broth in it. Well, not "real" beef broth, the label states "dried beef broth."

I am not sure why she was ordered to drink Beefamato. Maybe it contained an obscure vitamin she wasn't receiving in her regular diet, or an additional protein needed to preserve her ninety-year-old muscles. One thing's for certain—the doctor didn't make her drink Beefamato because it would be another tasty beverage alternative to her already-flavorsome lineup of liquid refreshment selections. Move over, Ensure, pass the Beefamato.

Beefamato is like North Dakota, you only go there if you have to. Tomato juice and beef do not belong side by side in a glass—on top of a mound of spaghetti, certainly, spread onto a pizza crust, maybe, but not in a glass with crushed ice and a cocktail napkin.

Mott's manufactures Beefamato. They also make a product called Clamato. Yes. Clamato—tomato juice and dried clam broth. I would give half a week's pay to have been a fly on the wall in that boardroom:

Suit #1: "You know, guys, this Beefamato stuff isn't selling too well."

Suit #2: "Well, Boss, its beef juice and tomato juice combined in a liquid. I tried to warn you."

Suit #3: "I know what we can do. Let's find an even worse ingredient to add to tomato juice. The buying public will be so repulsed by the new beverage that Beefamato will seem like sweet, cool, nectar in comparison."

Suit #1: "Number three, that's brilliant. I'm putting you in for a raise. Now, what foul, vile liquid can we add to our tomato juice? "

Suit #2: "How about the gooey liquid that comes inside the potted meat can?"

Suit #1: "Not vile enough."

Suit #3: "I've got it! How about clams! No. Wait. How about dried clam broth!"

Suit #1: "Perfect! Son, you'll be running this company one day."

According to my research, Clamato is a big deal in the northeastern states. Coincidentally, that's also where cranberries are grown.

Ocean Spray blends cranberries into several successful combinations. They bottle Cran-Grape juice, Cran-Apple juice, and even Cran-Tangerine and Cran-Mango. Maybe the folks at Mott's were jealous of the creative innovation occurring in the Ocean Spray test labs.

Suit #1: "I'm sick of those guys over at Ocean Spray. They get to have all of the fun. They're going wild with cranberries over there. I want some new beverage combinations, and I want them ASAP!"

Suit #3: "I've got it, sir. How about Cran-Beef, and Cran-Clam?"

Suit #1: "Number three, you're a genius!"

We're not talking about adding cherry juice or vanilla syrup to Coca-Cola, those combinations make sense. It's clam juice.

It's as if Mott's—makers of a fine applesauce, by the way—thought of the most disparate flavor combinations available. What's next? Grape juice and dill pickle liquid: Grapickle? Clam juice and orange juice: Clamorange? Turkey gravy and clam juice: Clamurkey?

I found a news article on the Internet that suggested that the new Clamato energy drink could also be used as an aphrodisiac. A sign of marketing desperation? Maybe.

Suit #2: "Boss, the Cran-Clam isn't selling, either."

Suit #1: "#$%@*&! I just knew that was our ticket into the beverage-blend big time!"

Suit #3: "What if we tell them that Cran-Clam is the next Viagra?"

Suit #1: "Brilliant, number three! Number two, why don't you ever come up with ideas like that?"

I don't drink tomato juice, but if I did, I would want my tomato juice to taste like tomatoes. Not pot roast, or mollusks, or cherries, just tomatoes.

Question: What is the one thought everyone has after taking a sip of Clamato?

Answer: Wow, I could've had a V8!

Haggis

I have often written that if I ever visited Scotland, I would eat haggis.

I have never been to Scotland, but I can now say that I have eaten haggis.

Yesterday, my family and I attended the twenty-third Scottish Highland Games and Celtic Music Festival on the Mississippi Gulf Coast. A friend was competing in the Highland Games portion of the event, so we traveled to Gulfport looking forward to watching the competition.

The festival was filled with activities and food. There were pale men in plaid skirts throwing rocks. There were pale men in plaid skirts playing bagpipes. There were pale men in plaid skirts herding sheep, and there were pale men in plaid skirts selling plaid skirts to other pale men.

There was also a storytelling stage with an open mic. I thought about getting up on the stage and telling the story of my most recent challenge as the parent of a second-grade boy.

Story: Two days ago my seven-year old-son was playing on the swing set during recess and fell out of the swing. The problem: His pants stayed in the swing. Typically that wouldn't be too big of a crisis, unless the son in question doesn't like to wear underwear. He apparently spent a few seconds buck naked on the playground, but the event wasn't a big enough deal to him when recounting the day's activities to his mother. "I made an A on my quiz, I had chicken for lunch, I played wallball at recess, and that's about it."

If I fell to the ground, naked, in front of my peers, it would take me years to get over. I have nightmares about it today, and it's never even happened. He barely even remembered it when the teacher relayed the story. Maybe we need to send him to school in a kilt.

I had never attended a Scottish-themed event. Scottish festivals might be a great place to watch time-honored sporting events, to learn about one's family crest, or hear Celtic music, but it's the last place one should visit when hoping to eat good food.

If you want food, go to the New Orleans Jazz and Heritage Festival or the Austin City Limits Music Festival. Never, I repeat never, go to an event that draws its culinary inspiration from any corner of the British Isles.

There were fried Mars bars, a culinary creation born in Scotland, Angus burgers (not so bad), and the ever-present funnel cake (an American creation, but more than likely a Scottish-American creation). My children ate Scotch Eggs for the first time.

A Scotch Egg is a hard-boiled egg covered with a layer of sausage, then battered and fried. They liked it. Go figure.

I visited Hamish's Kitchen, a booth that served haggis. I eat for a living so thought I'd give it a shot. Haggis is sheep's lungs, heart, and liver mixed with oatmeal, onion, and beef fat. It looks like a blackish gray porridge-from-hell and smells like dirty gym socks. Actually, that description would be doing dirty gym socks a disservice. Haggis smells like…well, just think of the worst thing you have ever smelled and then triple it. That, my friends, is haggis.

I have eaten many peculiar food items in my twenty-eight-year restaurant and writing career, and up until now, chitlins have been the main offender. Folks, chitlins taste like a sweet, moist slice of chocolate cake when compared to haggis.

I took one bite (actually one-half of one bite) and thought I was going to lose it on the spot. The couple working the booth—the evil people who sold me the haggis in the first place—were laughing. How cruel, I thought, for them to make this evil gruel, ask honest people to pay money for it, and then laugh while I gnarled my face in pain and distaste eating their concoction.

I love the Scots. I know I'll love visiting Scotland one day. Paul McCartney has land there. *Braveheart* is one of my favorite movies. Celtic festivals are a blast, but haggis should forever stay on the other side of the pond.

The Funky Food Trash Heap of History

Over the years there have been many funky foods introduced to the eating public.

A short list of funky foodstuffs that have hit our grocery store shelves over the years would include:

A dessert called "Garlic Cake" which happened to be the only dessert that followed you around for two days.

"Funky Fries" introduced by Heinz a few years ago. Funky Fries were flavored French fries. They were frozen in bags and were sold in the flavors of chocolate fries, sour cream fries, cinnamon fries, and blue fries. Somehow I can't see anyone dipping chocolate or cinnamon French fries into ketchup. Obviously others felt the same way, as Heinz pulled the product from production after a few years.

In 1974, Gerber, the baby food company, introduced "Gerber Singles" which were adult versions of vegetables, fruits, and entrees. Unfortunately Gerber Singles were served in baby food–style jars, and adults couldn't bring themselves to put on bibs again.

The biggest food faux pas in history would have to be the introduction of "New Coke." I remember the furor. The wolves were knocking at the door of the Atlanta-based soft-drink giant, and the company quickly reintroduced "Classic Coke," which we still enjoy today.

In the early 1990s, Pepsi introduced "Crystal Pepsi," which also flopped, even though they used one of my favorite Van Halen songs to introduce the product.

Last year a number of new food products were introduced to the market, most of which will end up in the funky-food trash heap of history.

Jones Soda Company, the same folks that introduced a turkey-and-gravy-flavored soft-drink, gave us a mashed-potato-flavored soda, a fruitcake-flavored soda, and a green-bean-casserole-flavored soda. All of these products are headed for the funky-food trash heap. No one eats fruitcake, so why would anyone drink a fruitcake-flavored soda? Green bean-casserole might be a big hit at covered-dish suppers, but who wants to eat a green-bean-casserole while drinking a green-bean-casserole-flavored drink?

Another drink that hit the market last year was Grapple, a combination of grape and apple flavors. I would imagine Grapple will soon be replaced by Crapple, a combination of cream soda and apple, which may be the only drink that actually tells the consumer how bad it is before he or she even pops the cap.

The good folks at Hostess introduced a Twinkie snack cake filled with a green goo, which leaves everyone wondering how, with such astute minds in the new product development department, the company could be in the middle of bankruptcy proceedings?

The Pringles potato chip company gave us potato chips with trivia questions printed on them. Milky Way introduced a liquid version of their candy bar, and someone found a way to produce black carrots, orange cauliflower, and miniature watermelons.

Viewed on their own, these products seem as though they might have potential, and one might understand that a food executive with stockholders breathing down his or her neck, living with the daily pressure to create more sales and larger market shares, could come up with some of them. But listed together in a food column, they seem way too funky.

While reading about last year's newly introduced foodstuffs, I was struck with an idea that someone should invite all of the major food company executives to an annual dinner party where nothing but the new and funky foods that were introduced in the previous year is served. Looking at last year's list, the meal would be filled with mostly snack foods and funky flavored drinks. In the end the annual meal would prove that it's hard to improve on the tried-and-true culinary staples that have endured the test of time.

If it ain't broke, don't turn it blue, or liquefy it, or miniaturize it, or stuff it with green goo.

The New Mississippi Oil Boom

Yesterday I spent $70 to fill my vehicle with gas.

Gasoline prices are at an all-time high and experts are forecasting even steeper prices in the near future. I am not worried.

With all of the recent talk of record-high gas prices affecting the economy, more information is now being released about biodiesel as an alternative fuel. Biodiesel is a reformulated diesel fuel that is produced from animal fat, vegetable oil, or recycled restaurant grease.

I won't worry about high gas prices because I live in Mississippi, the recycled-restaurant-grease, deep-fat-frying capital of the world. This biodiesel stuff is going to place us into the driver's seat for the twenty-first century, just as cotton did in the nineteenth century. Folks, we're back!

This is exciting. One can't throw a rock in Mississippi without hitting an all-you-can-eat catfish buffet or fried chicken franchise. Hell, we even fry biscuits, Twinkies, and Snickers bars down here. We've got more grease than any region on the planet.

Mr. Bush, we don't need more foreign oil, we need more fried catfish restaurants.

Iowa and Nebraska only thought they had a leg up on the alternative-fuel solution with their corn-made ethanol. Mississippi now has the edge with recycled restaurant grease. Though we need to speak to someone about a better name; "biodiesel" doesn't exactly roll off of the tongue.

I propose Lardinol. (Note: I hereby register the word Lardinol and want a percentage of all future sales for coming up with the catchy name.) Not only does Lardinol sound more elegant than ethanol, it does what all great product names should do—it tells the consumer what it's about. Lardinol is produced because we have "lard in all" of our food. Mississippi, it's us. It's here. It's now. It's brilliant. I'm proud.

The fossil fuels giants' best days are behind them. Move over, Saudi Arabia and Qatar, Mississippi is soon to become the petroleum capital of the planet.

The Nissan plant in Canton can do their part by retrofitting their automobiles to burn Lardinol®. Better still, maybe one of the Nissan engineers can develop an SUV with a built-in deep-fat fryer in the third-row seat. Americans could fry chicken gizzards while driving to and from work, never once having to stop at a gas station.

Ah, the possibilities.

So long "Black Gold," "Texas Tea," the Lone Star state's oil monopoly is over. The wells will run dry. The glass skyscrapers in Houston will empty. Movies such as *Giant* and TV shows reminiscent of *Dallas* are long gone. Look for the new nighttime soap opera *Tutwiler*—the riveting weekly saga of a catfish farming family's biodiesel dynasty in a small Mississippi Delta town—complete with the first season cliffhanger: Who shot Billy Earl?

And we thought being the fattest state in the union was a detriment. On the contrary, we have only been going back for seconds to do our part in helping solve the world's energy needs. From now on, each and every Mississippian should line up at the fried seafood buffet a minimum of three times a week. It is in our country's best interest. National security is at stake. Pile a few extra hush puppies on your plate; it's your duty as a patriotic American, and a citizen of the soon-to-be richest state in the union.

When the oil-rich nations' power began to increase, they formed the Organization of Petroleum Exporting Countries, better known as OPEC. As the Lardinol® craze catches on, and cars begin to burn recycled tater-tot grease, we will need to form our own alliance. Therefore, as of today, I am establishing the Federation for Lard Advancement through Biodiesel, FLAB. Again, a name that tells it all, and again, I want a cut for creating the catchy handle.

Our new state motto: Save gas, eat catfish. E Pluribus Eatum, Amen.

No Shirt, No Shoes, No Problem

I have written often about the quirkiness of some New York restaurants.

Last year I wrote about a Manhattan restaurant that serves blowfish ovaries. Blowfish ovaries, when prepared by a novice chef (and sometimes a skilled one), can kill the person eating them. I have also written about an Upper East Side restaurant that forced diners to eat in complete and total darkness.

Last week I read a Reuters story about a New York restaurant that holds a monthly "Clothing Optional Dinner." The term "Clothing Optional Dinner" is nothing more than a fancy twenty-first-century expression for eating naked.

The Reuters article had a photo that accompanied the piece. A man with a spare tire around his gut was sitting in a dining room eating food that was further inflating the spare tire around his gut. This would be an occasion where being in the restaurant where everyone eats in total darkness would come in handy.

I would like to declare, here and now, that we have officially gone too far with the theme-restaurant thing. Why do we need a restaurant where we can eat naked if we choose? Doesn't the health department in New York have enough on their plate? So much for the "No shirt, no shoes, no service" rule. Besides, I don't want to follow a diner who previously sat, bare-bunned, in my restaurant chair.

Your mother's etiquette lessons would most certainly come in handy during a clothing optional dinner, where having a napkin in your lap, would be a must. Of course, some would need larger napkins than others, but we won't go there.

The establishment wasn't named in the story. However, I wonder if the restaurant in question is a sidewalk cafe. If so, what do the other New Yorkers think when they walk by and look into the window of a restaurant with a bunch of naked people eating in it. Answer: Nothing. It's just the normal, everyday, run-of-the-mill craziness up there.

If someone opened a clothing-optional restaurant in South Mississippi, there would be a line around the block. Not a line to get in and eat, but a line to stand at the window and ogle the diners. Unfortunately no one in South Mississippi would dare go in and eat because we all have wives and girlfriends who can beat us up.

One of the naked guests, a woman named Carol Ordover, stated that it was impolite to stare, and that men must always look nude women in the eyes. To which I would reply: "What's the point?" Why not just keep your clothes on and eat wherever you want?

My first thought while reading this story was that this restaurant had to have been a table-service eatery and not a buffet-style joint. Have you ever noticed that the average customer in a buffet-style restaurant is approximately 675 pounds heavier than the average table-service patron?

Once I got that visual out of my mind, it hit me, and I thought that the naked-dinner event planners might be on to something. The weight-loss industry is a multibillion-dollar industry. What better way to lose weight than to go to a restaurant where middle-aged, out-of-shape people are eating buck-naked in the dining room.

Imagine being a waiter and having to work on clothing-optional night. Spilling the soup in someone's lap would be an entirely different offense.

Robert's Top 10 reasons why New York's nude dining will never catch on:

1. Vinyl and Naugahyde booths stick to your thighs
2. Most wives don't even like us watching too much football
3. February in New York
4. A compliment to the chef such as "Nice melons" will get you slapped
5. Hairy backs
6. Hot soup
7. Steak knives
8. "Waiter, there's a hair in my soup" takes on an entirely different meaning
9. Did I mention hairy backs?
10. Sausage is forever off the menu

When his or her restaurant is located in New York, home to approximately 2,385,931,659 restaurants, the run-of-the-mill restaurateur has to do something to make the place stand out. However, this shock-value thing has gone too far. What's left? Answer: There's nothing left. It's like having the final losing hand in a game of strip poker, when you've reached the totally nude point, game over.

Food Quirks

Everyone has food quirks. We all prefer certain foods over others. There are plenty of foods that I eat that some folks would never touch, and vice versa.

My daughter has a very versatile palate. She'll try anything once. My son—though not a soldier in the adolescent chicken-tender army—would live on yogurt and bananas, alone. Both children eat more grown-up cereals than their father. My wife prefers a steady diet of coffee and cheese.

In an essay I wrote five years ago entitled "My South," there is a line that reads: "In My South, people put peanuts in bottles of Coca-Cola and hot sauce on almost everything."

When I speak to a group or association, I usually end the speech by reading the "My South" piece. The peanuts/Coca-Cola line always generates chuckles and sighs. People seem always to remember dropping nuts into a soft drink, or they remember someone who did.

I never have put peanuts in Coke, but I had school friends with whom I sat in the lunchroom who did it every day.

Peanuts and Coke seem like a strange pairing. If I had to name the strangest food quirk that I possess, it would be my affinity for using applesauce as a dip for potato chips. The combination of the salty and sweet holds great appeal to me.

I know people who dump Milk Duds into their popcorn at the theater. Some food quirks are easy to understand: mustard on French fries, cornbread into buttermilk, and French dressing on pizza. Others are strange but seem palatable: potato chips on sandwiches. And some are just downright strange: pickles and peanut butter.

My children dip their fries into blue cheese dressing. I am not a fan of blue cheese dressing, but I can understand the pairing.

Some people's food quirks go to the extreme, and to the point where they eat hardly anything. I have one friend, I will call him the Web Guru, who eats almost nothing, and when I say almost nothing, I'm not talking about quantity, I'm talking about variety.

The first ten years I knew him, he ate mostly fried chicken tenders. As he grew older, he stepped away from fried food and limited his diet even more.

On a business trip to San Francisco earlier in the year, I took the Web Guru to the French Laundry in Yountville, California. The French Laundry is widely considered the best restaurant in the country. The things Thomas Keller does with food are fanciful to the point of mind-boggling. Lawrence Nadeau, the maître d', was expediting a twelve-course meal filled with foie gras terrines, caviar, and the like. The Web Guru passed on every course.

This was good and bad. Bad, in that I was responsible for bringing him there and putting him in a situation where he had to decline Keller's world-class food. Good, in that I got to eat the courses he was unable to eat (which amounted to every course except the bread course).

In the end, I paid $240 plus tax and tip so that my friend could eat a basket of bread. However, it is notable that once the bread basket arrived, the Web Guru covered it with both arms and pulled it in tight to his chest, hoarding the basket of freshly baked treats for himself.

The Web Guru and I were eating lunch last week. He ordered a sandwich with turkey and bread and a bag of potato chips. The sandwich was dry—no mayonnaise, mustard, lettuce, pickle. Nothing. As we sat visiting, I watched him place the potato chips—one by one—onto his turkey sandwich. There is hope yet.

Chapter 10

News

We the (Obese) People

My home state has made national headlines once again.

Three legislators in the Mississippi House of Representatives proposed a bill (HB 282) that would ban restaurants from serving obese people.

As a restaurateur and businessman, doing business in a state where more than 30 percent of the populace is obese, I am adamantly opposed to this law on many levels. As one who is considered, by the government's standards, obese, I am in opposition because I enjoy eating out, and eating out often (hence the obesity).

What are we restaurateurs to do? Keep a set of scales at the hostess stand and weigh each customer once they walk through the door? "Good evening, welcome to Bob's House of Pork. Three for dinner? OK, you two heifers come step on the scales, there's no way you're eating here tonight."

If this bill passes, be assured that there will be restaurants that don't weigh customers. All of the fat people (me included) will know where the non-weighing restaurants are located (probably all-you-can-eat buffets), giving them an unfair advantage in the marketplace. As a kid, I knew all of the places that didn't check I.D.s; as an adult I'll do the same, trading pitchers of cheap beer and grape-flavored malt liquor for catfish and hush puppies.

If HB 282 passes, I would like to propose a few pieces of legislation of my own:

HB 282A: The Hunting Law. Many Mississippians are shot in hunting accidents every year. I propose that IQ tests be administered at all locations that distribute hunting licenses. If the applicant's IQ is not 125 or above, he has no business walking around in the woods with a loaded shotgun. Talk about saving lives. HB 282A, my friends, will do just that.

HB 282B: The Driving Bill. HB 282B would require that all licensed Mississippi drivers retake the Mississippi driver's license exam every time they travel more than ten highway miles in the passing lane without passing another automobile. Somewhere along the way, our local driving instructors quit teaching the section in the manual that covers how the passing lane is supposed to work. It ain't hard, people: Once you pass someone, get back into the right-hand lane.

HB 282C: The National News Media Interview Law. This law would require a minimum of a sixth-grade education and a nominal grasp of the English language before anyone is allowed to speak to a reporter on national television. The state of Mississippi will also publish a list of approved adjectives and similes to be used in such interviews, so our citizenry can come up with better descriptions than how the tornado sounded "like a freight train" or how "harshly" the alien's probing methods were carried out once inside the UFO.

HB 282D: The Delta Heritage Law. HB 282D would require all citizens of the Mississippi Delta to limit their ancestral discussions to a minimum of forty-five minutes per dining period. During the allotted time period, said genealogy buff may only go back four generations without receiving a warning citation. If subject traces his or her lineage all the way back to the Civil War during one meal period, a $75 fine shall be levied (Revolutionary War descendant discussions will result in mandatory jail time). This law also applies to relations' choice of college, which sorority their grandmother joined, and which tract of land their family owned 150 years ago.

HB 282E. The Florence-Richland Bypass Law. This has nothing to do with the others, but while I am proposing laws, I would love to see the highway department build a bypass around Florence and Richland. I have nothing against these two communities, it's just that it takes me ninety minutes to get to Jackson and thirty minutes of it is spent in the last five miles of the trip.

HB 282F: The Potato Salad Allocation. No more than four batches of potato salad will be allowed in any home during a funeral or wake. The bill would also place a quota on green-bean casseroles (no more than three) at any single covered-dish supper.

Three cheers for good government, of the person (me), for the person (me), and by the person (me). Now pass the hushpuppies.

We're Number One! (Again)

In junior high school, pep rallies were mandatory. I never minded them, because they were a legitimate excuse to get out of class and hang out in the gymnasium. I never became too lathered up during these proceedings; call it lack of school spirit, absence of general enthusiasm about which grade could yell louder than the other, or uncooperative spirit fingers.

Various cheers came and went during my school years. Some were funny, "U-G-L-Y, you ain't got no alibi, you're ugly." Others were dull, such as "push 'em back"; some were obvious, "defense"; still others made no sense, "Two bits, four bits…," you know the drill.

The only cheer that is universal to every school, cheerleading squad, and professional sports team is the ubiquitous "We're number one!"

Everyone does the "We're number one," cheer, no matter where they are ranked or listed among the competition. A team can be in the cellar, forever dwelling in last place in their division or conference, but eek out one win against a better opponent, and suddenly all of the fans and players are screaming, "We're number one." It's the American way.

The Centers for Disease Control and Prevention has once again released their annual national obesity statistics, and my home state, Mississippi, is number one, again. We've been number one since 2004. In the sports world that's two more than a threepeat. We're a dynasty!

Mississippi was followed closely by Alabama, Tennessee, and Louisiana. Could it be that our food is better? It's no coincidence that the survey was released around the same time that Chilton County, Alabama peaches were coming in. Tennessee has great barbeque, Louisiana is the most culinarily diverse state in the nation, and Mississippi is the world capital of fried catfish.

Instead of a telephone-interview poll to decide which state is fatter, the CDC needs to rent the Georgia Dome and host an Olympic-style competition of all fifty states. We might not win the four-hndred-meter relay every time, but we could kick butt in the shot put, dead lift, and pie-eating contest.

We'll dust off all of the old high school cheers. When competing with Colorado—the nation's skinniest state—we can chant from the sidelines, "Two bits, four bits, gumbo roux, you better look out or we'll sit on you!"

We probably wouldn't have much of a chance in the pole vault, but when it comes to skeet shooting and archery, we'll place a few South Mississippi deer hunters on the roster and annihilate the competition.

While researching this column, I came across a piece written by *Los Angeles Times* health editor Tami Dennis, with the headline: "Yeah we're fat. But not as fat as Southerners." In a post on her newspaper's health blog, Dennis states, "Poor Mississippi. I'm sure it tries. Really, I'm sure it does. But have you had Southern food?"

Yes, Tami, we have "had" Southern food. It tastes great. That's why we're so fat.

Various readers commented on the newspaper's blog. One reader stated: "I don't buy the excuse about diet or weather... My family spends every summer in Italy or France eating like crazy and not working out all that much—we always come back slimmer and trimmer." Yes, but they don't serve jambalaya or etouffée in France or Italy, do they?

A man named Rick posted, "I now live in Ohio, but grew up in Mississippi and still go back 4–5 times every year. These 'fat' surveys always surprise me because I see many more grossly obese people in Ohio than in Mississippi. Many."

Note to self: Slip a mickey to the Ohio competitors at the CDC Olympics the evening before the pie-eating contest.

The California bloggers continued to pile on in post after post. A poster named Mike stated, "Along with poor performing schools and lackluster economies Southerners are a fat bunch to boot."

To Mike I say: U-G-L-Y, you ain't got no alibi. We may be fat, but weight can be lost. Ugly (manners, that is) lasts a lifetime. And, by the way, we're still number one!

Lawsuits Aplenty

A man in Morgantown, West Virginia, is suing fast-food giant McDonald's for $10 million because they put cheese on his hamburger.

According to a recent story in the *Charleston Daily Mail*, "The man says he bit into a hamburger and had a severe allergic reaction to the cheese melted on it. Jeromy Jackson, who is in his early 20s, says he clearly ordered two Quarter Pounders without cheese at the McDonald's restaurant in Star City before heading to Clarksburg."

"His mother Trela Jackson and friend Andrew Ellifritz are parties to the lawsuit because they say they risked their lives rushing Jeromy to United Hospital Center in Clarksburg."

According to the report, "the three drove to Clarksburg and started to eat the food in a darkened room where they were going to watch a movie, Houston said."

Anyone who has ordered fast food at a drive-through window in the last ten years knows to check their order at the window before pulling out of the line. There is a humorous scene in one of the *Lethal Weapon* films in which Joe Pesci delivers a profanity-filled rant about the high probability of having one's order messed up when using the drive-through window. I am not sure what movie the threesome was planning to watch, but if they would have rented *Lethal Weapon*, they could have save a little pain and suffering.

Mr. Jackson must be the most lactose-intolerant man on the planet. Actually, I didn't even know that McDonald's used real cheese on their hamburgers. I thought that they used one of those cheese-food type products.

In 1992, a lady received $2.9 million after spilling McDonald's coffee in her lap. In 2002, two overweight girls sued the largest burger chain in the world claiming that McDonald's food made them fat. Before long, McDonald's will have to change their corporate symbol from golden arches to a huge bulls-eye.

Everyone is suing everyone else nowadays. Maybe I'll find an open-minded judge, a few sympathetic jurors, a billboard lawyer, and sue some people, too.

In today's legal climate I could have a field day. There are tons of people who have caused me irreparable harm over the course of my life. I'll sue them all.

I will sue the Mattel toy company for using those evil twist ties when packaging Barbie dolls, requiring a mechanical engineering degree just to free Barbie from her box.

I will sue Led Zeppelin for the hearing loss I sustained while listening to their music with headphones on during high school. Add the Rolling Stones, Pink Floyd, and Van Halen to that list.

I will sue Sony because the clock on my DVD player is still blinking.

I will sue movie director Martin Scorsese for making movies so well that I have spent approximately 1,235 nonproductive hours in a sedentary state—time which could have been spent in community service or in the pursuit of world peace—watching his films.

I will sue all of the major disco groups of the 1970s because I never learned to do the Hustle.

I will sue Bobby Brown for messing up the life and career of Whitney Houston, and then I'll sue Whitney Houston for marrying Bobby Brown in the first place.

I'll sue the makers of mousse hair gel because I applied so much of it to my mullet-style haircut in 1986 that my hair began to fall out—a serious condition that continues to this day.

I will sue my wife for making my son and me sit through the movie version of the musical *Hairspray*. I will then sue John Travolta and the movie's producers to have those 177 minutes of my life given back to me.

I will sue the producers of the TV show *So You Think You Can Dance* because, at one time in my life, I actually thought that I could dance. It turns out that I was terribly terribly wrong.

I will sue the makers of Milk Duds—$1 million for each silver amalgam filling in my mouth.

I will sue the makers of amalgam fillings because they allegedly lead to a loss of memory.

I had other lawsuits in mind, but I have forgotten them.

If a lady can get almost $3 million for coffee burns and a guy can get $10 million because they gave him cheese on his burger, I should certainly be entitled to a cash award for all of the horrible atrocities that I have been forced to endure over the course of my life.

A Riot in the Cafeteria

The food police are at it again. This time they're targeting school lunch boxes.

The Center for Science in the Public Trust has recently issued a Lunchbox Makeover for school-age children, giving them what they believe are "10 tips for a healthy school lunch."

It is my belief that—to a person—everyone who works at the CSPI is childless. Here are their supposed "easy" suggestions for making over our children's lunch boxes:

1. **Encourage your child to choose 1 percent or fat-free milk.** The problem is not the milk, but how to keep the milk cold. It's already hard enough to get cold milk at school. I can remember the milk cart at my school used to arrive mid-morning, immediately after recess. There's nothing quite as unrefreshing as a glass of warm milk immediately after running for twenty minutes in the scorching Mississippi heat.

2. **Leave the cheese off sandwiches, unless it's low-fat or fat-free cheese.** My daughter inherited her cheese addiction from her mother. Their philosophy: "If it tastes good, it'll taste better with cheese." I'll let the CSPI try and fight that battle. Though I know the adversary, and they don't have a chance. My wife thinks cheese is one of the major food groups and should be reclassified as chewable calcium.

3. **Switch from fatty luncheon meats to low-fat alternatives.** If God would have wanted us to eat low-fat bologna, he would have made skinnier pigs.

4. **Include at least one fruit in every lunch.** I have no problem with this one. In elementary school, I used fruit as a bargaining chip to trade for other people's bologna-and-cheese sandwiches. An apple and two bananas were usually good for three chocolate chip cookies and a Pop-Tart.

5) **Sneak vegetables—like lettuce or slices of cucumber, tomato, green pepper, roasted peppers, or zucchini—onto sandwiches.**

What planet are these people living on? My wife, who is somewhere over the age of thirty, doesn't even eat cucumbers, tomatoes, or green peppers, how will she sneak them onto my child's bologna-and-cheese sandwich?

6. **Use whole-grain bread instead of white bread for sandwiches.** Amazingly enough, we're a step ahead of the game on this one. At our house it's always been 100 percent wheat bread since the children were born.

7. **Limit cookies, snack cakes, doughnuts, brownies, and other sweet baked goods.** Actually, my vote is for no sugar for anyone under the age of sixteen. When they're able to drive, we'll let them eat sugar. I'll support that legislation, tomorrow. At our house, we don't let our children eat sugar-filled foods before they go to school, and certainly don't want them eating processed sugar while they're at school. To our kids, sugar is like granulated amphetamine. My children are active enough; I couldn't imagine loading them up on doughnuts, cake, and brownies, and turning them loose on their teachers. Although, while babysitting, my mother seems to take great delight in feeding them a few scoops of ice cream just before she drops them off at our house. Once, I think I heard her laughing hysterically as she drove out of the driveway.

8. **Limit potato, corn, tortilla, or other chips.** At this point, I think we need a quick recap—warm milk, no cheese, low-fat processed turkey, kiwi, roasted pepper, cucumber, and tomato with a slice of wheat bread—no Fritos, no Ruffles, no Tostitos. Where's the benefit of being a kid, if you don't get to eat a few potato chips? I'm not talking about sitting in front of a television or video game and eating a large can of Pringles. We adults spend the rest of our lives watching what we eat. Kids run and play and spend all day burning calories. I say, "Pass the Doritos."

9. **If you pack juice, make sure it's 100 percent juice.** Good luck. Have you ever seen an all-out riot created by a nine- and five-year-old? It can turn nasty pretty quickly.

10. Don't send Lunchables. Do we actually need someone to tell
    us that?

Are these healthy suggestions? Yes.

Are they "easy" suggestions, as the CSPI states? No.

In a nutshell, be realistic. Don't load your children up on sugary and
fatty foods. Don't let them lounge in front of the television all day,
and for your own safety, wait until they're twenty-one to feed them
zucchini, green peppers, and cucumbers.

Beans, Beans, Good for Your Heart
(but not your arrest record ... or your pedicure)

Last week I read a story in the *Evening Standard* that opened with the sentence "Hugh Grant has been arrested after allegedly hurling a tub of baked beans at a photographer."

How can one read an opening line such as that and not continue?

The word "allegedly" is included in the sentence for the *Evening Standard*'s legal comfort. Though there is an accompanying photograph of Grant—the movie actor who starred in the quintessential chick flick *Four Weddings and a Funeral*—midway through his windup, a carry-out container of baked beans at the ready, seconds before they were "allegedly" hurled at the photographer.

It struck me as odd that a stuffy Brit such as Grant would not only have eaten baked beans, but enjoyed his serving of baked beans so much that he asked the restaurant for a doggie bag to bring home the half-eaten portion of tomato- and vinegar-spiked legumes.

This is how the *Evening Standard* reported the incident:

> The arrest followed a clash with the freelance paparazzi photographer outside Grant's Chelsea home on Tuesday morning.
>
> Mr Whittaker said he had turned up to take pictures of the actor's former girlfriend Liz Hurley, who lives in the same street. When Grant, 46, arrived in his car he asked him to smile as he took his picture.
>
> The film star allegedly snapped, swearing at Mr Whittaker, 43, and reportedly kicking him three or four times. Then, as Grant entered his house, he allegedly turned and threw a plastic container of baked beans at him.
>
> Mr Whittaker told a tabloid newspaper: "I said Give us a smile please and he looked really angry. I walked backwards and he walked after me. He kicked me hard three or four times then kneed me in the groin."

I don't have much sympathy for paparazzi types, but getting knocked upside the head by a pint of beans and then kicked in the groin by a middle-aged actor is certainly demoralizing and humiliating.

The second photograph included in the article was of Grant attempting to kick the photographer. His foot is four inches off of the ground and nowhere near the groin. I'll give Grant a pass on that count as he had no time to warm up and stretch before the bean-throwing, paparazzi-kicking exercise began.

Typically, I would spend the remaining column inches at my disposal on jokes that make fun of Grant, his movies, the blandness of British food, and beans in general. But as I was writing this, I remembered a humiliating baked-bean incident from my past.

During my college years, while waiting tables in one of those brass-and-fern style restaurants, I spilled an eight-ounce bouillon bowl of baked beans on a woman's foot.

I had just arrived at her table and the serving tray was still in a position high above my head. The beans fell from a height of approximately seven feet above the floor and landed upside down and squarely on her instep.

An eight-ounce bouillon bowl weighs over nine ounces. Filled with beans, it probably approaches one pound. Pardon my physics, but a one-pound bowl, falling from a height of seven feet, traveling at a velocity of… Well, you get the picture. The beans fell fast and they fell hard. The woman let out a shrill shriek and then a series of low-pitched sobs and moans.

She was wearing sandals and I stood speechless as I watched the steaming hot beans ooze through her toes and onto the floor. I almost lost my job due to the leguminous pedicure, but was saved by the woman's graciousness. Her husband, on the other hand, gave me the evil eye. When I asked if I could bring his wife another side order of beans, he asked for a towel, the manager, and a baked potato instead.

It seems that baked beans are quickly becoming a weapon of the future. It won't be too long before someone in this part of the country figures out how to kill a deer using them.

The photographer is lucky that Grant lives in London. Had the actor been a resident of Mississippi, he would have been coming home with a doggie bag full of fried chicken wings and catfish—both of which would be more effective hurling weapons than baked beans.

In the end, justice was served last week as every man who has had to sit through *Four Weddings and a Funeral, Notting Hill, Love Actually, Sense and Sensibility,* and both *Bridget Jones* movies in theaters, again on HBO, and then on DVD, every Valentine's Day, and every anniversary, exhaled a collective sigh of jubilant satisfaction. Karma can be a beautiful thing.

All You Can Eat

"Buffet Bans Fat People" was the headline I came across while surfing the Internet. OK, I'll bite.

According to a story on Breitbart.com, a man in Houma, Louisiana, was charged double for making too many trips to the buffet line. Ricky Labit, a 265-pound offshore worker, said he had been frequenting the Manchuria Restaurant in Houma for several months when, on his most recent visit, a waitress charged him double for taking too many trips to the buffet. The waitress told him, "Y'all fat, and y'all eat too much!"

The story is filled with all manner of juicy quotes such as Labit responding, "I ain't that fat, I only weigh 277."

Labit might have one of those wavy carnival midway mirrors in his bathroom, because the waitress said he looked as if he had a "baby in the belly."

Have you looked around an all-you-can-eat buffet lately? They're everywhere. You can't throw a rock without hitting one in South Mississippi. If they start banning fat people, they'll lose 75 percent of their business, including me.

"All-you-can-eat" was invented for fat people. I am chief among the sinners. Skinny people aren't interested in eating all of the food that they can cram into their gut. That's why they're skinny. They want healthy food, and small amounts of it. There are a few skinny people at the all-you-can-eat buffet, but they're usually sitting with a group of people wearing XXL shirts who talked them out of eating a salad at another restaurant.

Again, I am chief among the sinners. I weigh 247. I wear XXL shirts, and I feel like Ricky Labit—I ain't that fat (at least not too fat to go back for seconds, or thirds).

The name itself, "all-you-can-eat," is a challenge. *I'll show them just how much I can eat,* I think to myself. It's a psychological thing. I want to win. I want to beat the system. I always think that I can eat more than the amount I paid. It's the buffet-owner's hook. Keep bringing it out, I'll show you how many hush puppies I can swallow in one sitting.

There is a mood that permeates through approximately 20 percent of all-you-can-eat buffet customers. One can see it in their eyes. It's in my eyes when I eat at an all-you-can-eat buffet. It's a look of panic. It's the frenzied fear that the kitchen might run out of food, so I need to pile my plate so high that I can't easily walk back to the table without spilling half of the food that I was worried was going to be gone in the first place.

Last spring my publisher sent a photographer from New York to photograph food for my new grilling cookbook. He was interested in the dining customs of our neck of the woods, so I took him to a few of my favorite local "joints."

While looking at the menu in a fried catfish restaurant, I noticed him staring at the menu and speaking softly—to no one in particular—"All you can eat, all you can eat." The diminutive New Yorker looked up and asked, "You mean they'll keep bringing me food as long as I sit here?"

"Yep," I said. "But they're not too worried about you." He ate mostly cole slaw that night, further proving my point that skinny people eat too much green stuff. That goes double for skinny New Yorkers.

When I was in high school, I worked for a man who weighed over five-hundred pounds. At the time, my hometown of Hattiesburg, Mississippi, had one restaurant that served all-you-can-eat catfish.

The second Thursday of every month, my boss would take us to the all-you-can-eat catfish restaurant. After the first few months, I started to notice the look of dread on the faces of the servers as we walked through the doors of the restaurant. My boss was a bottomless pit and could keep eating until he got bored. As long as the servers brought more catfish, he could keep eating it. He didn't look as if he had a baby in the belly; he was carrying an entire litter.

That look of dread was probably the same one that was displayed by the waitress in Houma. Bottom line: If you're going to offer all-you-can-eat, you have to deliver on that promise (or challenge). Otherwise, skinny 247-pound people like me are going to be offended.

A sign in the Houma restaurant reads: "Food is for eating, not toys for your child." A handwritten addition is added to the bottom of the sign "Or 20% added." It looks as though the fat tax they've been warning us about for years is finally here. Quick, pass the hush puppies.

Freeze! This Is a Ham Up!

I read a news story a few weeks ago with this headline: "Robber Allegedly Holds Up Bar With Ham Sandwich."

OK, I thought, you've got my attention.

The story stated: "Police say a man used what they call a 'gun-shaped' object in his attempt to rob a Humboldt Park bar at 1013 N. Western Monday night. But a tipster tells CBS 2 the weapon was actually a ham sandwich molded into the shape of a gun. The ham-robber fell on his way out of the bar and was arrested. Brian Latuszek has been charged with aggravated robbery."

And people wonder why I never run out of things to write about.

So much for the carved-block-of-soap-and-black-shoe-polish trick; now we have moved into the realm of luncheon meat holdups

How drunk does one need to be to rationalize not only robbing a bar, but doing so with two pieces of Wonder bread, pressed ham, and a side of mayo as your weapon? Better still, how drunk would someone need to be to be threatened by a man holding a ham sandwich?

Granted, the robber should get marks for creativity, as I am sure that it is not easy to mold a ham sandwich into the shape of a .38-caliber handgun. I wonder if he used white or wheat.

If this incident would have taken place in New Orleans (and it certainly could have, and sometime in the past, might have), I believe that the robber's attempt would have been successful. First, they don't eat a lot of ham sandwiches down there. Most of the sandwiches that are consumed are po'boys. It would be much easier to shape a po'boy into a believable assault weapon than a ham sandwich. Second, there's no shortage of drunks in New Orleans. If they can elect Ray Nagin for another term, they could certainly fall for a po'boy being used as a firearm.

A po'boy would work, but so would many other foodstuffs. As a matter of fact, I could think of at least seven better weapons in the grueling fifteen minutes it took to write this column:

SPAM. A can of SPAM would certainly be a more effective weapon than a ham sandwich. One could still stay within the "ham" theme. Though a can of SPAM is compact and could be easily concealed. It is also heavy enough to hurl across a room and do some damage.

Vienna sausage goo. That gelatinous goo floating on top of Vienna sausages is deadly stuff when in the hands of a trained professional.

Here's more:

1. Boiled Brussels sprouts and cabbage. Walk into your neighborhood bar with a large pot of boiled sprouts and cabbage and watch the place clear out faster than a group of Marilyn Manson fans at a Barry Manilow concert.
2. A week-old bag of Krystal burgers with extra onions. In college, I left a bag of Krystals in my car by accident. They stayed there two days. I couldn't get a date for two years.
3. My wife's broccoli-and-blue-cheese casserole. One bite and they'll hand over all of their worldly possessions.
4. A potato gun. During downtimes in the early days of the Purple Parrot Cafe, we shot potatoes out of a homemade PVC cannon from the front door across the street to a large billboard that advertised trial lawyers.
5. A medley of the greatest hits from the Waffle House jukebox. Not a food weapon, but a deadly threat, nonetheless. A few choruses of "Waffle House Stomp" or "Waffle House Hash Browns, I Love You" and the patrons of any business will fork over all of the money in their wallets to stop the ear-bleeding misery.

We don't need stricter gun control laws in this country. We need more sandwiches. Now, if someone could just get Dick Cheney to use a ham and Swiss on rye the next time he goes quail hunting.

The Beer Barrel Belly Buster

When I was a child, fountain-dispensed soft drinks were usually served in the twelve to sixteen-ounce range. Today, more than a quart of beverage—in a cup the size of a small trash can—is the norm.

Soft drinks aren't the only culprits. Over the last few decades portion sizes of most commercial food items have grown out of control. Simultaneously our waistlines have gone along for the ride. We're passing everyone in the fast lane on the super-sizing autobahn and heading toward ... well, I'm not really sure what we're headed toward because I can't think of another clever, speeding-autobahn-meets-overweight-large-portion-eaters metaphor, but you get my drift.

Yesterday, a hamburger was a hamburger. Today, a hamburger can be a quarter-pound, half-pound, double, triple, quadruple, or even a Monster Thick Burger. How far will we go until we have reached the absolute biggest burger we can fit onto a plate?

That was actually a trick question, because, according to an article in the *Courier-Express* of Dubois, Pennsylvania, we're there.

The fine folks at Denny's Beer Barrel Pub in Clearfield, Pennsylvania, recently rolled out a fifteen-pound hamburger. No typo there, you read it correctly, a **FIFTEEN-POUND** hamburger.

According to the *Courier-Express*, the burger, christened the Beer Barrel Belly Buster, comes with "10.5 pounds of ground beef, 25 slices of cheese, a head of lettuce, three [whole] tomatoes, two [whole] onions, a cup-and-a-half each of mayonnaise, relish, ketchup, mustard, and banana peppers, and a bun."

That amount of ground beef in any dish is enough to send your average PETA member into full-bore convulsions. But while your vegan coworker is flopping around on the floor in petit-mal burger panic, try to wrap your brain around the phrase "a cup-and-a-half of mayonnaise." That's enough to send me into a nauseating seizure.

The burger is said to feed a family of ten. But it would have to be a very hungry family of ten, as dividing the burger into ten equal pieces still leaves twenty-four ounces of hamburger per person. That is equal to six Quarter Pounders for each and every member of that large, non-birth-control-practicing family of carnivores.

The Beer Barrel Belly Buster is actually the latest in a long line of size-topping monster sandwiches unveiled in the Great Ivy League Burger Wars of 2005. A few months ago Denny's Beer Barrel pub was offering a mere eleven-pound burger. Kate Stelnick, a one-hundred-pound Princeton, New Jersey college student ate the entire eleven-pound burger in one three-hour sitting.

Not to be outdone, the Clinton Station Diner in Clinton, New Jersey, introduced a 12.5-ounce burger. To which Denny's Beer Barrel Pub countered with the aforementioned fifteen-pound Beer Barrel Belly Buster.

No personal details were given of the diminutive Princeton student, Kate Stelnick, who, for all of her effort in eating eleven pounds of hamburger in one sitting, received nothing more than a certificate, a T-shirt, and—we can assume—a major case of gas and indigestion. Nevertheless, it's good to know that Ivy Leaguers aren't quite as smart as they would have us believe.

I have a friend who only eats hamburgers. When I say he only eats hamburgers, I don't mean that he eats a hamburger every once in a while in between other foods and snacks. He almost exclusively eats hamburgers. He won't even touch a piece of chicken.

Occasionally he will order a steak, but he'd rather have a hamburger.

His wife used to make spaghetti, and he ate it every once in a while, but he recently told her, "I don't like spaghetti anymore."

"You used to," she said.

"Well I don't anymore; let's go out for a hamburger."

He will eat an occasional scrambled egg for breakfast or the rare peanut-butter-and-jelly sandwich for lunch, but mostly he eats burgers. He would truly be in heaven at Denny's Beer Barrel Pub.

The story of the Beer Barrel Belly Buster broke on the same day that former President Clinton announced the formation of an initiative to combat childhood obesity. No word as of yet whether the former burger-loving ex-president had any particular Princeton coeds in mind when he released the initiative.

So what have we learned today, children? Soft drinks continue to grow larger, Bill Clinton's timing has improved, Ivy Leaguers have had their heads buried in books so long that they have resorted to devising clever ways to eat massive amounts of hamburger, autobahn-food metaphors don't grow on trees, and we all secretly delight just a little when a vegan coworker has a petit-mal burger panic.

Shhh! Don't Tell Charlie

Last week Congressman Charles Rangel, D-N.Y., was quoted in the *New York Times* as saying, "Mississippi gets more than their fair share back in federal money, but who the hell wants to live in Mississippi?"

The answer to the congressman's question as to who wants to live in Mississippi is: me and 2,844,657 of my friends and neighbors, not to mention a few hundred thousand expatriated Mississippians stuck in New York, California, and all points in between.

After reading the *Times* article, my first reaction was to fire off a letter to the congressman's office and various editors of national newspapers extolling the benefits of living in Mississippi: the friendly people, the stunning natural resources, the music, the art, the literature, the low cost of living, the beautiful women, the moderate climate (sans August), and the food—especially the food.

New York has its fair share of great cooking, but with all due respect to Mr. Rangel, I am talking about food with soul. Not soul food, although we certainly have plenty of that—and surely the best of that genre is served here in my home state—but food with soul. Food that was prepared with love as my grandmother did, as my wife does for our children. Food with soul infers a love, respect, and dedication to the preparation and dining process. It's food of love, with love, and for love.

It's the food, Charlie. On a 2005 nationally televised special for Hurricane Katrina relief, Morgan Freeman, the Academy Award–winning actor, said of his home state, "I'd live here for the food alone." Freeman knows what we know; Rangel knows not.

We know the joy of eating broiled speckled trout, salty oysters, and fresh shrimp from the warm Gulf waters, soft-shell crab and jumbo-lump crabmeat from Ocean Springs and Bay St. Louis. We know of the bliss that overcomes one in the middle of biting into a slab of sweet, smoky ribs from Leatha's in Hattiesburg, or a filet of crispy-fried catfish dotted with hot sauce at any one of the hundreds of quaint fish houses hidden away on lightly traveled country roads.

The rolls served at the Elite on Capitol Street in Jackson, and the comeback dressing at the Mayflower, are both worthy of anyone's citizenship, as is the gumbo at Hal and Mal's. We know tamales from Doe's in Greenville, cheesecakes from Jubilations in Columbus, and fried chicken at the hundreds of small diners and cafes located on town squares and roadside joints, not discounting the chicken served on your grandmother's dinner table—the true food of love.

We've know fine dining from the City Grocery in Oxford, to Nick's in Jackson, and the Purple Parrot Cafe in Hattiesburg. From organic beef and free-range poultry in Meridian to a world-class creamery south of Tylertown, we've got the resources to eat like royalty. From the Sweet Potato Capital of Vardaman to the Tomato Capital of Crystal Springs, down here the vegetables are fresher, the conversation is friendlier, and the politicians are more polite.

Life moves slower in Mississippi, but we'll not apologize for taking time to visit, to listen, and to help one another. After reading Congressman Rangel's statement, I was reminded of another Morgan Freeman statement. When asked by a reporter why he lives in Mississippi when he could live anywhere in the world, Freeman replied, "I live in Mississippi because I *can* live anywhere in the world."

So in the end, I will not fire off a letter to Mr. Rangel explaining why we enjoy living in Mississippi, for fear that the correspondence might sway his ill-informed opinion, subsequently changing his mind and enticing him to move down here—an act that would consequently put at risk our long-standing and hard-earned reputation for hospitality.

Subway 911

A man in Jacksonville, Florida, was arrested last week for making fraudulent 911 calls.

He wasn't calling the police station to ask if their "refrigerator is running?" and he wasn't asking the dispatcher if she had "Prince Albert in a can?" The Associated Press reported that Reginald Peterson was hauled off to the pokey because he called 911 to complain that the Subway restaurant had left the sauce off of his sandwich.

Peterson, forty-two, actually called 911 twice. The first call was to complain about his sandwich. The second call was to complain that the police weren't arriving fast enough. By that time Peterson had become belligerent about the lack of sauce on his sandwich and they locked him out of the store. My guess is that his third call was made from the jail to his lawyer.

The AP reported that when "officers arrived, they tried to calm Peterson and explain the proper use of 911. Those efforts failed, and he was arrested on a charge of making false 911 calls."

It baffles me that anyone would get so upset about a sandwich that they would call 911. But it baffles me even more that it happened at a Subway. It's one of my son's favorite restaurants. There's one two blocks from my house and we eat there often. They make your sandwich right in front of you. If you want more sauce, or no sauce, all you have to do is say so. There's no need to get the police involved.

Google and YouTube are filled with 911 calls of all types. Many of them have to do with food. One man called 911 because "Someone broke into my house and took a bite out of my ham and cheese sandwich." A lady called from inside a fast-food restaurant and complained to authorities, "They won't fix my taco...I ain't havin' no rice in it...he's holdin' my dollar and ten cents!" Another called asking, "Can you connect me to Domino's Pizza?"

We are passionate about food. It's one of the only things in life of which everyone has an opinion. Eating is universal. It's what we do, three times a day (more if you're me), 365 days a year.

YouTube has a lengthy 911 call from a woman who is sitting in the drive-through line at a Burger King waiting for her Western Bacon Cheeseburger.

The 911 archives are also filled with such non-vital emergencies as "I'm watching a movie and there's a guy beating another guy with a bat" and "What day of the week is this?" But the best ones are food-related.

It all falls back to the legendary Joe Pesci scene in one of the *Lethal Weapon* movies where he reels off a curse-laden diatribe as to why one should never use the drive-through window, but always walk up to the counter. That incident, by the way, was over a tuna sandwich at Subway.

Open Mouth, Insert a Giant French Foot

Last week French president Jacques Chirac started a verbal food fight with Great Britain on the eve of the G8 summit.

In a private chat with German chancellor Gerhard Schroeder and Russian president Vladimir Putin, President Chirac was overheard saying, "You cannot trust people who have such bad cuisine. It [Great Britain] is the country with the worst food after Finland."

Citizens of the British Isles were boiling over the comments. Actually, boiling might be a bad choice of adjective since the G8 Summit was to be held in Scotland, home to the magnificent dish haggis, a wonderful mixture of boiled sheep innards, boiled lamb liver, and boiled oatmeal.

Mr. Chirac stuck the culinary dagger in a little further when he quipped, "The only thing they [UK citizens] have ever done for European agriculture is mad cow disease."

The gloves were off!

In an obvious attempt to drag the Americans into the food fray, former KGB agent Putin tried to stir the pot further by asking, "What about hamburgers?"

"No, no," Chirac replied. "Hamburgers are nothing compared with British food."

Putin can say what he wants about American hamburgers, but in 1990, when the first McDonald's restaurant opened in Moscow, it broke the company's worldwide opening-day sales record for customers served. Fifteen years later, that same unit continues to be the busiest McDonald's in the world.

Also, someone might want to remind Mr. Putin that McDonald's operates 103 restaurants in Russia and has served more than 300 million customers (and more than 66 million Big Macs).

Putin's jab is akin to the Southern Mama Phenomenon. One can criticize their sweet ol' mama all day long, but when anyone else chimes in with a negative comment, the gauntlet is dropped.

My question for Mr. Putin would be. "If your citizens are such culinary connoisseurs, why are they so fascinated by twoallbeefpatties-specialsaucelettucecheesepicklesonionsonasesameseedbun?"

But let's not lose focus here. The original comment that started the rigmarole was "The only thing they have ever done for European agriculture is mad cow disease." If Chirac would have uttered a similar comment about American food, especially in the South, somebody, somewhere would have said, "Them's fightin' words!"

I, too, have made fun of British cuisine. But I'm not a world leader, and no one listens to me, anyway.

I would think that some good Southern cooking is exactly what Mr. Chirac needs. He might focus less on profiting from the Oil for Food Program and concentrate more on the food-for-the-starving-people-of-the-world program. The United States is spending billions to feed the world; it's time for the French and Germans to put their money where their insults are.

If it weren't for us (and the Brits), the French would be eating schnitzel and sausage every meal. How about a little gratitude, guys? I've been to Germany. You don't want anything to do with their food.

I once heard the great American writer Jim Harrison refer to the French as "cheese-eating surrender monkeys." I wouldn't go that far, but somehow I think that if these world leaders would visit the Piney Woods of Mississippi, we could settle these problems once and for all.

We'll fly the G8 leaders into the massive Pine Belt Regional Airport and introduce them to some *real* food. I would take Chirac to Leatha's BBQ Inn for a large smoky slab of fall-off-the-bone bbq ribs, baked beans, and sweet slaw. I would put Leatha's barbeque up against any of France's Michelin-starred restaurants.

We could pick up Gerhard Schroeder on the way to Rayner's Seafood House for some of the best fried catfish in the South. Then we'd stick Putin in the backseat and drive him out to the middle of nowhere on the banks of the Bouie River and sit down over a bowl of turnip greens and hush puppies at Cowboy Jim's restaurant (they make a mean hamburger, too). Maybe *then* we could make some progress in the world.

Why not? If London can host the Olympics, Hattiesburg could certainly pull off the next G8.

You guys want world peace? Come down here, have a seat, pour a glass of sweet tea, put your napkins in your laps, turn on the window unit, and get down to the business of solving the world's problems.

And if Chirac makes that type of remark while eating in Mississippi, we'll tell him—in the immortal words of the late Lewis Grizzard— "Delta is ready when you are."

Chapter 11

Travel

Spring Break Diary
Day One: Saturday

4:30 a.m.—I wake up early for a 9:30 a.m. flight out of Jackson. Last night I told my wife we needed to leave the house no later than 6:30 a.m. I organize luggage, locate airline tickets and condo confirmation numbers. The rest of my family sleeps peacefully.

6:23 a.m.—My wife is putting on makeup. Her hair is still wet. Did I mention that the Jackson airport checks no one in within thirty minutes of his or her departure time? My nine-year-old daughter is still asleep. For some reason, my five-year-old son slept under his desk last night. The 6:30 a.m. departure is not going to happen. I guess there is something that can be said for consistency.

6:52 a.m.—The St. John Scramble officially commences (as it does every time we try to get to an airport on time). No matter what time the flight, or what time I tell my wife we need to leave, we are forty-five minutes late. Being a master of the St. John Scramble, I had the foresight to tell my wife that we needed to leave at 6:30 a.m. when we actually didn't need to leave until 7:00 a.m. Wisdom comes with age.

7:24 a.m.—My wife refuses to get in the car unless we drive through Starbucks. I agree because I am the man of the house and I always call the shots.

7:29 a.m.—My wife forgot her ring at the house. We turn around. The kids are eating Starbucks pound cake for breakfast—megadoses of sugar. My son will be bouncing off of the car windows for the next ninety miles to the airport.

7:33 a.m.—We're on the road. Our flight leaves at 9:30 a.m. I consider calling my travel agent to check on later flights. My son is loudly singing jingles from cheesy commercials. My daughter is staring out of the car window. My wife is still unconcerned. I wonder how my son knows every word to the Forrest General Hospital television commercial.

8:47 a.m.—Tires squeal as we pull up to the curbside check-in at the airport. Skycaps scatter as I wildly throw suitcases and duffel bags out of the car in a practice with which I have become all too familiar, and at which I have become all too good.

8:58 a.m.—We check in ninety seconds under the wire and the four of us run through the airport like O.J. in a car-rental commercial. My daughter asks, "Who's O.J.?"

9:02 a.m.—My son loses his shoes in the security line. I learn that our fight's departure has been moved up fifteen minutes. We make it. Unbelievable. I still haven't eaten breakfast.

10:17 a.m.—On a small commuter jet, my son stands up, points, and yells out, "Momma, that man has a huge head!"

11:56 a.m.—After a mostly uneventful flight—one with no food service—we have a $92.78 meal at a so-called Tex-Mex cafe in the Dallas airport. The "house specialty" tortilla soup was nothing more than canned chicken noodle soup with the addition of limes, jalapeños, and Tostitos. My son spills his soft drink on his sister.

1:05 p.m.—Just before boarding the flight to Salt Lake City, I notice that we have seats 17B, 17C, 17D, and 17E. I say a heartfelt, silent prayer for the passenger who holds the ticket to seat 17A.

2:07 p.m.—At 35,000 feet, somewhere over West Texas, my wife notifies me that she left all of the ski school vouchers, lift tickets, and all other vital vacation stuff "in the box on the dresser, in the den." The den was still in Mississippi the last time I checked. The man in 17A is nice and skinny—a ray of hope

2:48 p.m.—Mr. 17A appears to have gastrointestinal issues. My daughter says, "Daddy, that man is making bad air."

5:15 p.m.—We check into the condo. The brochure advertised a "hot tub" in the unit. It looks more like a "hot bucket." My fourth grader might be able to fit inside.

6:49 p.m.—Sitting in my favorite sushi restaurant in the world—the Flying Sumo in Park City, Utah—eating Luxury Shrimp, Money Rolls, Utah Rolls, Samurai Rolls, Tuna Nachos, and Funky Rolls. The atmosphere is cool, the music is good, the food is great, and no one is making bad air. I'm watching my children eat food that I wouldn't eat until I was in my thirties. Sleep will come soon. Tomorrow we'll ski. All is forgotten. Life is good.

New York

NEW YORK, NY—I've just finished five days on the island of Manhattan with one goal: Eat well.

Being one who is passionate about food, and also one who travels to the nation's top restaurant city only once or twice a year, I usually have a lot of gastronomic ground to cover during my stay.

Ten years ago I developed a system for eating at my favorite New York restaurants. On a business trip I checked into my Midtown hotel and handed the concierge a list of eight restaurants that I hoped to visit during the course of my stay. He looked at the list, chuckled, and said, "Sir, there's no way you'll get in any of these restaurants. Some take months to secure a table."

I told him, "I don't care what time of day I eat. I'll be the first customer of the evening or the last customer to be seated at dinner. I'll sit at the lousy two-top by the kitchen door, the noisy booth by the kitchen, or at the bar. I just want to eat there. Give it a shot."

He gave me a smirk and said, "I'll try."

Thirty minutes later, the phone in my room rang, and with a note of surprise in his voice, the concierge informed me that he had secured seven out of eight reservations.

It's all about the food.

Before I left for this trip, I made my usual restaurant wish list. At the top of the list sat Per Se. Reservations at Per Se are typically booked two months in advance. Bypassing the hotel's concierge, I called Per Se as soon as we touched down, and gave the reservationist my standard I'll-eat-early-or-late-it-doesn't-matter routine. It didn't work. I was placed on a waiting list.

I began making the other reservations on my list with the knowledge that one of them might have to be canceled at the spur of the moment to make room for Per Se. I had five days—ten meal periods—and one goal: Eat at Per Se.

Per Se was opened by the French Laundry's Thomas Keller two

years ago. For lovers of art, there are local flea-market painters, then there are noted practitioners who are recognized in national publications and galleries, and then there are the masters. In golf, there are local hackers, pros on the tour, and guys like Nicklaus and Palmer. In basketball…Well, you get the picture. In the world of fine dining, there are guys like me, then there are guys like Emeril, and then there is Thomas Keller, and he stands alone behind the pulpit of the nation's foremost culinary cathedral. Ask the nations top twenty-five chefs to name the best chef in the country and twenty-three of them will say—without missing a beat—Thomas Keller.

Keller, a modern-day Michelangelo of food, is the chef/owner of the French Laundry in Yountville, California, widely acknowledged as the best restaurant in the country. On my only opportunity to eat there, I had my then two-year old daughter in tow, and though she would have been a model customer, children were out.

For me, Per Se—the French Laundry's New York cousin—is the pinnacle, the grail, the culinary summit of Everest, the restaurant where no other has gone before.

Over the course of the visit, I dined at all of the other restaurants on my list, yet Per Se remained a tough nut to crack. After yellowtail and jalapeño at Nobu, I called the Per Se reservationist, no dice. After lamb's tongue and beef cheek ravioli at Babbo, I called again, no luck. Hoping that the squeaky wheel would get the grease, I made calls during frisée salads at Gotham Bar and Grill and crispy rice with spicy tuna at Koi, to no avail.

I was down to my last full day in town and holding out for a cancellation at Per Se's 10 p.m. and final seating. Holding theater tickets for an 8 p.m. show, I made late lunch reservations at Union Square Cafe. We ordered multiple courses, assuming it was going to be very late before we ate at Per Se, if we were able to eat there at all. During our third course at Union Square Cafe, sometime around 2:30 p.m., I received the call I had been waiting for all week. We were in, but not at 10 p.m. Per Se's only opening was at 5:30 p.m.

I immediately hung up the phone and told my wife to drop her fork, we were about to eat a nine-course meal at Per Se in three hours.

Next week: New York Part II, Dinner at Per Se.

Per Se

NEW YORK, N.Y.—I have just eaten the best meal of my life. Hands down. No question.

That is a powerful statement for someone who eats for a living. Yet there is no other way to describe my dining experience at Per Se, as anything less than "perfect." From the service to the food to the atmosphere, it just doesn't get any better.

These days the Holy Grail of restaurants is the French Laundry in Yountville, California. Reservations are taken two months in advance and seatings fill instantly. I rarely travel to the Napa Valley, so Per Se, the French Laundry's New York cousin, is my East Coast Grail. Reservations at Per Se are hard to come by, too. I applied the "squeaky wheel theory" and received a table on the last night of my visit.

Per Se is located on the third floor of the newly constructed Time Warner building. The elegantly sparse but spacious dining room has only sixteen tables. The view overlooks Columbus Circle to the tree line of Central Park South with the Upper East Side skyline in the distance.

Never have I eaten such a worldly meal in one place. Eleven courses featuring jet-fresh foods flown in from all over the world. The first course was salmon crème fraîche in a tuile cone. The next course featured oysters from Greece, poached in butter and served over a savory sabayon of pearl tapioca with Russian Sevruga caviar.

The third course was a salad of Hawaiian hearts of peach palm. It was at this point that I realized that no component of the meal would be overlooked and all details would be covered, down to the two butters that were served with the bread. One came from a small creamery in France and another from an organic farm in California. The bottled water was shipped in from a small company in Wales.

The fourth course was a seared lobe of foie gras dusted with finely crumbled walnuts and served with a small compote of poached apples. I have resigned myself to the fact that I will never eat foie gras prepared as expertly as that one.

The fifth course was a sesame-crusted filet of hirimasa, a Pacific fish that might have been the mildest, whitest fish I have eaten. That was followed by a fricassee of Nova Scotia lobster with a confit of artichokes, picholine olives, oven-roasted Roma tomatoes, piquillo peppers, and a spicy lobster broth.

After a rabbit course, the server brought a pan-roasted sirloin of Australian Wagyu beef that was served alongside a Wagyu brisket that had been braised for forty-eight hours, a roasted potato gratin that was sixteen layers thick but less than one inch tall, a forest mushroom duxelles, and crisp haricots verts with sauce bordelaise.

The next course featured pickled Tristar strawberries from a farm in Upstate New York, paired with Tellicherry pepper shortbread, cheese from France, and Blue Moon Acres Mezza arugula. A pineapple sorbet course followed, and was served with a compressed pineapple and macadamia nut "nougatine," which, I see when I look at my notes from the meal, I described as "unbelievable," and since I am not allotted enough space in this column to do the dish justice, I will let that description stand.

Two more courses followed the sorbet course, but I was numb.

I was given a guided tour of the kitchen, unusually large by New York standards—actually, large by any standards. During the day, forty chefs do the advance work to prepare that evening's meal. At night it takes fourteen chefs to carry out the dinner service. That's a total of fifty-four chefs working to service a sixteen-table restaurant. Again, unbelievable.

On the kitchen wall was a sixty-inch plasma monitor with a live, closed-circuit camera focused on the French Laundry's kitchen, Per Se's Napa Valley cousin. the French Laundry, on the other hand, has a monitor in their kitchen showing the Per Se kitchen. Wherever Chef Thomas Keller is, he can observe his chefs at work.

The meal was perfect, down to the silverware, serving pieces, china, and crystal, each unique and of the finest quality. As I write this column and think back to my meal at Per Se, I am trying hard to be critical and think of something—just one thing—that was even slightly disappointing. I can't think of one thing. I guess when a restaurant goes to the trouble to import their water and butter from thousands of miles away, every other detail, whether large or small, is covered.

Will I eat a better meal sometime in the future? Maybe. I certainly hope so. I am currently trying to get a table at the French Laundry for my July visit to that area. Stay tuned.

The French Laundry

YOUNTVILLE, CALIF. —"I have just eaten the best meal of my life. Hands down. No question." Those were the opening sentences of a column I wrote just five weeks ago after dining at Per Se, in New York.

Stop the presses. I have just experienced a humbling, thirty-two-course culinary bacchanalia at the hands of Thomas Keller, and the statements made just five short weeks ago are now old news.

I have once again eaten the best meal of my life. Hands down. No question.

On a warm evening in July, I experienced a slight hint of what Sir Edmund Hillary might have felt when he reached the peak of Mount Everest. Though mine was a culinary pinnacle, it was a zenith, nonetheless. For years, the French Laundry has been my gastronomic Mecca. I have finally reached the summit.

The French Laundry in Yountville California, is widely considered the nation's finest restaurant, a reputation it has dutifully earned over the course of the last twelve years. At the French Laundry, excellence seeps from every nook and cranny and percolates from every personality. It exists—actually thrives—several strata above even the finest restaurants in New York. Nothing compares.

I arrived with three friends; an artist, an architect, and a CEO. Our reservation was scheduled for a 7 p.m. seating, but we arrived an hour early and were seated immediately. In an instant the server informed us that Chef Keller had developed a special menu for our party, and instructed us to sit back and enjoy the ride.

There were sixteen rounds of culinary brilliance on tap for our small group. I sat across the table from the architect. The artist and CEO faced each other to my right and left, respectively. When each course arrived, the artist and CEO were served the same item, which was an entirely different dish, though similar in flavor profile, to the course served to the architect and me. As I always do when dining out, we shared and tasted each dish, all thirty-two of them.

278

The wine pairings were made with the artist and CEO receiving a similar pour, while the architect was given a different wine to complement his course. I, as always, being the only teetotaler in the group, resigned myself to drinking distilled water and focusing on the food. Gladly, this would not suffice at the French Laundry. It was after the first course, when the sommelier learned that I would not be drinking, that I was blessed with one of the most brilliantly amazing "touches" I have ever witnessed in a restaurant.

Sensing that I would more than likely be turning down every wine offering, he asked, "Would you like me to design a non-alcoholic beverage tasting to be paired with your meal, sir?"

I have been eating professionally for eighteen years and not drinking for even longer—twenty-three years. Never had that question been posed. I had resigned myself to a life without pairings. Not if Thomas Keller's staff was going to have anything to say on the matter. Not at the French Laundry.

I'm not talking Shirley Temples and Roy Rogers. Before each course, after he had poured the wines, the sommelier presented me with some of the most unique and inventive beverages I have ever tasted. While the others drank rare French champagnes with their chilled avocado soup, I was served a sparkling apple cider that was the perfect accompaniment. When the artist, architect, and CEO were poured a fine Madeira with their White Truffle Custard, I was given a gourmet root beer with a truffle syrup reduction that paired with the dish perfectly. Other courses were accompanied by such inventive beverages as a lavender and chamomile mimosa, "Chaud Froid" corn and truffle cappuccino, and Golden Monkey Black Tea with porcini shavings. Each inventive, each a perfect pairing, and each created on the spot. Brilliant.

Typically, this column comes in at 750 words. I could use twice the column inches allowed and still not begin to breach the surface of the truly amazing aspects of this meal.

After eating a meal such as this, a food writer runs the risk of using overly flowery verbiage and exaggerated adjectives to describe the experience. The problem with this restaurant is that any description I would commit to paper couldn't do justice to actually sitting in the dining room and experiencing the actual meal. From the maître d' to the servers, to the kitchen staff with whom we visited after the meal, everyone was at the top of his or her game. I couldn't find one single negative in the entire experience, a rare treat, indeed.

It is the only meal I have ever eaten that needed a halftime break. After the tenth course, the maître d' asked if we would like to take a short break in the garden. We did, and the overly attentive service continued, even outside of the restaurant.

A quick tour of the kitchen, and an opportunity to thank Chef Keller in person ended, what will now be described as the finest dining experience of my life. While browsing through my notes of the meal, I see comments such as "extremely professional and informed staff," "perfect service," "best ever," and "truffles, truffles, truffles!"

In conclusion, thirty-two courses, five hours and fifteen minutes from start to finish, brilliant food, excellent service, good friends, and the country's greatest culinary institution made for a most memorable evening.

THE FRENCH LAUNDRY
CHEF'S TASTING MENU
JULY 17, 2006

SALMON TARTAR IN A TUILE CONE

CHILLED MELON SOUP
Summer Melons, Mint, and Yogurt

CHILLED HASS AVOCADO SOUP
Hass Avocadoes, Cilantro Shoots and Espelette
Laurent Perrier "Grand Siecle" MV
Sparkling Apple Cider, Sonoma Sparkler

BEET SORBET
with Granny Smith Apples and Black Pepper

"QUININE SORBET"
with Lime Scented "Gelée" and Fresh Juniper Berry "Tuile"

CAULIFLOWER "PANNA COTTA"
Beau Soleil Oyster Glaze and Russian Sevruga Caviar

"OYSTERS AND PEARLS"
"Sabayon" of Pearl Tapioca with Beau Soleil Oysters and Russian Sevruga Caviar

SOFT SHELL CRAB
Vanilla Mousseline, Bananas and Shaved Hazelnuts

"SASHIMI" OF SPANISH BLUEFIN "TORO"
Marcona Almonds, Globe Artichokes, "Mâche" and Pedro Ximenez Glaze
Manzanilla "La Guita"

CODDLED HEN EGG
Minced Périgord Truffles and Toasted Brioche "Soldiers"

WHITE TRUFFLE CUSTARD
with a "Ragoût" of Périgord Truffles
Barbeito, Sercial, Madeira 1978
Root Beer, Truffle Syrup

SALAD OF SUNCHOKES
with Apricot "Confit", Marinated Peppers, and Curry "Aigre Doux"

SALAD OF YOUNG GLOBE ARTICHOKES
Baby Leeks, Sweet Carrot "Ribbons," Red Pearl Onion "Petals,"
Spanish Saffron "Mayonnaise" and Garden Basil
Emmerich Knoll, Gruner Veltliner, 2004, Austria
Lavender and Chamomile "Mimosa"

"AGNOLOTTI" OF SWEET GOLDEN CORN
Black Truffles from Provence and Corn Pudding

BLACK TRUFFLE GNOCCHI
with Grated Périgord Truffles
Domaine Boillot, Meursault "Les Perrieres," 2004
"Chaud Froid," Corn and Truffle Cappuccino

ROASTED HAMACHI COLLAR
Artichokes, Wilted Arrowleaf Spinach and Lemon

SAUTÉED FILLET OF JAPANESE "SUZUKI"
French Laundry Garden Summer Squash, Niçoise Olives, "Fleur de Courgette"
and San Marzano Tomato "Marmelade"
Chateau Simone, Palette, 1998

"PEAS AND CARROTS"
Maine Lobster Tail "Cuite Sous Vide," Garden Pea Shoot Salad
and Sweet Carrot Buttons

SWEET BUTTER-POACHED MAINE LOBSTER "MITTS"
Green Grape "Confit," Melted Belgian Endive, Périgord Truffles and
Sauternes-Lobster Coral Emulsion

SAUTÉED MOULARD DUCK "FOIE GRAS"
Medjool Dates, Celery Branch and Pumpkin Seed "Vinaigrette"

MOULARD DUCK "FOIE GRAS AU TORCHON"
with Silverado Trail Strawberry Jam and "Frisée" Lettuce
Domaine Weinbach, Gewurztraminer, "Cuvee Theo" 2003

"PORK AND BEANS"
All Day Braised Hobb's Shore "Poitrine de Porc,"
with a "Cassoulet" of Pole Beans and a Whole Grain Mustard Sauce

WOLFE RANCH WHITE QUAIL "EN CRÉPINETTE"
"Ragoût" of Golden Corn, Applewood-Smoked Bacon, Piquillo Peppers
and "Béarnaise" Reduction
Radio Coteau, "Savoy," Pinot Noir, 2004

WAGYU
Spring Onion, Cèpes, French Laundry Green Beans and "Sauce
Bordelaise"

BOUILLON-POACHED TENDERLOIN OF SNAKE RIVER FARM
PRIME BEEF
"Nameko" Mushrooms, Broccolini, "Kohishikari" Rice
with Sweet Garlic and Ginger-Scented "Jus"
Modicum 2001
Golden Monkey Black Tea

"COBB SALAD"
Tomato "Confit," Applewood Smoked Bacon, Hard-Boiled Quail Egg
and Hass Avocado "Puree"

"MONTE ENEBRO"
Slow-Baked Heirloom Beet, Fennel Bulb "Relish" and Juniper Wood-
Aged Balsamic "Vinaigrette"

ROYAL BLENHEIM APRICOT SORBET
Marcona Almond "Streusel" and "Gelée de Noyaux"

VALRHONA ARAGUANI CHOCOLATE TART
Caramel Ice Cream and Butterscotch "Crunch"
Toro Albala, Pedro Ximenez, 1971

"MIGNARDISES"

Watershed

How far will a man travel for a good piece of fried chicken?
The answer: 383.75 miles.

While attending a party in Atlanta last year, I was approached by
numerous people on several separate occasions over the course of the
evening. All asked one question: Have you been to Watershed? Some
added...and have you eaten their fried chicken?

I had not been to the restaurant Watershed, although I was a fan of
Chef Scott Peacock and his collaborative cookbook project with Edna
Lewis, *The Gift of Southern Cooking.* The fact that all of these people
were separately talking about one thing, Watershed and its fried chicken,
roused my curiosity.

I told my traveling companions that after the cooking demo on the
following evening, we would travel east on Ponce De Leon Avenue into
neighboring Decatur, Georgia, and eat this fried chicken that everyone
was raving over.

After arriving at Watershed we learned two things: 1) The famed
chicken is only served on Tuesday nights. 2) We better get there early
because it sells out quickly.

It was Wednesday, we were twenty-four hours late, and though we
enjoyed an excellent meal of contemporary Southern cuisine in a very
modish atmosphere, we weren't able to order the fried chicken everyone
had been talking about.

The meal that evening was outstanding. I remember a butter bean
hummus that was served with a warm homemade pita. Someone in our
group—maybe me—ate trout, another ordered an organic pork chop
with greens and the most upscale macaroni and cheese I had ever tasted,
and another ate chicken—but not fried chicken.

For eleven months I have lusted after the fried chicken at Watershed. I
have talked to countless friends on numerous occasions of the three-day
process used to prepare the chicken. I have planned road trips and tried
to organize business meetings in the Atlanta area, all for naught.

Last week I was in Atlanta on a Tuesday. The day had finally come. I called Watershed and asked the receptionist for the earliest reservation available. She gave me a table for three at 6:45 p.m. "Will there be any chicken left at 6:45?" I asked.

"Probably," she said. I crossed my fingers.

We arrived at 5:30 p.m. and asked to be seated early. After 383.75 miles, I didn't want to risk missing out on the chicken, again. She saw the desperation in my eyes and complied.

We all ordered the fried chicken, which is served with mashed potatoes, garlic green beans, and two buttermilk biscuits. As I looked around the restaurant, everyone was eating fried chicken. The full menu is available on Tuesday nights, but no one seems to care. They, like us, came for fried chicken.

Every Sunday the chefs at Watershed begin preparing for Tuesday's fried chicken night by marinating fifty birds in a saltwater brine. On Monday, the chicken is transferred from the brine into a buttermilk marinade where it sits for the next twenty-four hours. On Tuesday, after three days of brine and buttermilk foreplay, all of the cooktops are lined with cast-iron skillets filled with lard, a little bit of butter, and a touch of bacon grease.

A half of a bird is served. Only a hundred orders are prepared; when they're gone, one must wait until the following Tuesday.

As we were waiting for the chicken to arrive, I asked my dining companions, "Can you remember the best mashed potatoes you have ever eaten?

"I can," I said. They were eaten on March 2, 2005, on my first visit to Watershed.

One would think that a mashed potato is a mashed potato is a mashed potato. Not so. Think about it. Have you ever eaten mashed potatoes that were so good that you remember exactly where and when you ate them?

The chicken arrived. Eleven months had passed since I first heard of the famous three-day fried chicken process at Watershed. The buildup had been significant. The pre-billing was considerable. Expectations were high. So many times these situations are ripe for a major letdown. Not so with the Watershed chicken.

Each piece was perfect. The meat was plump and juicy, the crust was light and crisp, just like my grandmother used to make.

Isn't that the gold standard for everyone's fried chicken—will it be as good as my grandmother's?

I am not prepared to say that the Watershed chicken was better than my grandmother's, but it was at least as good. And seeing that she passed away fifteen years ago, this is the closest I will ever get.

Was it worth traveling 383.75 miles? Absolutely.

Just the Boys

SNOWMASS, COLO.—I am on a father-son vacation with my six-year-old.

My family usually travels in a pack of four. This trip, prior commitments kept my wife and daughter at home and placed the two men, on their own, in a ski resort. It is the first time that he and I have ever spent any quality time away from home—just the boys. I am a happy daddy.

I love and adore my wife and daughter, but there is something special about two guys traveling alone. Things are different. Even though we are staying in a ski-in ski-out Colorado condo, it has taken on the feel of a Mississippi backwoods deer camp. Certain rules don't apply when the girls aren't around.

The clothes we wore yesterday, even the clothes we wore four days ago, are doing just fine piled up in the corner of the den. We both know that later in the week, if we run out of clean clothes, we might have to dig into the dirty pile to find something to wear. The kitchen island serves as a perfect luggage rack to keep the duffel bag that holds all of our ski clothes and jeans, so we don't have to bend down while digging for something clean.

There seems to be an unusual amount of empty space around the bathroom sink, and the toilet paper never seems to run out. There are always plenty of towels and washcloths available, and for some strange reason we are on time everywhere we go—early even.

The condo's refrigerator is stocked with all of the father-son essentials: milk, orange juice, bottled water, and Coke Zero. In the pantry are two boxes of Cheerios, a wide variety of protein bars, bananas, and a box of Pop-Tarts.

My son had never eaten a Pop-Tart. If my wife had a clue that I was letting him eat a Pop-Tart for breakfast, she would fly out here and fill the pantry with yogurt, turkey sausage, and fiber-laden cereals with strange European and vegetarian-sounding names.

When two guys are on their own, eating ends up in a lower place on the activity pecking order. That is a strange sentence for me to type, because, when I'm traveling, eating usually ends up at, or near, the top of the list.

We eat breakfast in the condo every morning, selecting from the aforementioned items. We eat lunch on the slopes, usually burgers, soups, or salads. We have eaten dinner, three nights out of six, at the restaurant located at our condominium.

This is new territory for me. Restaurants and food are usually a top priority when traveling. This trip it's all about my son. He learned how to snow ski, and on the final day-and-a-half, we skied together. Who needs food when a father and son are bonding?

Actually, we are both starting to miss the girls, all of the Pop-Tarts were eaten two days ago, the Cheerios are running low, and we are out of clean clothes.

My father died when I was six years old. I had never been on a father-son vacation in my life; that is, until now.

I am skiing with my son. I am a happy daddy.

Ravioli and Sweet Tea in NYC

I bit the bullet. Actually, I bit the Big Apple and took the kids to New York.

Over the last eighteen years, my visits to the island of Manhattan have focused on one thing: eating. Each year my schedule is dictated by restaurants, business meetings, and theater, in that order. Every detail of every minute of every visit is planned, plotted, mapped out, and determined by restaurant reservations.

I spend hours devising my restaurant strategy so as to squeeze in every possible dining experience available. I eat for a living. I love food and I love restaurants, they're my hobby, so when one is in the top restaurant city in the world one must make every meal and every moment count.

This visit my wife and I had three extra passengers on board: my daughter, son, and mother-in law (actually, the boy should be counted as two people). Priorities change, restaurants change, and theater schedules change. Change is good, right?

I have now seen New York restaurants through the eyes of a nine- and five-year-old (make that two—very active and energetic—five-year-olds rolled into one).

Theater, not restaurants, was the main focus of this visit. Our hotel was in Times Square; therefore all of the restaurants surrounding Times Square were fair game.

Twice we ate fairly good Chinese food at a restaurant named Ollie's on 44th and Broadway where my daughter—a devout sweet tea drinker—had her first experience with hot tea. On the second visit, a late-night meal after a show, there was no iced tea available and the waiter poured hot tea over ice and watched intensely as my daughter tried to choke the watery liquid down with the addition of several sugar packets. A spicy orange-flavored chicken dish was the highlight of that meal. It was a dish that could hold its own in any joint in Chinatown.

My daughter never gave up on her quest for sweetened tea in Manhattan. At every meal at every restaurant, deli, and cafe, she asked the server for "sweet tea," only to have the request denied each time.

More than anything else this visit will be known as the trip my son learned about ravioli and gnocchi. In Carmine's, a bustling, tourist-laden, family-style Italian restaurant (also on 44th), my son ate a platter of ravioli large enough to feed a family of four. He talked about it for the rest of the trip. Whether we were in a deli, bakery, or toy store, he asked whoever would listen, "Do you have ravioli here?"

In Danny Meyer's Union Square Cafe, he fell in love with gnocchi. Union Square was the one "nice" restaurant we braved with the kids. I had two business meetings away from the family that mostly satisfied my craving for fine dining: Meyer's Eleven Madison Park; and Asiate on the thirty-fifth floor of the Mandarin Oriental Hotel, where I ate from the most creative and stunning bento box I have ever seen.

Every time I visit the city, I like to sneak away one morning and walk the streets. I'll usually have breakfast at a locals-only joint and "take in" the city. I feel like a New Yorker for a brief moment, and then it's out of my system until the next visit. This trip I took the subway to SoHo, where I ate breakfast at Balthazar. I have spent several late-night dinners at that French bistro on Spring Street. Some of the city's top chefs dine there after their restaurants have closed. However, I had never eaten breakfast there.

I enjoyed a breakfast of brioche French toast, applewood smoked bacon, freshly baked croissants, and scrambled eggs with mushrooms and asparagus in puff pastry. The latter being the culinary highlight of the trip.

Was it fun? Was this trip worse than others due to the limitations? In the end, I learned a lesson that should have known from the outset. I would much rather eat in New York tourist joints with my children than alone in any of that city's finest restaurants.

Late at night, driving home from the airport after a grueling day of travel, the car was quiet. Separately, we were all reflecting on the previous six days. As we passed a highway sign that stated the remaining mileage to Hattiesburg, my hometown, an excited voice broke the silence. It was my daughter. "Sweet tea, hallelujah, thank you, Lord!"

Pilgrimage

In a non descript building, on U.S. 411 outside of Madisonville, Tennessee, in the foothills of the Smoky Mountains, sits a little smokehouse. Over the past few years it has become the porcine capital of the known universe. It is a place I have wanted to visit for a long time. Last week I made my pilgrimage.

Do you know the feeling of "let down" when you've anticipated something all of your life, or looked forward to visiting a person or place, and once you finally get there, or meet the person, it—or they—don't quite live up to your longtime romanticized expectations? A young boy worships a pro athlete during his youth and meets him later in life to find him rude and obnoxious. The idolized rock musician is nothing more than a hack in person. Dorothy and the Scarecrow meet the Wizard and he's a charlatan behind a curtain. Well, that didn't happen, far from it.

Allan Benton and his smokehouse operation were everything I'd expected and more. The man behind the curtain was the real deal. The visit was a culinary field trip of the first order.

Benton grew up poor. So poor he didn't even know what "poor" was. His family lived in the mountains of rural Virginia without running water, electricity, or indoor plumbing. Smoking and curing meats was a way of survival. Necessity is the mother of perfection. Benton now produces the country's best bacon, the Holy Grail of pork.

With a master's degree in psychology, Benton taught high school before becoming a master of cured meats. During our visit, he was humble and knowledgeable. I don't know if I have ever met anyone in the food industry who is as passionate about his work as is Benton.

Benton gave my wife and me a guided tour of his operation. He cures and smokes bacon, hams, and prosciutto which he ships to fine restaurants and food lovers from New York to Napa.

Benton also makes sausage. But he can't ship the sausage. I have wanted to try his smoked sausage and hot sausage for the last two years. While I was there, I loaded up on sausage and kept it iced down for the next six days while on the road. It currently sits in my freezer in a place of reverence waiting for the next special-occasion breakfast.

Bacon and ham are what put Benton on the foodie map. He smokes and cures bacon as our ancestors did two-hundred years ago. The end result tastes the way bacon is supposed to taste.

Mass-produced commercial bacon is injected with a chemical brine in a packing house, quick-smoked in a smoke room, and—twenty-four hours later—packaged and shipped. It's quick, it's easy, it's profitable, and the result tastes nothing like bacon did years ago.

The Allan Benton process for curing and smoking bacon takes time—at least five weeks. Benton explained the bacon curing process as he walked us through the operation. First he mixes together a blend of salt, pepper, and brown sugar, rubs the pork bellies, and stacks them in a thirty-eight-degree cooler for two weeks. The dry rub recipe is one passed down from his grandfather. Next he transfers the bellies to another cooler where they hang in a forty-five-degree environment for a week-and-a-half, then to an aging room for another two weeks.

Once the bacon leaves the aging room, it is transferred to a smokehouse. The smokehouse is a simple ten-foot-by-fifteen-foot structure located behind the main building. As Benton opened the door, a thick cloud of hickory and applewood smoke billowed out.

I was amazed by the size of the stove that generates all of the smoke for Benton's meats. It was about three feet tall, one foot wide, and well used. The smokehouse is in operation 24 hours a day, 7 days a week, 365 days a year. Even on his one day off, Benton visits the smokehouse several times to add a log or two to the wood-burning stove.

I loaded up on bacon, ham, prosciutto, and sausage, and as soon as I got home, I put some bacon in the skillet.

Cooking cured bacon is much different than cooking regular store-bought bacon. I overcooked the first two batches I prepared when I ordered Benton's bacon several years ago. Curing removes moisture, so during the frying process, lower heat must be used to cook the bacon, and one must remove the bacon from the pan earlier than when cooking store-bought bacon. It might not look cooked, but it is, and it is very, very, very good.

Over the years I have traveled from coast to coast meeting and eating with some of the kings of the culinary world. Some of the meetings were good and some were letdowns. This time the man behind the curtain surpassed my expectations.

Save the emails and phone calls: www.bentonshams.com, 423-442-5003.

Notes and Comments from a Fourth of July Vacation

The following are notes and ramblings from a Fourth of July vacation:
I have to go to the beach once every four or five years to remind myself why I only go to the beach every four or five years. My family is not like most families. I go to Destin, Florida, to check out the restaurants, my wife goes to shop, my children go because they don't have a vote.

I love the beach. I spent the summers of my youth in boats and on beaches. My wife is not a beach person. Her skin is extremely fair. Nicole Kidman's complexion looks like George Hamilton's next to my wife's. Her family comes from a long line of Northern Europeans who lived in the cold, overcast, rainy, and sun-forgotten climates of places like Norway, Sweden, and Scotland. Actually, I have always believed that her ancestors originated in a faraway land called Caucasia. My wife could be the spokesmodel for Caucasia.

Luckily both of my children look like their mother. Consequently, their complexions are so fair that their skin is almost transparent. Taking this group to the beach requires mountains of patience and gallons of sunscreen.

In another stellar example of good timing, I picked a week to vacation at the beach in which three shark attacks occurred. As if it weren't going to be enough of a struggle to get these little fair-skinned sun zombies out on the beach, we now had the challenge of getting them to put a toe in the water. (I don't know why I used the word "we" in the previous sentence…my wife never left the condo.)

Food Notes:
The Acme Oyster Bar of Destin needs to sue the Northwest Florida Yellow Pages for listing them as the "Acne Oyster Bar."

Breakfast is my favorite meal of the day. Luckily I have found a new restaurant to add to my list of favorite breakfast restaurants. Another Broken Egg Cafe is everything that a breakfast restaurant should be. It has a comfortable, civilized, and relaxed atmosphere, a staff of cheery and accommodating waitresses, and—most of all—great food.

I ate at the Another Broken Egg Cafe every morning of my vacation.

While the descendants of Caucasia were fast asleep, I was having some of the best breakfasts I have enjoyed outside of my home kitchen.

Finally, I have found a place where when one asks for scrambled eggs "lightly scrambled," they actually do it. Most places scramble eggs to death. Overcooked scrambled eggs are one of the greatest tragedies of the morning breakfast table.

"Scrambled light" is the process of scrambling eggs to the stage where the eggs are almost cooked. They are removed from the skillet while they are still wet and have a light sheen on them. Eggs will continue to cook (out of the skillet), so they must be removed before they appear fully cooked.

I am not a fan of omelets, but the Another Broken Egg Cafe menu listed eight of them. My brother ordered an omelet on two consecutive mornings and was pleased both times.

For non-omelet-eating egg lovers, the Another Broken Egg Cafe serves dishes that they call Breakfast Scramblers. The Breakfast Scrambler was a skillet filled with two or three scrambled eggs and other tasty items thrown into the scramble. I ate one with crisp, chopped bacon, spinach, onions, and melted Monterey Jack cheese. It was excellent.

The owners might want to rethink the Blackberry Grits, a dish that surely has Lewis Grizzard spinning in his grave, but everything else was perfect. The menu is large and varied and there are four locations: two in Destin, one in Tallahassee, and the flagship unit in Mandeville, Louisiana.

In Conclusion:

Family vacations are fun despite all of the quirks and idiosyncrasies. Creating memorable experiences for my children is one of my primary goals these days. In the process of my trying to create memories for them, they are unintentionally creating memories for me.

This most recent vacation yielded four new entries into my "Things I Never Thought I Would Say (or Hear) Until I Became a Parent Journal." They are:

"From now on, put your clothes on before you go outside."

"Please don't throw the hairbrush into the toilet."

And…last but certainly not least…

"I'm sorry I poured coffee into your ear."

Chapter 12
My South

My South

Thirty years ago I visited my first cousin in Virginia. While I was hanging out with his friends, the discussion turned to popular movies of the day. When I offered my two cents on the authenticity and social relevance of the movie *Billy Jack*, one of the boys asked, in all seriousness, "Do you guys have movie theaters down there?" To which I replied, "Yep, and we wear shoes, too."

Just three years ago, my wife and I were attending a food and wine seminar in Aspen, Colorado. We were seated with two couples from Las Vegas. One of the Glitter Gulch gals was amazed, amused, and downright rude when I described our restaurant as a fine-dining restaurant. "Mississippi doesn't have fine-dining restaurants!" she insisted, as she snickered and nudged her companion. I fought back the strong desire to mention that she lived in the land that invented the 99-cent breakfast buffet, but I resisted.

I wanted badly to defend my state and my restaurant with a fifteen minute soliloquy and public relations rant that would surely change her mind. It was at that precise moment that I was hit with a blinding jolt of enlightenment, and in a moment of complete and absolute clarity it dawned on me—my South is the best-kept secret in the country. Why would I try and win this woman over? She might move down here.

I am always amused by Hollywood's interpretation of the South. We are still, on occasion, depicted as a collective group of sweaty, stupid, backward-minded, and racist rednecks. The South of movies and TV, the Hollywood South, is not my South.

- My South is full of honest, hardworking people.
- My South is color-blind. In my South, we don't put a premium on pigment. No one cares whether you are black, white, red, or green with orange polka dots.
- My South is the birthplace of blues and jazz, and rock and roll. It has banjo pickers and fiddle players, but it is also has B.B. King, Muddy Waters, the Allman Brothers, Emmylou Harris, and Elvis.

- My South is hot.
- My South smells of newly mown grass.
- My South was the South of *The Partridge Family, Hawaii Five-0,* and kick the can.
- My South was creek swimming, cane-pole fishing, and bird hunting.
- In my South, football is king, and the Southeastern Conference is the kingdom.
- My South is home to the most beautiful women on the planet.
- In my South, soul food and country cooking are the same thing.
- My South is full of fig preserves, cornbread, butter beans, fried chicken, grits, and catfish.
- In my South we eat foie gras, caviar, and truffles.
- In my South, our transistor radios introduced us to the Beatles and the Rolling Stones at the same time they were introduced to the rest of the country.
- In my South, grandmothers cook a big lunch every Sunday.
- In my South, family matters, deeply.
- My South is boiled shrimp, blackberry cobbler, peach ice cream, banana pudding, and oatmeal cream pies.
- In my South people put peanuts in bottles of Coca-Cola and hot sauce on almost everything.
- In my South the tea is iced, and almost as sweet as the women.
- My South has air-conditioning.
- My South is camellias, azaleas, wisteria, and hydrangeas.
- My South is humid.
- In my South, the only person that has to sit on the back of the bus is the last person that got on the bus.
- In my South, people still say "yes, ma'am", "no, ma'am", "please" and "thank you"
- In my South, we all wear shoes...most of the time.

My South is the best-kept secret in the country. Keep the secret...it keeps the jerks out.

My South II

While channel-surfing on the television the other day, I came across another clichéd programs about the South. A group of supposed Southerners were talking about eating a possum.

As long as I have lived in the South, I have never eaten a possum. No one I know has ever eaten a possum. I have never been to anyone's house who served possum. I have never seen possum offered on a restaurant menu, and I have never seen possum in the frozen meat section of a grocery store.

I have, however, seen possums running through the woods. And I have seen a few possums (who weren't good runners) in the middle of the road.

In the South, we might eat strange foods, but possum isn't one of them.

As far as Hollywood is concerned, the South is still one big hot and humid region full of stereotypes and clichés. We are either Big-Daddy-sitting-on-the-front-porch-in-a-seersucker-suit, sweating and fanning while drinking mint juleps beside a scratching dog—or—the poor-barefooted-child-in-tattered-clothes, walking down a dusty dirt road beside a scratching dog. There is no middle ground. Most of the time, we are either stupid or racist or both.

A year ago I wrote a column titled "My South." In light of yesterday's possum experience I would like to add to the list of things that make up my South. The South of movies and TV, the Hollywood South, is not my South.

- In my South, no one eats possum. We do, on occasion, accidentally run over them.
- In my South, little girls wear bows in their hair.
- In my South, banana pudding is its own food group.
- My South doesn't have hoagies. In my south, we eat po'boys.
- In my South, the back porches are screened and the front porches have rocking chairs and swings.

- In my South, the ham is as salty as the oysters.
- In my South, everyone waves.
- In my South, we know the difference between yams and sweet potatoes.
- In my South, we eat every part of the pig, just like they do in Paris.
- In my South we use knives, forks, and spoons, but we let cornbread and biscuits finish the job.
- My South has tar-paper shacks but it also has tall glass skyscrapers.
- In my South, people will put crabmeat on almost anything.
- My South has tire swings hanging under live oak trees.
- In my South, grandmothers will put almost anything inside a mold filled with Jell-O.
- In my South, "cobbler" is a dessert, not a shoemaker.
- In my South, the only things that "squeal like a pig" are pigs.
- In my South, ice cream is made on the back porch instead of in a factory.
- In my South, grandmothers always have a homemade cake or pie on the counter.
- My South has bottle trees.
- In my South, we give a firm handshake.
- In my South, "sopping" is an acquired skill and could be an Olympic sport.
- My South is oleander and honeysuckle.
- In my South, we celebrate Easter a month-and-a-half early with a two-week-long party called Mardi Gras.
- In my South, fried chicken is a religion with its own denominations.
- My South has sugar-sand beaches, pine forests, plains, hills, swamps, and mountains.
- In my South, we still open doors and pull out chairs for ladies.
- In my South, we eat hush puppies instead of wearing them on our feet.
- In my South, it's OK to discuss politics and religion at the dinner table. As a matter of fact, it is required.
- In my South, we don't hold Elvis's movies against him.

- My South has shrimp boats and multicolored sunrises.
- In my South, we move slowly because we can.
- My South has covered dish suppers and cutting-edge fine
  dining restaurants.
- In my South, young boys still catch fireflies in washed out
  mayonnaise jars.
- In my South, 50 percent of the dinner conversation deals with
  someone's genealogy.
- In my South, we don't burn crosses, we worship them.
- In my South, the dogs are still scratching.

My Mississippi

In the Spring of 2009 I was asked to speak to the Governor's Conference on Tourism in my hometown of Hattiesburg. I wrote and read the following verses at the end of the speech.

- My Mississippi is where we all gather to share a meal. It's a neighbor coming over with a freshly baked pie when you've suffered a loss.
- My Mississippi is full of literary giants and coffee-shop storytellers.
- In my Mississippi, we put hot sauce on everything, and hotter hot sauce on everything else.
- In my Mississippi, the coffee is as bold as the women, as smooth as the babies, and strong as the men.
- In my Mississippi, it's "pecan" (*puh-cahn*). A pee can is something one uses in a bathroom emergency.
- My Mississippi has music that will make you take a dirt road home.
- In my Mississippi, fried chicken is a religion and the holy church of cast iron is the sanctuary.
- In my Mississippi, grandmothers always have a cake under glass or a pie on the counter.
- In my Mississippi, we never use one syllable to say something that would sound so much sweeter when using two.
- In my Mississippi, we use knives, forks, and spoons, but we let cornbread and biscuits finish the job.
- In my Mississippi, slowing down is not a choice, it's a way of life.
- My Mississippi is hand-cranked ice cream with fresh peaches and a brain freeze.
- My Mississippi is small-town Christmas parades and pancake-breakfast fund-raisers
- In my Mississippi, grandfathers tell stories—mostly true—while peeling peaches with pocketknives.
- My Mississippi is crickets in the grass, lightning bugs in jars, and neighbors on the sidewalk.

Where is my Mississippi? It's more than a place on the map, it's in your heart, it's in your soul, and it's in your stomach. My Mississippi is your Mississippi. Food is the common link that we share; it is the catalyst that brings us together.

North vs South Weddings

While reading the July 27 edition of the <u>New York Times</u> I came across this wedding announcement:

"Coleen Mary Jennings and Bethany Ann Mills affirmed their partnership on Wednesday night at Full Moon, a resort in Big Indian, N.Y. Tim Hughes, a friend from San Francisco, and Randy Schwartz, a friend from Manhattan, led the commitment ceremony, which included a neo-pagan ritual called handfasting, where the couple's hands were bound together with ribbons."

Today's column is not about Coleen and Bethany. I wish them all of the best things in life. It's also not about a commitment ceremony presided over by Randy from Manhattan. It's not even about a neo-pagan ritual.

This column is about the difference between the North and the South. I keep hearing reports of the homogenization of our country and how "alike" we are all becoming. "There's not a dime's bit of difference between the North and the South," they'll say.

Let's contrast the Northern commitment ceremony with a recent Georgia wedding as reported in the <u>Gwinnett Daily Post</u> on July, 5. The headline read: "Couple Marries at Waffle House."

The <u>Post</u> stated, "The lucky couple, George `Bubba' Mathis and Pamela Christian - both 23 and employees at the Dacula diner (Waffle House) located at the Ga. Highway 316/U.S. Highway 29 interchange... For years, the couple tried to marry on their Independence Day anniversary. But the bride was always scheduled to work. Instead of waiting any longer - she got the day off at the last minute; Mathis had to report for the morning shift - the couple of nine years decided to seal the deal at work."

The <u>Post</u> continued, "The result was what a NASCAR tailgate might be like if Hank Jr. himself stopped by with all his rowdy friends: Loud and proud - country music, storytelling and plenty of Dale Earnhardt paraphernalia"

A Waffle House wedding makes one long for a neo-pagan ritual of handfasting. I happened upon the Waffle House news story on the Internet the same morning I was reading the <u>New York Times</u>. There was no formal announcement in the Georgia newspaper, but had there been one, I imagine it would have read something like this:

George `Bubba' Mathis and Pamela Christian were married at the Waffle House on Highway 29 in Dacula, Georgia, between the breakfast and lunch shifts last Saturday. The couple exchanged their vows on the asphalt just beside the handicapped parking spot near the new entrance. The bride wore a flowing white gown which she had just changed into in the ladie's room after working the graveyard shift. The groom wore his standard-issue Waffle House uniform, resplendent with black apron, non-slip shoes, and paper cap, as he was scheduled to man the flat-top griddle during the reception.

Guests were entertained by the Waffle House jukebox while waiting for the bride to walk down the aisle (sidewalk). The processional, "Honky Tonk Badonkadonk," by Trace Adkins, played loudly over cries of, "Patty melt plate on two, scattered, covered, and diced," and "Someone needs to clean the coffee spoons," coming from inside the diner.

The bridesmaids were all sisters of the bride who also served waffles and patty sausages at the reception. The groomsmen were fellow employees who were busy covering the groom's shift inside the diner while the couple exchanged vows.

A quick reception was held at booths six, seven, and three as Bubba finished his scheduled shift. The couple then drove to Gatlinburg with their three children for the honeymoon.

In the end, I guess it's all about love. Whether one is having their hands wrapped in ribbon, or saying "I do" while eating a scrambled egg sandwich. Just don't ever let anyone tell you that there's no difference between the North and South.

Of course, this is all coming from a guy who was remarried by an Elvis impersonator at the Graceland Wedding Chapel in Las Vegas the day after his church wedding. Love knows no bounds (of taste, that is).

Small-Town Pancakes

I love living in the South.

As far as my literary agent in New York is concerned, I live in a small Southern town. In reality, I live in a medium to large-sized town by Southern standards.

Whether my metropolitan area is large, medium, or small, there are two events each year that make me feel as if I am living in the smallest of the small-town South: my local Christmas parade and the annual Kiwanis Club pancake breakfast.

Both events occurred on the same day this year. The Hattiesburg Mississippi Christmas Parade is small, even by small-town standards. There are no large Macy's-style helium-filled balloons, Broadway lip-syncers, or elaborately decorated floats, but there is a spirit to the event that evokes a comforting sense of community.

There is something about small-town Southern Christmas parades that transports me to the innocence of a Norman Rockwell–painted America. I try to never miss a local parade.

The Kiwanis Club pancake breakfast has been a local event for as long as I can remember. The pancakes are OK. The syrup is an inexpensive generic variety, and the sausage is passable. But it's not the food, or the quality of the food, that makes the event memorable. It's the people. It is citizens from all walks of the community that gather together to share a meal, and a morning meal at that. Young, old, black, white, Protestant, Catholic, rich, poor—the only link connecting all of the people in the room is that they all bought a $5 ticket from a Kiwanis Club member. Nevertheless, there is a common bond that is shared during a meal that breaks down all barriers.

It's not the food, it's the fellowship. Sharing a meal together is a very biblical thing. Food is used throughout the Bible. Whenever two or more are gathered in His name, there is usually a loaf of bread, a few fishes, and some wine. Food is the common link we all share; it is the catalyst that brings us together.

Pancakes were a common link in bringing my family together on many occasions. My grandmother made excellent pancakes. We never woke up in her home without eating pancakes. Her pancake recipe was one of the components that defined her place in the family structure—my grandfather was the avid sportsman who could fix anything, my grandmother made great pancakes. Of course their personalities and talents were deeper and more complex than that, but when broken down into their simplest forms, those were the roles and labels. We all lived up to them. I was the hyper wild kid, my mother was the single-mom art teacher, and my grandmother cooked great pancakes.

Whenever the family gathered on vacation and breakfast was served, my grandmother—"Muz" we called her—prepared pancakes. She cooked them at her home, at our home, and away from home. Muz showed her love for us through the simple act of cooking pancakes.

A few years ago, while eating pancakes with my daughter, it struck me that no one had ever cooked pancakes for Muz. Every time we were together, she did all of the cooking. At the time she was living in an assisted living home. We called her and made arrangements for a pancake breakfast the next morning. I cooked the pancakes this time and it was one of the more memorable breakfasts I can remember.

I have never joined a civic club. Most of them meet at lunch, which is the height of my workday. And I don't know a whole lot about what they do other than cook pancakes once a year. However, one has to be a fan of any organization whose motto is "Serving the children of the world." In addition to serving the children of the world, once a year, they are feeding the citizens of my town.

Here's some unsolicited advice from a formerly jaded southerner: Never let a small-town parade, a pancake-breakfast-fund-raiser, or a chance to cook for your grandmother pass you by, ever.

The Mint Julep

Rule number 237 of the 362 Undeniable Truths of the Deep South Restaurant Business is: True Southerners never drink mint juleps.

When a customer steps up to the bar in a Southern restaurant and orders a mint julep, we already know five things about him:

1. He comes from north of the Mason-Dixon line. Usually a state such as Rhode Island or Connecticut.
2. He is amazed that everyone is wearing shoes down here.
3. He thinks he is hearing a foreign language when the bartender uses the terms "ma'am," and "sir."
4. He will try to slip the word "y'all" into a sentence, but use it in the singular.
5. He will make a hilarious lemon-squinted face once he tastes the mint julep.
6. He will then order a glass of white zinfandel or a strawberry daiquiri and ask when the next Civil War reenactment is scheduled.

Some Northern tourists believe the South is still nothing more than *Gone with the Wind* and Jim Crow. To those people, the Southerner falls into one of two categories: the poor, barefooted child walking down a dirt road, or Big Daddy in his seersucker suit sitting on the front porch of an antebellum mansion sipping a mint julep.

It's ridiculous, and akin to saying that everyone from California is a surfer, everyone from Texas is a cowboy, and everyone from New York is rude. Well, two out of three…

Outside of Louisville, Kentucky, on Derby Day, no one from the South drinks mint juleps (even on Derby Day, Kentuckians don't enjoy them). People who say they like to drink mint juleps only enjoy the romantic thought of drinking mint juleps. At any rate, Kentucky is barely in the South and its proximity to Ohio leaves it suspect.

My aunt Virginia occasionally drank mint juleps, but she moved to Maryland in her youth and took to drinking scotch and milk later in life. I always supposed that anyone who could mix milk with scotch was suffering from lifeless taste buds to begin with. To her, mint juleps probably tasted fine.

In a word, mint juleps…suck. Maybe that's three words, or it could be six, nevertheless, you get the picture.

Therefore, I submit for your perusal, The 10 Irrefutable Truths of Mint-Julep-Drinking Tourists from the North:

1. They will order a Coke by calling it a "pop."
2. If they muster the courage to order grits, they will put sugar on them.
3. Even though their mother has a double last name, they will make fun of the waitress's double first name.
4. They will be surprised when the iced tea arrives at the table already sweetened—and heavily so.
5. They have more than likely contemplated vegetarianism at least once in the last three months.
6. The waitress will think that they, too, talk funny, but will be too polite to say so.
7. At least twice during the course of the meal, they will call a crawfish a "crawdad."
8. They will remove the three cheeses, fried croutons, and all of the ham and bacon from the restaurant's heart-healthy salad offering.
9. They will have no clue that catfish is truly the other white meat.
10. They will quickly learn that the best parking space was not the one closest to the door, which was puzzlingly available when they arrived, but the one way across the parking lot in the shade.

Chapter 13

The Top 40
(plus a few more)

Purple Parrot Corn and Crab Bisque

½ tsp clarified butter
⅓ cup medium-dice yellow onion
¼ cup medium-dice green bell pepper
¼ cup medium-dice celery
1 tsp minced garlic
1½ tsp dried basil
1 tsp white pepper
¼ tsp cayenne pepper
½ tsp thyme
¼ cup white wine
1 Tbl brandy
1½ quarts chicken stock (or low-sodium chicken broth), hot
2 tsp Worcestershire sauce
2 tsp hot sauce
3 cups fresh corn kernels, scraped with pulp
  (or 2 cans whole-kernel corn, drained)
½ cup canola oil
½ cup flour
3 cups heavy cream
1 cup half-and-half
1 Tbl Creole seasoning
2 lbs jumbo lump crabmeat, picked of all shell

   In an 8-quart saucepan, sweat onion, bell pepper, and celery in clarified butter over medium heat until soft. Add garlic, basil, pepper, cayenne, and thyme. Stir well, making sure that spices are incorporated. Add wine, brandy, and stir well. Add stock, Worcestershire, and hot sauce. Cook on high heat 7–10 minutes, then reduce heat to medium. While stock is boiling, make a light peanut butter–colored roux with the oil and flour. Add the roux to the hot stock and stir thoroughly. Add heavy cream, half-and-half, Creole seasoning, and crabmeat. Serve hot and garnish with freshly chopped parsley. Yield: 1 gallon.

Crescent City Grill Seafood Gumbo

5 cups shrimp stock
5 cups chicken stock
5 gumbo crabs
3½ cups diced tomatoes, with juice
⅔ cup tomato sauce
2 Tbl Worcestershire sauce
1 tsp black pepper
2 bay leaves
2½ tsp basil
1 tsp oregano
1¼ cups corn oil
1½ cups flour
2 cups okra
3 cups medium-dice onion
1½ cups medium-dice celery
1 cup chopped green onion
1 cup medium-dice bell pepper
½ cup chopped parsley
3 Tbl minced garlic
2 Tbl Creole seasoning
3 Tbl hot sauce
2 lbs medium shrimp, peeled
1 lb claw crabmeat, picked of all shell
1 lb lump crabmeat, picked of all shell
1 lb oysters, with juice

Bring first 10 ingredients to a boil. Reduce heat to a brisk simmer and continue to cook, skimming the tomato-like foam from the top of the stock.

While the stock is simmering, make a dark roux using the corn oil and flour. To the roux add the okra, stirring constantly. Once the okra is incorporated into the roux, add the onion, celery, green onion, bell pepper, parsley, garlic, Creole seasoning, and hot sauce, stirring well to incorporate. At this point you should have something that resembles a black gooey mass. Add the shrimp and continue stirring until shrimp turn pink. Add the crabmeat and oysters.

Turn up the heat on the simmering stock. Transfer the seafood-roux mixture to the hot stock and stir until the roux is completely dissolved. Bring the stock to a boil once more and then reduce to a simmer.

Remove the gumbo crabs and serve over rice. Yield: 1½ gallons.

Potato Soup

½ lb bacon, diced
1 Tbl (plus ½ cup) butter
1 cup small-dice onion
½ cup small-dice celery
½ cup small-dice carrot
2 tsp minced garlic
2 tsp salt
1 tsp freshly ground black pepper
2 lbs potatoes, peeled and cut into ½-inch cubes
1½ quarts chicken broth
¾ cup flour
3 cups heavy whipping cream
1 cup sour cream
1 cup shredded Monterey Jack cheese
1 tsp hot sauce
½ cup freshly chopped green onion

Place bacon and 1 Tbl butter in a 6-quart stockpot over medium heat and cook bacon until golden brown. Drain fat and add vegetables, garlic, salt, and pepper. Cook for 4 to 5 minutes. Add potatoes and chicken broth and bring to a slow simmer. Cook until potatoes become tender, about 15 minutes. In a separate skillet, melt ½ cup butter and stir in flour to make a roux. Cook until the roux is light blond and gently whisk roux into soup mixture. Try to be careful not to break up the potatoes. Add remaining ingredients and bring to a simmer once more. Remove from heat and serve. Yield: 1 gallon.

Vegetable Beef Soup

3 Tbl olive oil
1½ lbs beef shoulder, small dice
1½ tsp salt
1 tsp pepper
1 cup small-dice onion
1 cup small-dice carrot
1 cup small-dice celery
1 Tbl minced garlic
½ tsp dried thyme
2 tsp steak seasoning
1 bay leaf
15-oz can diced tomato
1½ quarts beef broth
1 cup bloody mary mix (or V8 juice)
1 cup corn, fresh, scraped from the cob
1 cup peeled and diced potato
1 Tbl Worcestershire sauce
1 Tbl Kitchen Bouquet

Heat 1 tablespoon of oil over high heat in a large skillet. Season the meat with half of the salt and pepper. Brown the meat in olive oil. Do not overload the skillet. Overloading the skillet will cause the beef to steam instead of brown. Brown meat in batches, add more oil when necessary, then place cooked meat in a large stockpot.

Add 1 tablespoon of oil to skillet and sauté the onion, carrot, celery, and garlic for 5 minutes over medium heat. Add thyme, steak seasoning and bay leaf. Deglaze the pan by adding the canned tomatoes (with the juice) using a wooden spoon to remove any stuck-on proteins. Cook 5 minutes on high, and add to the meat in the stockpot. Place beef broth in the stockpot and cook over low heat. The soup should just barely simmer. After 1 hour, add bloody mary mix, corn, and potatoes. Continue cooking another 45 minutes. Remove from heat and stir in remaining salt, pepper, Worcestershire and Kitchen Bouquet. Yield: 1 gallon.

My Favorite Chili

1 Tbl olive oil
1 Tbl bacon fat
2 pounds beef sirloin, cut into ½-inch cubes
2½ tsp kosher salt
1½ tsp fresh-ground black pepper
3 cups medium-dice yellow onion
1 cup finely shredded carrot
¼ cup freshly minced garlic
1 Tbl ground cumin
2 tsp ground coriander
1 tsp oregano
1½ Tbl chili powder
1 6-oz can tomato paste
2 28-oz cans diced tomatoes
1 quart V8 juice
1 quart hot chicken broth
2 bay leaves
2 14-oz cans kidney beans, drained and rinsed
2 Tbl corn flour
½ cup water
1 Tbl freshly squeezed lime juice
¼ cup chopped fresh cilantro

Heat the oil and bacon fat in an heavy-duty 8-quart, sauce pan over high heat. Sprinkle the meat with salt and black pepper. Place half of the meat in the very hot oil. DO NOT MOVE THE MEAT FOR 3–4 MINUTES, you want to achieve a nice golden brown sear. Turn the meat over and brown the other side the best you can. Remove the meat with a slotted spoon and place it on a paper towel to drain. Repeat this process with the remaining meat.

Turn the heat to medium and add the onion, carrot, and garlic to the pot. Cook for 3–4 minutes. Using a wooden spoon, stir in the cumin, coriander, chili powder, and tomato paste. Cook for 10 minutes, stirring constantly to prevent burning. This step is very important; caramelizing the sugars in the tomato paste and vegetables will make a huge difference in the outcome of the chili.

Return the meat to the pot. Add the canned tomatoes, V8 juice, chicken broth, and bay leaves. Simmer VERY slowly for 2–3 hours. Stir often to prevent sticking. Add the beans and simmer for 15 more minutes.

Turn up the heat up so that the chili reaches a slow boil. Combine the corn flour with the water to make a paste. Stir the corn-flour mixture into the chili. Allow the chili to cook for 2–3 more minutes. Remove from heat and stir in the lime juice and cilantro. Yield: 1 gallon.

Crabmeat Holleman

1 cup Hellmann's Mayonnaise
2 egg yolks
1 Tbl sherry
1 Tbl Creole mustard
1 Tbl freshly squeezed lemon juice
1 Tbl Creole seasoning
1 Tbl Worcestershire sauce
1 Tbl hot sauce
⅓ cup small-dice red bell pepper
⅓ cup small-dice green bell pepper
1 lb jumbo lump crabmeat
½ lb backfin lump crabmeat
2 8-oz wheels Brie or Camembert cheese, cut into ½-inch cubes
6 Tbl seasoned bread crumbs
8 oven-proof ramekins or 1 scallop shell

Preheat oven to 375 degrees. Combine the first 8 ingredients and mix thoroughly with a wire whisk. Stir in peppers. Gently fold crabmeat into liquid mixture making sure not to break up the crabmeat lumps. Place a layer of crabmeat mixture into a 6-oz ramekin, then 2 cubes of Brie and another layer of crab. Top with seasoned breadcrumbs and bake for 10–12 minutes or until bubbly and bread crumbs are brown. Garnish with chopped parsley. Yield: 8.

Southern Hummus

2 tsp minced garlic
1 tsp salt
2 cups black-eyed peas, cooked
1 cup tahini, stirred well
2 Tbl freshly squeezed lemon juice
¼ cup olive oil
½ cup water, plus extra if needed
¼ cup chopped fresh parsley leaves
¼ cup pine nuts, lightly toasted

Using a blender, puree all ingredients except for the parsley and pine nuts. Add the water only as needed to keep the puree from becoming too thick.

Store in an airtight container in the refrigerator.

Before serving, garnish with chopped parsley and toasted pine nuts. Serve with herbed pita triangles. Yield: 5 cups.

Black-Eyed Pea Dip

2 cups black-eyed peas, cooked
1 Tbl bacon fat or canola oil
½ cup minced yellow onion
1 Tbl minced garlic
½ tsp salt
2 tsp Creole seasoning
1 10-oz can Ro-Tel tomatoes
½ cup grated pepper jack cheese
½ cup cubed Velveeta Cheese
½ cup diced roasted red bell peppers
¼ cup minced green onion

In a small sauté pan, heat the bacon fat over medium-high heat. Cook onions for 3–4 minutes. Add in the garlic, salt, Creole seasoning, Ro-Tel tomatoes and black-eyed peas. Simmer for 5 minutes. Cool slightly. Puree the peas mixture in a blender.

Combine the pureed mixture with the cheeses and heat over a double boiler stirring often. When cheeses have melted, fold in roasted red pepper and green onion.

Serve warm. Yield: 1 quart.

Crabmeat Martini

¼ red onion, small dice
1 lb jumbo lump crabmeat, gently picked of all shell
⅔ cup lemon-flavored oil
2 Tbl olive oil (not extra virgin)
1½ tsp Absolut Citron Vodka (optional)
½ cup white balsamic vinegar
1/4 cup ice-cold water
1 tsp salt
1 tsp freshly ground black pepper
1 tsp Crescent City Grill Cayenne and Garlic Sauce
2 tsp cilantro
2 tsp parsley

   In a large mixing bowl, combine all ingredients and gently toss with a rubber spatula, being careful not to break up any of the lumps of crabmeat. Cover and store in refrigerator 12 hours (tossing every hour or so) to let flavors marry. Gently toss (or turn over) just before serving, as the lemon vinaigrette will separate. Divide crabmeat mixture between 4 lettuce-lined martini glasses. Drizzle excess vinaigrette over the crabmeat to wet the lettuce. Garnish with a skewered olive for a light and cool first course, or double the recipe and serve on a lettuce-lined plate for a luncheon salad. Serve the leftovers in a decorative bowl on the coffee table, to be spooned atop your favorite cracker as an hors d'oeuvre. Yield: 6 servings, appetizers; 4 servings, salad.

Seared and Chilled Yellowfin Tuna with Mojo Mustard and Wasabi Cream

1–2 Tbl sesame oil
1½ lbs yellowfin tuna, fresh, preferably 1 large elongated piece
    the size of a rolling pin
1 Tbl kosher salt
½ Tbl freshly ground black pepper

In a large sauté pan, heat the sesame oil until smoking. Season the tuna with the salt and pepper, and sear each side in the hot oil. You should cook the tuna just long enough to achieve a subtle brown color on each side. The tuna should not be cooked to more than medium-rare. Cool the tuna immediately and prepare the sauces.

Yield: Appetizers for 10-12.

Mojo Mustard

⅓ cup sweet chili pepper sauce (found in Oriental markets)
⅓ cup Dijon mustard
1 tsp minced ginger
2 tsp soy sauce

Mix together all ingredients and chill before serving.

Wasabi Cream

2 Tbl dry wasabi powder
3 Tbl hot water
⅓ cup sour cream
2 tsp freshly squeezed lime juice
½ tsp salt

In a small mixing bowl, blend together the Wasabi powder and hot water to form a thick paste. Add in the remaining ingredients and blend well.

To serve the tuna:

Use a very sharp knife to cut very thin cross-section pieces of the tuna (¼-inch discs). Arrange the sliced tuna on a serving platter (as you would when spreading a deck of cards) and drizzle with the two sauces.

Note: When drizzling the sauces, do not cover the bright red tuna completely. The presentation is best when the bright red of the tuna is visible. Yield: 6-8 people.

Sensation Salad Dressing

3 Tbl freshly minced garlic
½ cup white wine vinegar
½ cup freshly squeezed lemon juice
⅔ cup olive oil (not extra virgin)
3½ cups cottonseed or canola oil
Salt to taste

Combine garlic, vinegar, and lemon juice, and slowly whisk in oils. Add salt to taste. Store in refrigerator 6–8 hours before serving. Stir well before dressing the salad. Yield: 5 cups.

Sensation Cheese Mix

2 cups freshly grated Romano cheese
¼ blue cheese, crumbled

Combine cheeses and store in an airtight container until ready to use.

To prepare Sensation Salad:
For the greens, use a mixture of 2 parts iceberg lettuce, 2 parts romaine lettuce, and 1 part spinach. Make sure and stir the dressing well, as the garlic tends to linger at the bottom of the bowl. Place salad greens in a mixing bowl and add just enough Sensation Dressing to wet the greens. Once the greens are dressed, add enough of the cheese mixture to generously cover all of the greens in the bowl. Place individual portions of the salad on chilled plates and serve immediately.

Crescent City Grill 1000 Island Dressing

2 cups mayonnaise
½ cup chili sauce
2 Tbl small-dice bell pepper
1 Tbl minced onion
3 Tbl sweet pickle relish
pinch salt
1½ boiled eggs, chopped

Combine all ingredients thoroughly. Yield: 3 cups.

Purple Parrot Cafe Blue Cheese Dressing

1¾ cups Hellmann's mayonnaise
4 ounces blue cheese crumbles
¼ cup sour cream
½ cup half-and-half
½ tsp paprika
2½ tsp lemon juice
2 tsp granulated garlic
¼ tsp Worcestershire sauce
¼ tsp white pepper

Blend first four ingredients with a wire whisk. Blend thoroughly. Add remaining ingredients and mix well. Yield: 3½ cups.

Breakfast Casserole Number 1

1 lb spicy breakfast sausage
¾ cup diced onion
¼ cup sliced green bell pepper
¼ cup sliced red bell pepper
1 tsp garlic
1 tsp Creole seasoning
1 tsp cayenne pepper
10 eggs, beaten
1 cup half-and-half
1 tsp dry mustard
6 pieces white bread, crusts removed
6 pieces wheat bread, crusts removed
¼ cup soft butter
1 cup shredded sharp cheddar
1 cup shredded Monterey Jack cheese
1 tsp hot sauce

Preheat oven to 325 degrees.

Brown sausage in a large skillet and drain most of the fat. Add vegetables, garlic, and seasoning and cook 5 minutes. Set aside.

Mix together eggs, half-and-half, and dry mustard in a mixing bowl. Using the softened butter, butter both sides of each slice of bread. Cut the bread into small cubes. Fold the bread, cheeses, and sausage mixture into the eggs. Mix well and place in a buttered 2-quart baking dish.

Bake for 40–50 minutes. Allow to rest for 15 minutes before serving. Yield: 8 servings.

The World's Last Meat Loaf

1 Tbl bacon grease or canola oil
1 cup minced onion
¾ cup minced celery
¾ cup minced bell pepper
1 tsp minced garlic
⅛ tsp thyme, dry
¼ tsp oregano, dry
2 tsp steak seasoning
1 Tbl salt
1 cup milk
1 Tbl Worcestershire sauce
½ cup ketchup
3 eggs
2 lbs ground beef
1 cup bread crumbs, coarse

Preheat oven to 325 degrees.

Heat the bacon grease in a large skillet over medium heat. Sauté vegetables and garlic with salt and dry herbs and seasoning until tender. Allow to cool.

Combine milk, eggs, Worcestershire, and ketchup and mix well. Place ground beef, cooled vegetables, and egg mixture into a large mixing bowl. Using your hands, squish the meat loaf until you have mixed everything together and all is well incorporated. Fold in the bread crumbs last.

Shape the meat mixture into the form of a loaf on a baking sheet. Using your hand, make an indentation down the center of the loaf. (This is where the glaze goes.) Bake 50 minutes.

While meat loaf is cooking, make the glaze. Remove from the oven and spoon glaze down the center of the meat loaf and spread over the sides. Return meat loaf to oven, lower heat to 300 degrees, and bake 30 minutes more. Allow meat loaf to rest 15 minutes before serving. Yield: 8–10 servings.

Baked Shrimp and Squash

6 cups ½-inch cubes squash
¼ cup clarified butter, canola oil, or bacon grease
1 Tbl minced garlic
1 tsp salt
1 tsp freshly ground black pepper
1 Tbl Creole seasoning
½ cup chopped green onion
3 cups fresh shrimp (36–42 count), peeled and deveined
¼ cup clarified butter or canola oil
1 Tbl Old Bay Seasoning
1 Tbl garlic
½ cup medium-dice onion
¼ cup medium-dice red bell pepper
¼ cup medium-dice green bell pepper
4 Tbl butter, cubed
¾ cup parmesan cheese
1 cup grated cheddar cheese
1 cup sour cream
¼ cup sliced green onion
1 Tbl hot sauce
1 cup crumbled Ritz Cracker crumbs
2 Tbl chopped parsley

Preheat oven to 350 degrees.

In a large skillet, sauté the squash, butter, garlic, salt, pepper, Creole seasoning, and green onion over medium-high heat until the squash is cooked. Place squash in a colander and press out excess moisture with the back of a spoon. Pour all into a stainless steel mixing bowl.

In the same skillet sauté the shrimp, butter, Old Bay, garlic, onion, and bell peppers until the shrimp are pink and cooked through. Transfer shrimp to the mixing bowl with the squash.

Immediately add butter, ½ cup parmesan cheese, cheddar cheese, sour cream, green onion, and hot sauce to the bowl with the hot shrimp/ squash mixture. Gently stir until butter and cheeses are melted. Pour the mixture into a 9×13 casserole dish.

Mix together the Ritz crumbs, ¼ cup parmesan, and parsley. Top casserole with the cracker crumb mixture and bake for 20 minutes or until bubbly. Yield: 6-8 people.

Whole Roasted Citrus Chicken

Brine

1 quart water
1 cup sugar
⅓ cup kosher salt
2 Tbl freshly ground black pepper
2 oranges
2 lemons
2 limes

For the Bird

1 whole chicken (3½–4 lbs)
1 orange, cut into quarters
1 lemon, cut into quarters
1 lime, cut into quarters
½ cup small-dice yellow onion
1 tsp minced fresh garlic
1 Tbl chopped fresh thyme
2–3 Tbl olive oil
2 tsp poultry seasoning

Place the water, sugar, salt, and, 1 Tbl black pepper in a saucepan and bring to a simmer to dissolve sugar and salt. Remove from heat. Using a vegetable peeler, remove only the outer skin from the first 2 oranges, lemons, and limes; be careful not to get any of the pith (white part of the peel). Add the peelings to the brine. Squeeze all of the juice from the peeled citrus and add the juice to the brine. Place the brine in the refrigerator and allow to cool completely.

Remove giblets and neck from the chicken and submerge the chicken in the brine. Cover and refrigerate overnight.

Remove chicken from the brine and, using a paper towel, dry all surfaces of the chicken, including the cavity area.

Combine the quartered orange, lemon, and lime with the diced onions, minced garlic, and fresh thyme. Stuff the citrus-onion mixture into the cavity of the chicken.

Brush the skin of the chicken with olive oil and sprinkle the skin with poultry seasoning and 1 Tbl black pepper. Tie the legs together and bend the wings back to secure them. Prepare the grill. Cook with the breast side up over indirect medium heat until the juices run clear, or until an internal temperature of 170 degrees is reached, approximately 1¼–1½ hours.

Place the chicken on a cutting board and allow it to rest for 10-12 minutes before carving. Serve hot. Yield: 4 servings.

Cioppino Tomato Stock

½ cup olive oil
½ cup butter
3 cups medium-dice onions
3 cups hand-chopped leeks (chopped fine, white part only)
3 cups medium-dice green bell pepper
2⅔ cup small-dice carrot
2 cups medium-dice celery
½ cup finely chopped fresh fennel
5-qt canned crushed tomatoes, highest quality
1 cup tomato paste
5 qts water (or stock)
¼ cup salt
3 Tbl tabasco
2 Tbl dried oregano
2 Tbl dried basil
2 Tbl dried thyme
6 bay leaves
2 Tbl Creole seasoning

Sautee onions in olive oil and butter. Do not brown. Add leeks, green pepper, carrot, celery, and fennel and cook 5–10 minutes until soft. Add remaining ingredients, bring to a boil. When stock begins boiling, immediately reduce heat. Cover and simmer 2 hours, stirring frequently. This stock must be made ahead of time and refrigerated (preferably 1 day ahead of time). Yield: 2½ gallons.

To prepare 1 portion of Cioppino:

2 swordfish pieces, 1 oz each
2 redfish pieces, 1 oz each
4 scallops
4 large shrimp (16–20 ct), last tail joint remaining
seasoned flour
2 oz butter

2 oz olive oil (not extra virgin)
1 Tbl garlic
2 oz white wine
6 mussels (optional)
1 oz lump crabmeat
2 cups cioppino stock

Lightly dust seafood in seasoned flour. Shake off excess flour. Sautee in olive oil/butter mixture. Add garlic. Deglaze with white wine and cook approximately 1 minute to reduce liquid. Add mussels and sautee. Add crabmeat and cippino stock and continue to cook for 5–6 minutes. Transfer to a serving bowl and garnish with fresh fennel. If you don't have one or more of these seafoods, substitute one or more of the others.

Pork Tenderloin with Muscadine Glaze

3 pork tenderloins (about 1½ pounds)
2 tsp kosher salt
1 tsp freshly ground black pepper
2 Tbl olive oil
1¼ Tbl unsalted butter
2 Tbl minced shallot
½ tsp minced garlic
¼ tsp salt
¼ cup brown sugar
½ cup Riesling wine, or muscadine wine if you can find it
¼ cup balsamic vinegar
1 cup chicken broth
1 bay leaf
¾ cup muscadine jelly
¼ cup minced red bell pepper
2 Tbl chopped parsley

Season the pork with the salt and 1 tsp pepper.

In an ovenproof skillet, heat the olive oil over high heat. Once the oil is hot, add in the butter and the pork tenderloins. Sear each tenderloin on all sides and place the skillet and tenderloins in the oven.

Cook 8–10 minutes. Remove the skillet from the oven and place the tenderloins on a plate and hold them in a warm place. Drain the excess oil from the skillet.

Place the skillet over low heat. Cook the shallots, garlic, and salt for 2–3 minutes. Add the brown sugar and cook until the sugar is melted. Turn the heat to medium and add the wine and balsamic vinegar. Cook until the mixture has reduced by half. Add in the chicken broth and bay leaf, simmer until the mixture has reduced by 70 percent. Stir in the jelly, ¼ tsp black pepper, and red pepper and simmer for 5–6 minutes. Stir often to prevent sticking and burning. Remove from the heat and stir in the fresh parsley.

Slicing on a diagonal, cut each tenderloin into 6–8 pieces. Arrange the slices on a serving platter and pour the glaze over the pork. Serve immediately. Yield: 6–8 servings.

Redfish Orleans

6 redfish filets, 6–8 ounces each
1 Tbl kosher salt
¼ tsp freshly ground black pepper
¼ cup olive oil
¾ lb shrimp, peeled and deveined
2½ cups sliced mushrooms
2 tsp minced garlic
¾ cup sliced green onion
¾ cup Creole Cream Sauce (recipe below)
¼ cup chopped parsley

Season the fish with the kosher salt and black pepper.

Prepare the grill. Place the fish on direct high heat and cook 4–5 minutes. Turn fish and cook another 4–5 minutes or until opaque in the center.

Heat olive oil in a large sauté pan over high heat. Sauté shrimp for 2–3 minutes, until they begin to turn pink. Add mushrooms and cook until tender. Add garlic and green onion and cook an additional 2–3 minutes. Add crawfish cream sauce and bring to a simmer. Remove from heat. Divide evenly and spoon over fish. Garnish with fresh parsley.

Yield: 6 servings.

Creole Cream Sauce

2 cups heavy cream
1 Tbl Crescent City Grill Creole Seasoning
2 Tbl Worcestershire sauce
2 Tbl Crescent City Grill Hot Sauce
1 tsp paprika

Place all ingredients in a double boiler over medium-high heat and reduce by half until thickened. Yield: 1 cup.

Old Bay Grilled Shrimp with Creole Beurre Rouge

When grilling shrimp, either skewer them or use a grill screen so they don't fall through the grates.

36 large shrimp, peeled and deveined
½ cup no-stick grilling marinade for shrimp (recipe in *New South Grilling*)
2 tsp Old Bay seasoning
1 Tbl freshly ground black pepper
1 recipe Creole Beurre Rouge (recipe on p. 339)

Using a pastry brush, coat the shrimp evenly with the marinade. Allow shrimp to marinate for 20 minutes. Sprinkle the shrimp with the Old Bay Seasoning and black pepper.

Prepare the grill. Place a grill screen on top of the grill and preheat. Place the shrimp on the grate over direct high heat and cook for 6–8 minutes, turning once.

Place the cooked shrimp on a bed of Dirty Rice (recipe on p. 338) and top with the Creole Beurre Rouge. Yield: 6 servings.

Dirty Rice

1 Tbl bacon fat or canola oil
2 oz ground beef
2 oz ground pork
½ cup diced onion
¼ cup diced celery
¼ cup diced bell pepper
2 tsp minced garlic
1 bay leaf
1 Tbl poultry seasoning
1 tsp dry mustard
1 cup rice
2 cups pork stock, hot

Heat the bacon fat in a 1-quart sauce pan over high heat. Add the ground beef and pork and brown. Stir in the vegetables and garlic and continue to cook 5–6 minutes. Stir in the seasoning and rice and cook until the rice is thoroughly heated. Stir in the pork stock and reduce heat to low. Cover the sauce pan and cook 18 minutes. Yield: 3 cups.

Creole Beurre Rouge

1 Tbl olive oil
2 Tbl small-dice green pepper
¼ cup small-dice yellow onion
1 Tbl minced garlic
¼ cup small-dice celery
2 tsp Creole seasoning
1½ cup medium-dice tomatoes
1 cup white wine
1 cup chicken stock
2 Tbl white vinegar
1 bay leaf
1 tsp dried oregano
1 Tbl chopped fresh thyme
1 cup unsalted butter, cubed and kept cold until needed
1 tsp freshly ground black pepper

In a medium sauce pan, heat olive oil over medium-high heat. Sauté peppers, onion, garlic, celery, and Creole seasoning for 5 minutes. Add tomatoes and cook 5 minutes longer. Add wine and reduce by half. Add chicken stock, vinegar, bay leaf, oregano, thyme and simmer 15–20 minutes, until the sauce turns into a thick paste.

Lower the heat and, using a wire whisk, begin incorporating the butter cubes, 2–3 at a time. Stir constantly to prevent the sauce from separating. Once all butter is added, stir in the black pepper and remove from the heat.

Store in a warm place (120 degrees) until needed. Yield: 6–8 servings.

Black-Eyed Pea Cakes with Crab Pico di Gallo

3 cups black-eyed peas, cooked
½ cup finely sliced green onion
⅓ cup small dice red peppers
½ teaspoon cumin
1 teaspoon Crescent City Grill Creole Seasoning
1 egg
¼ cup shredded Romano cheese
1 cup finely ground bread crumbs
2–3 tablespoons clarified butter or canola oil
½ cup Seasoned Flour
Crab Pico di Gallo (recipe opposite)
1 cup Seafood Remoulade (recipe opposite)
¼ cup chopped cilantro

With your hands or a potato masher, smash the black-eyed peas, leaving a few pieces whole. Add green onion, red pepper, spices, and egg. Mix thoroughly. Add cheese and bread crumbs and mix well. Divide the mix into twelve 1½-inch balls. Flatten balls to 2 inches in diameter and about ½ inch thick. These may be done a day ahead of time, covered, and stored in the refrigerator.

To cook the cakes, preheat oven to 425 degrees. Heat butter over medium-high heat in a large skillet. Lightly dust both sides of the cakes with seasoned flour and place them in the skillet to brown. Leave enough room between cakes to be able to flip them over. When cakes are brown on both sides, place them on a baking sheet and put them in the oven for 7 minutes, or until heated through.

Arrange 2 cakes on each serving dish so that one is flat and one is resting at an angle against the flat one. Divide the Pico di Gallo evenly over the cakes. Using a squirt bottle, garnish the plate with Seafood Remoulade. Sprinkle with freshly chopped cilantro and serve hot. Yield: 6 people.

Crab Pico di Gallo

1½ cups small-dice tomatoes, seeds removed
¼ cup small-dice yellow onion
1½ Tbl small-dice jalapeño pepper, seeds removed
3 Tbl lime juice
1 tsp white vinegar
2 tsp salt
⅓ cup chopped cilantro
½ lb jumbo lump crabmeat (backfin meat will also work for this recipe)

Mix all ingredients and allow to marinate in the refrigerator, gently stirring occasionally, for 2–4 hours prior to serving. Yield: 6 servings.

Seafood Remoulade

1 large stalk celery
½ medium sized onion
1 cup ketchup
3 Tbl fresh lemon juice
¼ cup prepared horseradish
1 cup mayonnaise
3 Tbl Crescent City Grill Creole Seasoning
2 tsp Lawry's seasoning salt
1 tsp minced garlic

Chop onion and celery in the food processor until they are small but not completely pureed. Place onion and celery into a mixing bowl. Add remaining ingredients and mix well. Can be made and held for up to 1 week before using. Remoulade sauce tastes better if made at least 1 day in advance. Yield: 1 quart.

Deep South Cornbread Dressing

1 Cornish (game) hen
2 quarts chicken broth
½ onion
½ carrot
1 bay leaf
1 Tbl bacon grease or canola oil
¼ cup diced bell pepper
1 cup diced celery
1 cup diced onion
2 tsp celery salt
2 tsp poultry seasoning
2 cups mushroom béchamel sauce (recipe opposite)
2 cups heavy cream
1½ cups chicken broth, strained from cooking hen
4 eggs
2 hard-boiled eggs
1 recipe cornbread, crumbled

Place the hen, broth, onion, carrot, and bay leaf in medium-sized stockpot. Simmer 1 hour and 20 minutes over medium heat. Remove hen and strain the broth. Allow hen to cool and pull meat from the bones. Chop meat.

Preheat oven to 325 degrees.

In a medium-sized skillet, melt bacon grease over low heat. Add vegetables and seasoning and cook slowly for 10 minutes. Pour into a mixing bowl. Add Mushroom Béchamel Sauce, cream, broth, and hard-boiled eggs, mixing well. Add crumbled cornbread and hen meat. Mix until all is well incorporated. Pour into a three-quart baking dish. Bake 1 hour 15 minutes. Do not overcook dressing (it should be moist but not runny). Yield: 8–12 servings.

Mushroom Béchamel Sauce

2 tsp olive oil, light
2 Tbl minced onion
1 Tbl minced shallot
1 Tbl minced celery
½ tsp salt
3 oz mushrooms, cleaned, sliced (1 cup)
1 cup chicken broth
¼ tsp granulated garlic
⅛ tsp dry thyme
3 Tbl butter
¼ cup flour
⅓ cup whipping cream

Heat oil in a 3-quart saucepan over low heat. Add onion, shallot, celery, and salt. Cook vegetables until tender. Add mushrooms and increase heat to medium. Cook 10 minutes, stirring often. Add chicken broth, garlic, and thyme. Bring back to a simmer and cook 10 more minutes.

In a separate skillet, make a light-blond roux by melting butter and stirring in flour. Add to simmering broth mixture. Cook 3–4 minutes and add cream. Freezes well. Yield: 3 cups.

The Ultimate Green-Bean Casserole

1 qt chicken broth
4 14.5-oz cans green-beans, drained
¼ cup diced bacon
1 cup medium-dice onion
2 tsp caraway seeds
1½ tsp salt
1 tsp pepper
2 cups Mushroom Béchamel Sauce (previous recipe)
4 oz can sliced water chestnuts, drained
1 cup shredded swiss cheese
6 oz can French's fried onions, divided

Preheat oven to 350 degrees.

In a large saucepan, bring chicken broth to a boil. Place green beans in the broth and simmer 10 minutes. Drain the green beans.

Meanwhile, in a separate skillet, render bacon until it just becomes crisp. Drain excess bacon grease from the skillet and add the diced onions. Cook over medium heat for 5 minutes. Stir in caraway seeds, salt, pepper, and Mushroom Béchamel Sauce. Remove mixture from the heat and fold in the green beans, water chestnuts, cheese, and half of the canned fried onions. Place mixture in a 3-quart baking dish and bake 30 minutes. Remove from the oven, sprinkle the remaining fried onions over the top of the casserole, and return to the oven an additional 12–14 minutes. Allow to cool slightly before serving. Yield: 10-12 servings.

Jill's Sweet Potatoes

4 cups cooked, peeled, and mashed sweet potatoes
3 cups sugar
4 eggs, beaten
1 cup heavy cream
3 sticks butter, divided
1 tsp cinnamon
1 tsp nutmeg
1 cup Rice Krispies
1 cup chopped pecans
1 cup chopped walnuts
1 cup brown sugar

Preheat oven to 350 degrees.

Grease a 13×9 casserole dish. Combine hot sweet potatoes, sugar, eggs, cream, half of the butter, cinnamon, and nutmeg in a bowl; mix thoroughly. Put sweet potato mixture in greased casserole dish.

Combine Rice Krispies, pecans, walnuts, remaining butter, and brown sugar in a bowl. Mix until crumbly. Sprinkle over sweet potato mixture.

Bake 40–45 minutes or until center is hot. Yield: 10–12 servings.

Wild Mushroom Risotto

5 Tbl whole unsalted butter
3 Tbl minced shallots
2 cups Aborio rice
4–6 cups hot mushroom stock
1 Tbl salt, added to the mushroom stock
¾ oz dried morels or 3 oz fresh, sliced into ¼-inch-thick slices (if using dry, cover the mushrooms completely with hot water, soak until softened, then slice)
1 cup cream
½ cup freshly grated Parmesan cheese
1 teaspoon freshly ground black pepper
2 Tbl chopped fresh parsley
2 tsp chopped fresh thyme
2 Tbl truffle oil

In a very large skillet, heat 3 tablespoons of butter over medium heat and add shallots. Cook until onions become soft. Add rice. Stir constantly to prevent rice from browning. The grains of rice need to get hot. Add 1½ cups of stock and turn heat down so that the stock is just barely simmering. Continue to stir constantly. As the stock is absorbed, add more stock in small amounts. Continue this process until the grains have become slightly tender. In a separate skillet, place the other 2 tablespoons of butter over a medium heat. Add sliced mushrooms and sauté until soft. Add the mushrooms to the risotto. When rice is almost completely cooked, add the cream and again stir until the moisture is absorbed. Remove from heat and stir in cheese, pepper, and fresh herbs. Drizzle the truffle oil over the risotto just before serving. Serve immediately. Yield: 6–8 servings.

Black Strap Molasses Muffins

¾ cup hot water
½ cup molasses
¼ cup milk
2 cups whole wheat flour
2 cups all-purpose flour
1 tsp baking soda
1 tsp salt
¾ cup sugar
3 Tbl baking powder
1½ cups pecans, roasted, cooled

Preheat oven to 325 degrees.

These muffins come out best if the batter is made at least 8 hours in advance.

Combine the molasses with the hot water and stir well. Add milk to the molasses mixture and set aside.

Sift together the two flours, baking soda, baking powder and salt. Add nuts and sugar to the sifted flours.

Gently fold the wet ingredients into the flour/nut mixture. It is very important not to overmix this batter (it is fine if there are small clumps of dry mixture still visible). Store batter in refrigerator until ready to bake.

Using a nonstick muffin pan, fill each muffin mold with ⅓ cup of the batter. Bake 15–18 minutes.

Let muffins cool slightly before removing them from the muffin pan. Serve warm. Yield: 12–16 muffins.

Fig Butter

1½–2 cups fig preserves
⅛ tsp cinnamon
Pinch of nutmeg
1 tsp vanilla extract
¼ cup unsalted butter, softened

Place half of the fig preserves, the spices, vanilla, and butter in a food processor. Puree until smooth. Add the remaining figs and pulse 6–7 times, just enough to slightly break up the whole figs.

Store in an airtight container in the refrigerator. Yield: 2 cups.

Comeback Sauce

1 cup mayonnaise
½ cup ketchup
½ cup chili sauce
½ cup cottonseed oil
½ cup grated yellow onion
3 Tbl lemon juice
2 Tbl minced garlic
1 Tbl paprika
1 Tbl water
1 Tbl Worcestershire sauce
1 tsp pepper
½ tsp dry mustard
1 tsp salt

Combine all ingredients in a food processor and mix well. Yield: 3½ cups.

The Denomination of Punch

Baptist Punch

2 cups cranberry juice cocktail
2 cups apple cider
1 cup pineapple juice
1 cup orange juice
¼ cup freshly squeezed lemon juice
2 quarts ginger ale

Combine first five ingredients, mix well. Just before serving add ginger ale. Yield: 3 quarts.

Mrs. Lampkin's Methodist Punch

1 48-oz can pineapple juice
1 pkg lime Jell-O
2 cups sugar
1 cup freshly squeezed lemon juice
1 small bottle almond extract

Mix all in gallon container and fill with water to make 1 gallon.

Catholic Punch

½ gallon burgundy wine
1 pint gin
2 quarts ginger ale
½ cup granulated sugar
¼ cup lemon juice

Mix two cups of the wine with the sugar to dissolve. Combine all into a large punch bowl.

Episcopalian Punch

⅕ bourbon, 100 proof
⅕ brandy
⅕ sherry
⅕ sparkling red wine
Juice of 12 fresh lemons
2 cups sugar
⅕ soda water

Combine all except soda water. Add soda just before serving.

Chocolate Decadence

3 lbs semisweet chocolate, best quality, chopped fine (may substitute
chocolate chips; if so, chopping is not necessary)
¾ cup strong brewed coffee or espresso
2 Tbl Taster's Choice coffee crystals
¼ cup hot water (to dissolve instant coffee)
¾ cup egg yolks
¾ cup egg whites
¼ cup sugar
2 cups heavy whipping cream

Combine the chocolate, coffee, and Taster's Choice in a double boiler
and heat until the chocolate is melted. In a large mixing bowl, beat egg
yolks slightly and slowly add the melted chocolate, being careful not to
cook the eggs. Set chocolate mixture aside.

Thoroughly clean and dry a separate mixing bowl and a whip
attachment for an electric mixer. It is important when whipping egg
whites that all utensils be very clean. Place egg whites in the clean bowl
and begin to whip on the high speed of an electric mixer. When they
begin to become foamy, slowly add in sugar and beat until stiff. Set egg
whites aside. In a separate bowl beat whipping cream until it has doubled
in volume.

Fold ⅓ of the stiff egg whites into the chocolate mixture and mix
gently. Add remaining egg whites. Once the egg whites are incorporated,
use the same technique to fold the whipped cream into the chocolate.
Pour the mousse mixture into a brownie-lined springform pan (recipe
opposite). Place in the refrigerator.

It will take 8–10 hours for the mousse to set up. This cake is best when
made a day in advance. Once set, cover tightly with plastic wrap to avoid
absorbing refrigerator odors. To serve, use a hot, damp knife and cut into
12–15 portions.

Brownie Crust

4 squares Baker's Semisweet Chocolate (4 oz.)
¾ cup salted butter
4 eggs
1½ cups sugar
1 cup flour
1 tsp vanilla extract
1 cup chopped pecans
Pinch of salt

Preheat oven to 325 degrees. Melt the chocolate and butter together over a double boiler. In a large bowl, cream sugar and eggs together. Slowly add the chocolate mixture. Add the remaining ingredients, but do not overmix. Line a 10×16 cookie sheet with wax paper. Pour batter onto cookie sheet, making sure it is evenly distributed. Place in preheated oven. Bake for 30–35 minutes or until a toothpick comes out clean. Allow to cool for 5 minutes, then turn brownie cake out onto a clean, dry surface and allow it cool a bit more, until it is cool enough that you can handle it.

Using the bottom circle of a 10 inch springform pan as your guide, cut a springform-pan-sized circle toward one end of the brownie cake. Next, assemble the springform pan and lock into place. Place the round brownie cake circle in the bottom of the springform pan, and then cut the rest of the brownie into strips to line the sides of the plan. You will probably end up with some odd-sized pieces, but the cake is moist enough that you can press them together for a solid crust. Allow this to chill while you make the mousse recipe. Yield: 12–16 servings.

Pumpkin Cheesecake

1½ lbs cream cheese, room temperature
1 cup brown sugar
Pinch salt
5 eggs
4 egg yolks
2 tsp vanilla extract
1½ cups pumpkin puree
1 tsp cinnamon
¼ tsp nutmeg
⅛ tsp allspice

Preheat the oven to 275 degrees.

Place softened cream cheese in large mixing bowl and beat using paddle attachment on medium speed until VERY smooth. Scrape sides and beat again to ensure there are no lumps.

Add sugar and mix well. Add in eggs and yolks a few at a time, allowing them to incorporate well before adding more.

Place the mixer on slow speed and add vanilla, pumpkin puree, cinnamon, nutmeg, and allspice. Blend well for another 2–3 minutes.

Crust

2¼ cups graham cracker crumbs
1 tsp cinnamon
¾ cup melted butter
½ cup sugar

Combine crumbs, cinnamon, and sugar and mix by hand. Add butter in stages, mixing well before each addition.

Evenly distribute the crust in a 10 inch springform pan, pressing it firmly onto the bottom of the pan and building crust up 2 inches on the sides of the pan.

Pour in the cheesecake batter and bake for 1–1½ hours. The cheesecakes should jiggle slightly when tapped.

Remove and refrigerate overnight before serving.

To cut, run a thin knife under hot water before cutting each slice. Yield: 10–14 servings.

King Cake Bread Pudding

2 cups milk
2 cups heavy whipping cream
¾ cup sugar, divided
4 egg yolks
8 eggs
2 tsp vanilla
⅛ tsp salt
1 tsp cinnamon
1 8–10-inch-round cream cheese–filled King Cake

Put the milk, cream, and half of the sugar in a small sauce pan and place over medium heat. Bring this mixture to a simmer, stirring occasionally to prevent the sugar from burning. While the milk mixture is heating, place the remaining sugar, egg yolks, whole eggs, vanilla, and salt into a stainless steel mixing bowl. Using a wire whisk, beat the egg mixture until it become light yellow in color. Slowly begin adding the hot milk to the beaten eggs, whisking constantly to prevent the eggs from cooking.

Cut the King Cake into 2-inch-thick slices. Pour half of the custard into a 2-quart round Pyrex baking dish (9-inch diameter). Submerge the King Cake slices in the custard. Pour the remaining custard over the top, cover the baking dish, and refrigerate over night.

Preheat oven to 325 degrees.

Remove the covering from the refrigerated bread pudding and gently press down the King Cake so that the custard completely covers the surface. Cover the bread pudding with a piece of parchment paper, and then cover the paper with a piece of aluminum foil.

In a roasting pan large enough to hold the Pyrex dish, place 2 inches of hot water. Place the Pyrex dish in the water and bake for 40 minutes. Remove the foil and parchment paper and bake for 10 additional minutes.

Remove from the oven and allow the pudding to rest for 1 hour before serving. Serve with Brandy Crème Anglais. Yield: 8–10 servings.

Brandy Creme Anglaise

1 cup cream
½ cup half-and-half
¼ cup brandy
¾ cup sugar, divided
4 egg yolks
1 tsp vanilla extract

In a stainless steel pot bring the cream, half-and-half, brandy, half of the sugar and vanilla to a simmer. While it is heating, combine the yolks and remaining sugar in a mixing bowl and whip until pale yellow in color.

Slowly begin adding the cream mixture into to yolks, stirring constantly until all the milk has cream mixture has been added. Pour the mixture back into the saucepan and cook over a low-medium flame stirring constantly. Cook until the mixture becomes thick enough to coat a spoon or spatula.

Remove from the heat and cool down in an ice bath. This sauce may be made 2 - 3 days in advance. Yields : 8-10 servings.

Sweet Potato Brownies

½ lb butter
2 cups sugar
1½ cups flour
1 tsp salt
4 eggs
2 tsp vanilla
2 cups grated potatoes
1 cups toasted pecans

Preheat oven to 350 degrees.
In an electric mixer, cream together butter and sugar until light and fluffy. Add remaining ingredients in order, stirring after each is added.
Pour into a buttered and floured 9×12 baking sheet.
Bake for 30–40 minutes.
Allow brownies to cool completely before cutting.

Glaze

2 Tbl butter
¼ cup orange juice
1 tsp cinnamon
1 cup confectioners' sugar

Melt butter and add remaining ingredients. Let cool. Glaze brownies after they have been cut. Yield: 15 brownies.

White Chocolate Bread Pudding Purple Parrot Cafe

5 oz white chocolate
4 egg yolks
1 egg
¼ cup sugar
2 tsp vanilla extract
1½ cups heavy whipping cream
½ cup milk
¼ tsp salt
Sourdough bread as needed (crusts cut off, and cut into 1-inch cubes)

Melt white chocolate in the top of a double boiler.

In another double boiler over moderate heat, combine eggs, sugar, vanilla, whipping cream, milk, and salt. When blended and warm, add melted chocolate. Place bread in buttered custard cups and pour some of the white chocolate mixture over. Allow mixture to settle and pour more over bread, pushing bread that floats to the top down with a spoon. There should be just enough liquid to soak into bread without any excess. Place cups in a shallow baking dish and fill dish with water halfway up the sides of the cups. Cover with a sheet of parchment paper and bake at 350 degrees for 1 hour. Remove paper and cook an additional 15 minutes, until the tops reach a light golden brown. Use a pairing knife to remove bread pudding from custard cups and serve on individual plates topped with White Chocolate Sauce (below).

White Chocolate Bread Pudding can be held in the refrigerator for 2 or 3 days and reheated in the microwave until just warm. This recipe can also be made into a larger batch in a casserole dish, instead of individual portions, and scooped out with a spoon and placed into a bowl. Yield: 8-10 servings.

White Chocolate Sauce

8 oz white chocolate
½ cup heavy whipping cream

Melt white chocolate in a double boiler, add heavy cream, and blend thoroughly. This sauce will hold in the refrigerator and can be reheated in the microwave until just warm.

Chapter 14

The Next 20

Mississippi BBQ Shrimp

2 cups white wine
1 qt shrimp stock
¾ cup Creole Seasoning
½ cup Worcestershire sauce
½ cup lemon juice
3 Tbl paprika
2 Tbl minced garlic
2 Tbl liquid crab boil
¾ cup Creole mustard
4 bay leaves
1 Tbl hot sauce

6 oz butter
1 lb large shrimp, head-on, unpeeled
2 Tbl black peppercorns, cracked

Bring all but the last 3 ingredients to a boil, immediately remove from heat and cool (can be made 2–3 days ahead of time).

When preparing the final dish, make sure to stir the cold BBQ Shrimp stock vigorously before adding it to the skillet.

To prepare a single order of BBQ Shrimp: Melt 6 ounces butter in a skillet and add the shrimp. Sauté until the shrimp begins to turn pink. Add cracked black peppercorns and sauté 1 minute. Add 2 cups of the BBQ Shrimp stock and cook until shrimp are just done.

Serve with plenty of toasted French bread for dipping. Yield: 4 servings.

Shiitake-Tasso Quiche

2 Tbl butter
1 Tbl extra virgin olive oil
3 cups thinly sliced leeks, white part only
1 cup large-dice tasso ham
1½ cups shiitake mushrooms, rough chopped
2 tsp fresh thyme
2 tsp minced garlic
2 tsp Creole Seasoning
½ tsp freshly ground black pepper
1 tsp hot sauce
½ cup heavy cream
6 large eggs
1½ oz smoked cheddar, grated plus 1½ ounces
1 Pie Crust

Preheat oven to 350 degrees.

In a 12-inch sauté pan, combine the butter and olive oil over medium-high heat. Once butter is melted, add leeks and cook, stirring occasionally, until the onions are lightly caramelized, 6–8 minutes. Add the ham, mushrooms, thyme, and garlic to the pan and season with thyme, Creole seasoning, and black pepper. Cook the mixture until most of the moisture has evaporated, approximately 8 minutes. Remove from the heat and allow to cool.

In a medium bowl, combine the heavy cream, eggs, and the remaining mix well. Add the cheese and the mushroom mixture and stir well. Add into pie crust.

Bake until set, 35–40 minutes. Rotate the pie every 10–15 minutes while cooking. Yield: 1 quiche.

Pineapple Pico *(grilled fish topping)*

1½ cups small-dice fresh tomatoes
¼ cup small-dice red onions
2 Tbl thinly sliced green onion
½ tsp minced fresh garlic
2 Tbl chopped cilantro
2 tsp seeds removed and minced fresh jalapeños
1 cup small-dice pineapple
1 tsp lime juice
½ tsp salt

Combine all ingredients and refrigerate until ready to serve. Best if made 2–3 hours in advance. Serve atop grilled fish. Yield: 3 cups.

Asparagus Bread Pudding

1 cup asparagus, cut into one-inch long pieces
1 Tbl olive oil
½ cup diced white onion
½ cup diced red pepper
1 tsp salt
1 tsp freshly ground black pepper
½ cup Riesling wine
12 Tbl chopped fresh basil
1 tsp dry mustard
1 cup sour cream
1 cup half-and-half
½ cup whole milk
4 egg yolks
2 eggs
6 cups crust removed and small-dice French bread

Preheat oven to 325 degrees.

Place three cups of water into a small saucepan and bring to a boil. Place the asparagus pieces in the boiling water and cook for 45 seconds Strain the asparagus and run it under cold water until cooled completely. Drain and dry the asparagus pieces and set aside.

In a medium-sized sauté pan, heat the oil over medium heat. Sauté the onions and peppers for 2–3 minutes. Add the cooked asparagus, salt, and pepper and cook for 1 more minute. Add the wine and allow it to reduce by half. Remove this mixture from the heat and set aside.

In a large mixing bowl, combine the basil, dry mustard, sour cream, half-and-half, milk, and eggs. Blend them together and fold in the cooked vegetables and French bread. Cover and allow the mixture to set for one hour before baking.

Place the pudding mixture into a lightly buttered 2-quart Pyrex baking dish. Cover the pudding with a piece of parchment paper, and cover the parchment paper with a piece of aluminum foil. Bake for 35 minutes covered. Remove the foil and paper and cook for an additional 10 minutes.

Allow pudding to rest for 10 minutes before serving. Yield: 8–10 servings.

Blackened Shrimp Pie

3 Tbl canola oil, separated
1 lb small shrimp
1 Tbl blackening seasoning
¾ cup chopped, medium-dice yellow onions
¾ cup chopped, medium-dice bell peppers
½ cup chopped green onions
2 Tbl Creole Seasoning
2 Tbl minced garlic
2 cups shredded Pepper Jack cheese
Puff pastry sheets (4×4) homemade or frozen

Heat 1 Tbl oil in a medium-high skillet. Sprinkle blackening seasoning on shrimp. Cook shrimp until cooked through. Remove from the skillet. Cool.

In the same skillet, add the remaining 2 Tbl oil. Sauté the onions, bell peppers, green onions, Creole Seasoning, and garlic until the vegetables are soft. Let cool completely.

In a bowl, combine the cooled shrimp, cooled vegetable mixture, and Pepper Jack cheese and mix well.

Place a 4"×4" puff pastry square on a dry surface and brush the top edges of the pastry with a small amount of butter (this serves as a glue to hold the pastry together while baking). Place a half cup of shrimp mixture in the center of the pastry and fold the ends together to form a triangle.

Hold cold until ready to bake. To cook, brush the top of the pastry with a light egg wash and bake in a 350-degree oven until lightly browned and the center is warm. Serve immediately on a warm plate lined with Beurre Blanc sauce (see recipe, next page). Yield: 8 pies.

Beurre Blanc

½ cup medium-dice shallots
½ cup white wine
½ cup white wine vinegar
¼ cup heavy cream
1 lb unsalted butter (cut into 1-inch cubes)
Salt to taste

Simmer the shallots, white wine and vinegar until almost all liquid has evaporated. Add the heavy cream and reduce by half. Do not brown the shallots. Incorporate the butter cubes slowly into the sauce, stirring constantly. Add salt to taste. Strain through a chinois or fine-mesh sieve and hold warm. Yield: 3 cups.

Kickin' Crab Cakes

8 whole eggs
8 egg yolks
¼ cup lemon juice
2 cups mayonnaise
2 cups sour cream
1 Tbl hot sauce (preferably cayenne and garlic hot sauce)
2 Tbl Old Bay seasoning
1 tsp salt
4 tsp Creole Seasoning
1½ cups green onions
½ cups chopped parsley
2 pounds claw meat
2 pounds backfin
2½ cups Japanese bread crumbs, separated

Whisk together eggs and egg yolks. Add lemon juice, mayonnaise, sour cream, and hot sauce and mix well. Add Old Bay seasoning, salt, Creole Seasoning, green onions, and parsley. Stir well.

Gently fold in both crabmeats. Add bread crumbs until the mixture begins to bind together. Form into 12 patties. The crab cake mixture should be wet but still hold together.

Place remaining bread crumbs on a plate. Lightly coat both sides of crab cakes in remaining bread crumbs.

Sauté in small batches in a skillet over medium heat until browned on both sides (don't overcrowd skillet). Serve immediately. Yield: 12 crabcakes (6 people).

Corn and Crab Cake Bisque

For each serving of Corn and Crab Cake Bisque: Sauté 3 oz lump crabmeat in one ounce of butter. Add green onions. Cook until just warm. Place 6 oz Corn and Crab Bisque (page 311) in the bottom of a wide, shallow 16-oz bowl. Place two crabcakes in the bottom of the bowl. Top with sautéed crabmeat.

Crab Cakes Monica

12 crab cakes
4 Tbl canola oil
½ lb peeled and deveined shrimp
2 Tbl Old Bay seasoning
2 Tbl minced garlic
1½ cups sliced green onions
2 cups Creole cream sauce

Preheat oven to 375 degrees.

Heat clarified butter in a large skillet over medium heat. Brown both sides of the crab cakes. Remove from heat. Place crab cakes on a baking sheet and bake in oven for 8–10 minutes.

While crab cakes are baking, return skillet to heat. Drain excess butter, leaving 2 tablespoons. Season shrimp with Old Bay Seasoning and sauté for 1–2 minutes until shrimp start to turn pink. Add garlic and green onions and continue cooking for several minutes. Add crawfish cream sauce. Bring to a simmer and cook for 2–3 minutes.

Remove crab cakes from oven and place on serving dishes. Divide topping evenly over crab cakes. Yield: 6 servings.

Creole Sauce

1 cup unsalted butter
4 cups diced onions
4 cups diced bell pepper
4 cups diced celery
2 Tbl garlic
3 bay leaves
1 Tbl dried oregano
1 Tbl salt
2 tsp white pepper
2 tsp cayenne pepper
2 Tbl paprika
1 Tbl thyme
1 Tbl basil
6 cups canned tomatoes, drained, rough chopped
4 cups chicken stock
¼ cup tomato sauce
2 Tbl sugar
2 Tbl hot sauce
2 cups Robert St. John's Bloody Mary Mix (or similar, can substitute V8)
¾ cup water
¼ cup cornstarch

3 lb large shrimp, peeled, deveined
2 tsp Creole Seasoning
3 Tbl canola oil

Melt butter. Add onions, celery, and peppers, and sauté until soft. Add garlic, bay leaves, oregano, salt, white pepper, cayenne pepper, paprika, thyme, and basil. Cook 5–8 minutes on medium-high. Add tomatoes and cook 10–15 minutes, until tomatoes break down.

Add stock, tomato sauce, sugar, hot sauce, and Bloody Mary Mix. Bring to a boil. Reduce heat and simmer for 30 minutes.

Add water to cornstarch and and stir well. Add to Creole Sauce and bring to a boil to thicken. Cool.

To make 4 portions of Shrimp Creole: Sprinkle shrimp with Creole Seasoning. Add oil to a large, medium-high skillet. Add shrimp and cook 3–5 minutes. Add 5 cups of creole sauce. Cook until hot and shrimp are done. Serve over warm white rice. Yield: 1½ gallons.

Étouffée

2¼ cups olive oil blend
2¼ cups flour
¼ cup tomato paste
1½ cups diced onions
1½ cups diced celery
1½ cups diced peppers
2 Tbl salt
1 Tbl + 1 tsp cayenne pepper
1 Tbl white pepper
1 Tbl + 1 tsp black pepper
2 Tbl basil
1 Tbl thyme
3 qt Seafood Stock
3 Tbl hot sauce

Heat oil, add flour, make brownish red roux. Cool 10 minutes.
Add tomato paste, veggies, and seasonings. Cook ten minutes.
Heat stock and add roux mixture to stock. Simmer for 10–15 minutes.

To prepare a single portion of Shrimp Étouffée: Sauté 12–14 large shrimp sprinkled with 1 tsp of Creole Seasoning in 2 Tbl canola oil until cooked through. Add 8 oz. étouffée sauce. Serve over 1 cup of warm white rice. Yield: 1 gallon.

Chicken and Andouille Fettuccini

⅓ cup canola oil
½ cup medium-dice red bell pepper
½ cup medium-dice green bell pepper
1 cup medium-dice yellow onion
1 lb andouille sausage, rough cut
3 Tbl minced garlic
2 cups sliced mushrooms (shiitake or button)
1½ Tbl Creole Seasoning
2 cups grilled chicken breasts diced into ½-inch cubes
2 cups Creole Cream Sauce
1 cup heavy cream
1 lb cooked fettuccini

   Heat clarified butter in a heavy sauté pan. Add peppers and onion.
Cook until soft and translucent. Add andouille and stir well. Add garlic
and mushrooms. Cook until mushrooms are soft. Add Creole Seasoning
and cooked chicken, stirring well to incorporate. Add crawfish cream
sauce stirring continuously. Add heavy cream to reach desired thickness.
Once heated through, serve over heated fettuccini. Yield: 6 servings.

Pepper Jack–Black Pepper Biscuits

2 cups flour
1 Tbl sugar
1½ tsp baking soda
1 tsp baking powder
1 Tbl kosher salt
2 tsp freshly ground black pepper
½ cup shredded Pepper Jack cheese
½ cup frozen butter
¾ cup + 2 Tbl buttermilk
1 egg
3 Tbl melted unsalted butter

Preheat oven to 375 degrees.

In a large mixing bowl, combine the flour, sugar, baking soda, baking powder, salt, pepper, and Pepper Jack cheese. Gently mix to combine the ingredients.

Using a cheese grater, carefully shred the frozen butter into the flour mixture. Lightly toss to incorporate. Work fast as it is very important to keep butter as cold as possible.

In a separate bowl, whisk together the buttermilk and egg. Add the buttermilk mixture to the flour mixture and, using your hands, blend the dough. Blend only long enough to moisten all of the flour. Do not overmix.

Place the biscuit dough on a lightly floured surface and roll out to ¾-inch thickness. Cut biscuits using a 2-inch round cookie cutter (do not twist when cutting, use a straight and quick up-and-down motion).

Place biscuits on a cookie sheet. Using a pastry brush, brush the tops with the melted butter. Bake 12–14 minutes. Yield: 10–14 biscuits.

Quick Biscuits

4 cups Bisquick
4 oz sour cream
1 cup club soda (room temperature)
¼ cup butter, melted

Preheat oven to 375 degrees.

Gently mix Bisquick, sour cream, and club soda together. Pour onto floured surface and knead very lightly. Roll out to about ½-inch thickness and cut with cutter. Brush a small amount of melted butter onto a sheet pan. Place biscuits on pan and brush remaining butter over top of biscuits.

Bake 8–10 minutes, or until golden brown. Yield: 12 biscuits.

Garlic-Buttermilk Salad Dressing

1 cup mayonnaise
⅔ cup sour cream
½ cup buttermilk
2 Tbsp sugar
1 tsp minced garlic
1 tsp paprika
1 tsp freshly ground black pepper
1 tsp mustard powder
1 tsp Creole Seasoning
1/2 tsp salt

Place all ingredients in a blender and process until smooth. Refrigerate immediately. Best when made one day in advance. Yield: 2 cups.

Creole Honey-Mustard Dressing

1 egg yolk
⅓ cup Dijon mustard
⅓ cup Creole mustard
⅓ cup honey
½ cup Balsamic vinegar
¼ tsp Crescent City Grill Hot Sauce
⅓ cup olive oil
1 cup cottonseed oil (or canola oil)

Place egg yolks, mustards, honey, vinegar, and Hot Sauce in a food processor. Blend thoroughly. With the machine running, slowly add oils. Store in refrigerator until ready to use. yield: 2½ cups.

My South Tea

2 mint leaves
2 thin slices of orange
2 thin slices of lemon
2 oz simple syrup
2 oz Firefly Sweet Tea vodka
1 oz Stoli O vodka
1 oz Smirnoff Twist
1 oz Peach Schnapps,
3 oz Sweet and Sour Mix
4 oz liquid iced tea concentrate

In a carafe filled with ice, combine all ingredients. Stir well.

Mahogarita

1 oz Grand Marnier
1 oz Jose Cuervo,
4 oz Sweet and Sour Mix
splash of orange juice
1½ oz 1800 tequila

Combine Gran Marnier, Jose Cuervo, Sweet and Sour, orange juice, and ice in a stainless bar shaker. Shake well. Pour into a salt-rimmed glass and float 1800 tequila on top.

Muz's Fudge Cake (Brownies)

4 squares Baker's chocolate
2 sticks butter
4 eggs
2 cups sugar
1 cup flour
1 tsp pure vanilla extract
1 cup chopped nuts
Pinch of salt

Preheat oven to 350 degrees.

Melt chocolate and butter together in a double boiler. Once incorporated, let cool slightly. Cooled chocolate should still be in liquid form.

Mix together the 4 eggs and gradually add the 2 cups of sugar until completely incorporated. *Slowly* pour the slightly warm chocolate mixture into the egg/sugar mixture, making sure not to scramble the eggs.

Carefully incorporate the flour into the chocolate/egg mixture. Add vanilla, nuts, salt, and mix.

Line a pan with wax paper or parchment. Pour in the chocolate mix. Bake at 350 degrees approximately 30 minutes, or until an inserted toothpick comes out clean.

Remove from oven. Let cool 5 minutes. Carefully flip the fudge cake and finish cooling. Once cooled completely, remove wax paper and cut into squares. Yield: 12-14 brownies.

Chocolate–Peanut Butter Cheesecake

1½ lb cream cheese, room temperature
1 cup sugar
Pinch salt
5 eggs
4 egg yolks
2 tsp vanilla extract
¾ cup heavy cream
½ cup peanut butter (creamy)
4 oz semisweet chocolate (melted)

Preheat the oven to 275 degrees.

Place softened cream cheese in large mixing bowl and beat using paddle attachment on medium speed until *Very* smooth. Scrape sides and beat again to ensure there are no lumps.

Add sugar and mix well. Add in eggs and yolks a few at a time, allowing them to incorporate well before adding more.

Place the mixer on slow speed and add vanilla and cream. As soon as the cream is incorporated, stop mixing.

Divide cheesecake batter into two separate bowls. Fold peanut butter into one batch. Fold melted chocolate into the other batch.

Crust

1½ cups graham cracker crumbs
¾ cup melted butter
½ cup sugar

Combine crumbs and sugar and mix by hand. Add butter in stages, mixing well before each addition.

Evenly distribute the crust in a nine-inch spring form pan, pressing it firmly on the bottom of the pan and building crust up 2 inches on the sides.

Pour in the cheesecake batter— alternating layers between chocolate batter and peanut butter batter until all is used (4 layers)— and bake for 1–1½ hours. The cheesecakes should jiggle slightly when tapped.

Remove and cool. Refrigerate overnight before serving.

To cut, run a thin knife under hot water before cutting each slice.

Yield: 12-14 slices.

Orange Crepes

Crepe Filling

1½ lb cream cheese, softened at room temperature
¾ cup sugar
2 Tbl finely grated orange zest
2 Tbl fresh orange juice
2 tsp vanilla extract
12 crepes

   Combine all ingredients (except crepes) and blend until smooth. Preheat oven to 325 degrees. Fill the crepes by placing the cream cheese mixture in a pastry bag and piping a 1"×1" tube down the center of each crepe. Roll the crepes and place them on a lightly buttered baking sheet, nonstick is preferable. Cover the crepes with a sheet of wax paper and cover the entire wax paper–covered baking sheet with a sheet of aluminum foil. Bake for 6–7 minutes, just until center is warm. While crepes are baking, make the sauce.

Orange Sauce

½ lb unsalted butter
½ cup sugar
2 Tbl freshly squeezed orange juice
¼ cup brandy

   In a medium-sized skillet, melt butter over medium-high heat. Add sugar and cook until it begins to dissolve. Add orange juice and whisk together ingredients. Add the brandy and carefully ignite. When flame subsides, lower heat slightly and cook for 4–5 minutes, until thick and creamy.
   Place warm crepes on serving dishes and spoon the heated sauce over them. Garnish with fresh mint. Yield: 6–8 servings.

ABOUT THE AUTHOR

Robert St. John, a native of Hattiesburg, Mississippi, is a twenty-eight-year veteran of the restaurant industry. For The last twenty-two years he has served as executive chef, president, and CEO of the Purple Parrot Cafe, the Crescent City Grill, and the Mahogany Bar in Hattiesburg and Meridian.

St. John is a restaurateur, chef, food writer, author, and a true original. One of the nation's only food/humor columnists, he began self-syndicating his weekly newspaper column in 1999 and quickly amassed a loyal and fanatical readership. The *Lexington Herald-Leader* called him a "Jeff Foxworthystyle chef with an opinion on all things culinary."

St. John's column is published weekly in thirty newspapers. Everyone from *Time* magazine —"St. John explores the roots of Southern hospitality with witty essays and quietly sophisticated recipes"—to National Public Radio —"The Mississippi restaurateur, food columnist, and chef treats his subjects with humor and a lot of down-home conversation"—has chimed in on St. John.

He has written and released eight books in the last seven years. A recent *Booklist* review stated, "If he had accomplished nothing more, St. John deserves kudos for making Hattiesburg, Mississippi, a restaurant destination. His Purple Parrot Cafe updated Southern cooking for a new generation."

St. John has appeared on the Food Network, the Travel Channel, and the Turner South network. He has two television projects in development and owns a gourmet food business which distributes products under the Robert St. John label. He writes a regular column for *Y'all* magazine and is a contributing writer to *Taste of the South* magazine.

St. John is the founder of Extra Table, an organization created to help restaurants end hunger in America. He serves on the board of the Mississippi Arts Commission and the Mississippi Museum of Art, on the advisory board of the Lauren Rogers Museum of Art, and on the National Chef's Council of the Chef's for Humanity organization.

A self-taught cook, St. John has been named the state's top chef by *Mississippi* magazine in 2006, 2007, and 2008. Additionally, the former Mississippi Restaurateur of the Year's restaurant—The Purple Parrot Cafe—was recently named the best fine dining restaurant in Mississippi and received a four-diamond rating from the *AAA Travel Guide* in 2008.

St. John is married with two children who worship the ground he walks on (as long as that ground is in Toys "R" Us or The Gap).

Visit Robert St. John's NEW website to:

Read Robert's weekly column and blog
View the latest photos and blurbs of Robert's culinary excursions
Watch videos of cooking demonstrations
Look up Robert's famous recipes
Book Robert for guest appearances and speeches
Links to Robert's restaurants
Follow Robert on Facebook and Twitter

www.robertstjohn.com

Book Robert St. John as a Guest Speaker

Robert St. John is a restaurateur, chef, author and a weekly food columnist. He has written and released eight books in the last seven years and has made appearances on the Food Network, the Travel Channel and the Turner South network.

A self-taught cook, Robert has been named the state's top chef by *Mississippi Magazine* in 2006, 2007, and 2008. Additionally, the form Mississippi Restaurateur of the Year's restaurant— The Purple Parrot Café— was recently named the best fine dining restaurant in Mississi and received a Four-Diamond rating from the *AAA Travel Guide* in 2

Robert is an entertaining public speaker willing to travel and speak organizations as diverse as:

Mississippi Association of the Self Insured
Starkville Arts Council (Starkville, MS)
Louisiana/Mississippi Bed and Breakfast Association
National Governor's Association
Mississippi Banker's Association
National Association of Junior Auxiliaries
Pensacola Symphony Guild (Pensacola, FL)
Tyler Women's Building Celebrity Chef Event (Tyler, TX)
Mississippi Main Street Association
Viking Range Corporation/Viking Culinary Group
Epcot International Food and Wine Festival
Natchez Literary and Cinema Celebration
Mississippi Development Authority
Southern Cultural Heritage Foundation (Vicksburg, MS)
Travel South USA

To book Robert St. John to speak at an upcoming event, contact Stacey Andrews at 601-264-0672, toll-free 1-888-315-6774 or email sda@nsrg.com.

"St.John is a hoot, a sort of Jeff Foxworthy-style chef with an opinion on all things culinary."
– *Lexington Herald-Leader*

"The Mississippi restaurateur, food columnist, and chef treats his subject with humor and a lot of down-hon conversation."
– National Public Radio

"A wicked sense of humor and a straightforward approach to cooking."
– *Roanoke Times*

"Like most great cooks, Robert St. John is a briiliant observer of human nature and of the culture at large."
– Julia Reed, contributing writer for the *New York Times Book Review*

www.robertstjohn.com
www.nsrg.com